MW00776502

Backpacking
New York

0 11557 01318 4

Backpacking New York

37 Great Hikes

Jeff Mitchell

STACKPOLE BOOKS

Published by
STACKPOLE BOOKS
5067 Ritter Road
Mechanicsburg, PA 17055
www.stackpolebooks.com

Printed in the USA

10 9 8 7 6 5 4 3 2 1

FIRST EDITION

Cover design by Caroline Stover
Front cover photo: Ian Strever and Matt LaRusso on the summit of Slide Mountain, Catskills. Photo by the author.
Back cover photo: View from Mt. Skylight, High Peaks, Adirondacks. Photo by the author.

Hiking and backpacking are inherently risky activities, with ever-changing conditions and numerous natural and man-made hazards. Please choose trails that are appropriate for your ability. Many trails in this guide have dangerous natural conditions demanding respect and experience. All persons using the trails in this guide do so at their own risk, and this guide is not a substitute for your own common sense, caution, and taking necessary safety precautions. The author and publisher disclaim any and all liability for conditions along the trails and routes of the hikes, occurrences along them, and the accuracy of the data, conditions, and information contained herein.

Library of Congress Cataloging-in-Publication Data

Mitchell, Jeff, 1974–
    Backpacking New York : 37 great hikes / Jeff Mitchell. — First Edition.
        pages   cm
    ISBN 978-0-8117-1318-4
    1. Backpacking—New York (State)—Guidebooks. 2. Hiking—New York (State)—Guidebooks. 3. Trails—New York (State)—Guidebooks. 4. Natural resources—New York (State)—Guidebooks. 5. New York (State)—Guidebooks. I. Title.
GV199.42.N652M57   2016
796.5109747—dc23
                                                      2015023687

To Christian, Kaitlyn, and Leigh Ann

Contents

Preface

Why do I enjoy backpacking? What's the point of hauling a big, heavy pack up and down mountains, across rocks and streams, while being dirty, sweaty, wet, and tired? The reasons are plenty.

There is something special about observing wildlife in the wilderness, climbing a mountain to behold a gorgeous view, or following a stream to a stunning waterfall. To view nature away from a car window is something to relish. To carry everything I need to survive on my back for a few days reinforces my appreciation of the convenient life I live. I feel a sense of pride and accomplishment when I traverse the wilderness under my own power and determination. It's amazing what our bodies are capable of when given the opportunity to explore. The astonishing beauty of our world is best realized by simply walking through it. So many incredible places bear witness to the grandeur of our state, nation, and world. By respectfully visiting and experiencing these places, we can appreciate and protect them.

Mainstream America may view backpackers as antisocial oddities. After all, what kind of psychosis is required to hike through the woods while being stalked by bears and snakes, only to sleep on the ground, in a tent, without a bed or bathroom? The reality is that the people you'll find along the trail are almost always the most selfless, gracious, interesting, and genuine people you'll ever meet. Backpacking reintroduces people not only to nature, but also to each other.

I hope this guide enables you to explore and enjoy the beautiful world with which you have been blessed.

Acknowledgments

Special thanks to all my friends and family: my parents, Joe and Tessa Mitchell, Ryan Koerber, Wes Atkinson, Steve Davis, Diana Krewson, Jen and Tim O'Brien, Melissa Jennings, Florian Diarra, Bill Paggio, Jay Lewis, Dan Wrona, Jeff Sensenig, Bob Holliday, Matt LaRusso, Ian Strever, Bryan Mulvihill, Carissa Longo, Paul and Paula Litwin, Rick and Nadine Dixon, Charles Pirone, Warren Renninger, Ruth Rode, Ed Kintner, Ashley Lenig, Bob Roache, Rob Danner, Mike Juskelis, Michael Merry, Jodi Reimer, Rick Ostheimer, Amanda Debevc, Kevin Skilskyj, Mike Servedio, and Kyle Weaver.

This book would not be possible without the assistance and support of Brittany Stoner and Stackpole Books.

Finally, I express my appreciation to all the trail organizations and volunteers who have made these trails a reality through their hard work and determination.

Introduction

New York is an exceptional place. No other state east of the Mississippi can rival New York's incredible diversity of terrain and natural features. The Empire State has it all—alpine summits, vast lakes, towering waterfalls, pristine wilderness, broad river valleys, gorges, canyons, plateaus, and rolling farmlands. Not surprisingly, New York is a premier hiking and backpacking destination, with trails that suit every interest and ability.

The state has a long and proud history in environmental conservation and preservation. It is home to the first state park. Wilderness protection is written in its constitution. Some of the first large-scale bequests of land for conservation happened in the state. New York has also created the largest state-owned wilderness areas in the entire country, covering over 1.3 million acres. This environmental heritage has laid the foundation for a vast system of world-class hiking and backpacking trails.

There have been countless guides written about New York's hiking trails. Yet few, if any, focus solely on the state's backpacking opportunities. Guidebooks about the Empire State have taken a segmented approach, where intense focus has been given to a particular region of the state, but not the state as a whole. Backpackers may be surprised to learn that New York is much more than the Adirondacks or Catskills. From east to west, trails explore the gorgeous Taconics, the glaciated plateaus and gorges of the Finger Lakes, and the deep woods of Allegany State Park.

This guide provides a descriptive overview of the trails included. It does not provide turn-by-turn or mile-by-mile descriptions. For more detailed descriptions, you should purchase a guidebook and map of that trail, if they are available. The intent of this guide is to include a variety of trails that may interest backpackers, and to describe what to expect on the hike. This guide also showcases less popular trails, in the hope they will be used and survive for future generations of backpackers.

This is now the sixth outdoors book I have written. I write because I feel a need to share. It is my hope people will want to experience the incredible world that surrounds them, and to protect that world for not only future generations, but also their own. People will only protect what they know. By writing about these beautiful trails, I hope that people will learn about them, experience them, and protect them and the landscapes through which they pass.

New York's Backpacking Trails

New York has one of the most extensive systems of backpacking trails in the East, potentially rivaled only by Pennsylvania. While Pennsylvania has an extensive network of single-name trail systems, New York's system tends to be a web of smaller, individual trails, particularly in

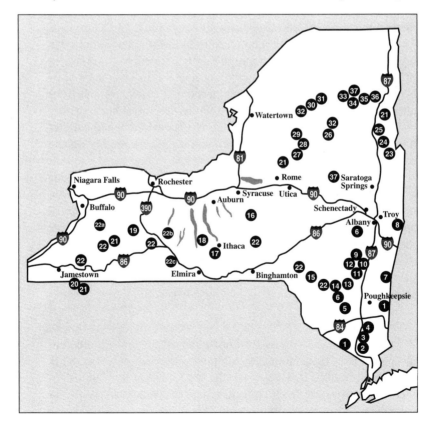

the Adirondacks and Catskills. These trails can be combined for backpacking trips.

There are also long, single trails. The famous Appalachian Trail crosses the southern Hudson Valley. The Long Path is over 350 miles long and stretches from the Palisades to near Albany, traversing Harriman State Park, the Shawangunks, and the Catskills. The Finger Lakes Trail is the longest in the state as it explores the southern foothills, nearly crossing the length of New York. The North Country Trail will extend from Lake George to North Dakota and, when complete, will become the longest trail in the state. Much of the North Country Trail also follows the Finger Lakes Trail; both of these trails cross a lot of private property and follow or cross many roads. The Northville–Placid Trail may be New York's premier, long-distance single trail, exploring the valleys, lakes, streams, and rivers of the Adirondacks.

While I have not hiked the North Country Trail, Finger Lakes Trail System, and the Long Path in their entirety, I felt it was important to include those trails in this book due to their length and importance, and because I felt backpackers should be aware of them. Summarized descriptions of these trails are included.

Trail Conditions

Trail conditions are constantly changing. Trails are often rerouted, blazes are repainted or changed, and side trails may be built, expanded, or abandoned. A trail that was in excellent condition might be severely damaged by floods and blowdowns after a storm. Trails may also be severed by private property owners and have to be rerouted. Bridges may be washed away in a flood, or a trail can be flooded by beavers. It is impossible for this guidebook to identify all changes that may have occurred along New York's numerous trails since they were last hiked or researched. For this reason, this guide offers descriptive overviews of the trails. For current trail alerts, go to the website of the trail organization that covers the region where you intend to hike.

Camping Regulations

Trails in New York cross a variety of public lands owned and controlled by various agencies. The camping rules and regulations vary from agency to agency.

State Parks: Backcountry camping is generally prohibited, unless at an approved shelter, lean-to, or campsite.

Wildlife Management Areas: Backcountry camping is prohibited, unless approved by the regional supervisor.

State Forests, Adirondack Park, Catskill Park: Backcountry camping is permitted. The campsite cannot be within 150 feet of a road, stream, trail, spring, pond, lake, or other water body, unless it is at an approved site, shelter, or lean-to. Camping is prohibited in the Adirondacks at elevations higher than 4,000 feet from April 30 to December 15. Camping is prohibited in the Catskills at elevations higher than 3,500 feet from March 21 to December 21.

Private Land: Naturally, you should not camp on private land unless you have permission. However, the Finger Lakes Trail system does have a few approved campsites and lean-tos on private land that backpackers can use.

Backpacking during Hunting Season

Every trail passes through public or private land where hunting takes place. During hunting season, wear fluorescent orange. Try not to disturb a hunt or wildlife, and be considerate of hunters. It is important for backpackers to be respectful of other outdoor enthusiasts.

Trailhead Parking

Many trailheads are located in isolated areas, and vandalism of vehicles does occasionally occur. To protect your vehicle, make sure it is locked, all windows are closed, and anything of value is placed out of sight. Taking commonsense precautions will help keep your property safe.

New York often has larger trailheads in the Adirondacks and Catskills. These trailheads generally have road signs and a register. Trails in other areas of the state tend to cross and follow more roads and do not have trailheads that are as clearly established.

Sign Trail Registers

Trail registers are a common sight along New York's trails, particularly at trailheads and parking areas. It is important to sign them for several reasons:

- *Safety*. If something were to happen to you on the trail, it would be easier to determine your location and direction if you had signed the register.
- *Government assistance*. It is easier for parks or agencies to acquire grants and funding to preserve and maintain trails that are being

used. The most accurate way to determine use is by the number of names in a register.

- *Trail conditions and warnings.* Previous backpackers often write about trail conditions, give warnings, and note experiences on the trail, which can be helpful to subsequent backpackers.
- *Camaraderie.* Registers create a sense of kinship and camaraderie on the trail.

Backpacking Etiquette

Always show respect toward nature and your fellow backpackers. Please observe the following:

- Pack out everything that you carried in. If you can, also pack out litter left by others.
- Do not pick vegetation or disturb, harm, or feed wildlife.
- Do not take shortcuts, particularly through switchbacks, as this causes erosion.
- Do not deface, carve into, remove, or damage anything.
- Follow all rules and regulations established by the park, forest, or other agency.
- Be considerate to other hikers along the trail, particularly when you share campsites or shelters.

Respect Private and Public Property

Several trails in this guide cross private property at some point. To maintain good relations with the owners, backpackers must treat private property with the highest respect. When crossing private property, do not litter, camp without permission, build fires, loiter, or damage property. Pass through as quickly and quietly as possible. If camping is permitted, follow all rules and do not become a nuisance; keep the noise level down, and change your clothes and relieve yourself discreetly.

Anyone involved with trail organizations knows that working with private property owners to permit a trail crossing is a constant source of concern. To ensure the survival of many of New York's backpacking trails, the cooperation and trust of these owners is absolutely critical. If the owners were to withdraw permission for a trail crossing, the trail would be severed and its existence threatened. Put yourself in the shoes of a private landowner: Would you want a stranger causing problems or being a nuisance on your property?

Public lands must also be respected. Too many people feel they have the right to use, pollute, and exploit public land in any way they see fit. Always follow regulations of public agencies regarding the use of their lands, and help pack out litter or clear dump sites. We all need to be more appreciative of the public land that has been provided for our benefit.

Bears

The black bear calls New York home and can be found across the state and along all backpacking trails. For the beginning backpacker, no other animal causes more stress or worry. For the experienced backpacker, seeing a bear is often a highlight of a trip because bears are rarely encountered.

As a general rule, bears are shy and retiring; they often try to avoid humans. There is one area where this rule does not apply, and that is the High Peaks region in the Adirondacks. Here, bears have become accustomed to humans and seek out their food. They are a presence at some camping areas and shelters. Some bears are almost famous for their ability to steal food from properly hung bags and even canisters. It is imperative you follow all regulations for food storage while in the High Peaks. In other areas of New York, store your food by hanging it or keeping it in a canister, and never feed bears.

Black bears do not need to be feared; they need to be treated with intelligence and respect. Always avoid cubs and keep your distance from them, because their mother will be protective and more likely to be aggressive. Make noise while hiking through thick brush; surprising a bear can result in aggressive behavior. I often clap. Always store your food properly, along with soap, toothpaste, and utensils. Never keep food in a tent, shelter, or sleeping bag.

If you do find yourself faced with an aggressive bear, back away slowly, avoid eye contact, and wave your hands and arms to make yourself appear larger. Never run. If a bear does charge you, it will typically be a bluff. If a black bear attacks you, however, you must fight back. The strategy of playing dead applies to brown or grizzly bears, which do not live in New York.

Snakes

New York is home to seventeen species of snakes, of which only three are venomous: the timber rattlesnake, copperhead, and massasauga. All three species are fairly uncommon in New York and scarce in most of the Adirondacks. In all my backpacking trips, I've seen venomous snakes about six or seven times, and never while backpacking in New York.

The timber rattlesnake grows to 35 to 74 inches, is most active between April and October, and occurs in two phases: the common black-brown phase and the rare yellow phase. It often enjoys sunning on rocks. The timber rattlesnake has the widest habitat of New York's venomous snakes, with a primary range in the southeastern part of the state, but also can be found across the southern tier to the western areas of the state. Isolated populations are found as far north as Lake George.

The copperhead grows to 22 to 53 inches and also enjoys sunning on rocks. It lives in the lower Hudson Valley, with some isolated populations in the Catskills. This snake does not have a rattle.

The massasauga is the rarest of New York's venomous snakes, found in only a few large wetlands near Syracuse and Rochester. It is unlikely you will ever see one. It grows to 18 to 39 inches and generally lives in swamps, bogs, and wetlands.

Snakes tend to be shy creatures that are afraid of humans. Snakebites are rare and typically occur when people harass or try to handle a snake. When you approach a snake, always give it a wide berth and observe it from a safe distance. Do not harm snakes, as they are becoming increasingly rare and may be protected by law. Most snake encounters will be on ledges and rocks with sun exposure. Rattlesnakes almost always let you know you are getting too close with a shrill rattle. If you hear the rattle, freeze and locate the snake before proceeding.

If a snake does bite you, seek medical attention immediately. Stay calm and hydrated. The venom of these snakes is generally not fatal to an adult, but it can kill a small child. Keep the wound below the level of the heart, clean, and immobilized as best you can.

Need a reason to like snakes? Here's one: They are our allies in the fight against Lyme disease. The bacteria that causes the disease can only form in rodents, and only ticks can transmit the disease. When a snake eats an infected rodent, the disease is destroyed, never to be transmitted again. Because snakes are so crucial to our ecosystems and our health, please respect and protect them.

Black Flies

Of all of New York's annoying insects, none can rival the black fly. This tiny purveyor of pain can bring entire communities to a standstill and even affects the outdoor tourism industry. Black flies are most problematic in the Adirondacks where there are extensive lakes and wetlands; however, these insects can be found across the state. They seem impervious to most insect repellents and love to crawl under clothing—or under belts and straps that are pressed against skin—to bite. They will happily bite through t-shirts. In spring, hikers pay close attention to when they begin hatching. While the hatch varies from year to year, black flies generally become a nuisance beginning in early to mid-May and continuing until late June or early July. The peak of the black fly "season" is late May to early June. They often swarm a person and bite relentlessly. Unlike mosquitoes, they are silent. Their numbers are suppressed by wind or by hot, dry weather, and they are not active at night. The lifespan of a black fly is about three weeks, and only females bite, since they require a blood meal to develop their eggs for the next generation.

Lyme Disease

Lyme disease is a bacterial infection transmitted by the bites of infected deer ticks. Very few tick bites actually lead to the disease. When a person is bitten by an infected deer tick, symptoms usually develop in a few days or weeks. A circular rash envelops the bite and flu-like symptoms may result. If caught early enough, the disease can be successfully treated with antibiotics.

The risk of infection increases when the tick is attached for thirty-six to forty-eight hours. Most people will find a full-grown tick within that period of time, so the greatest risk of infection comes from tiny ticks in the nymph stage, which are about the size of the period at the end of this sentence.

Deer ticks are found in the woods, but they tend to be most often encountered in grassy and brushy areas. While some insect repellents are effective against ticks, the best defense is to wear long, light-colored, pants and sleeves and inspect your body for ticks at the end of the day.

Ticks are common throughout New York, with the exception of the Adirondacks. However, over the last few years, ticks have been encountered with greater frequency in the Adirondacks, particularly in the southern portions of the Adirondack Park.

Giardiasis

Although some hikers drink directly from springs and streams, this is not advisable. The risk of being infected with giardiasis or another water-borne bacterial or microbial infection is too great, and the consequences will easily end your hike and require medical attention. Safe water is within easy reach of any hiker thanks to a variety of water filters and chemical or ultraviolet purifiers.

Backpacking for Beginners

Many dayhikers are interested in backpacking, but are too intimidated to give it a try. Making the transition is surprisingly easy. Follow these simple tips for your first trip:

- Choose a relatively easy and short trail offering a one-night trip.
- Acquire a map, brochures, or Internet information to learn everything you can about the trail you intend to backpack.
- Purchase or rent the proper equipment. At a minimum you will need a backpack, tent, sleeping bag and pad for ground insulation, water treatment supplies, and footwear.
- Don't pack too heavy. Keep a close eye on your pack weight and bring items that have multiple purposes. You will be surprised by how little you actually need while backpacking.
- Bring a friend who is familiar with backpacking.
- Learn about "Leave No Trace" ethics and how to hang or store your food at night.

The abilities of beginners can vary greatly; these trails, or sections thereof, are good choices for those looking to start backpacking:

- Appalachian Trail
- Morgan Hill State Forest
- Connecticut Hill Wildlife Management Area and Robert H. Treman State Park
- Finger Lakes National Forest
- Letchworth Trail
- Allegany State Park
- West Canada Lakes Wilderness Loop
- Woodhull–Bear Lake Loop
- Remsen Falls–Nelson Lake Loop
- Ha-De-Ron-Dah Wilderness
- Dog Pond Loop
- High Falls Loop

Trail Maintenance and Support

Almost every New York backpacking trail is primarily maintained by volunteers or nonprofit organizations. A few trails have their own maintaining and governing organizations, such as the Finger Lakes Trail Conference. Other organizations focus on different trails in a region, such as the Adirondacks or Catskills, as compared to a particular trail system. New York does not have a statewide hiking organization.

Keep in mind that a trail is much more than a path through the woods. Creating a trail required incredible work and determination. Maybe easements had to be negotiated with private landowners, or permission acquired from a state agency to cross public lands. There were probably several scouting missions and meetings to determine where to locate the trail, as well as the work to construct the trail; dig sidehills, switchbacks, and drainage; and build bridges and shelters. A trail you hiked for a few hours likely required others to donate hundreds of hours of their time to create and maintain.

While hikers often take trails for granted, they shouldn't. We all can, and should, do more. Please consider volunteering some time or supporting the organizations that make these trails a reality.

Trail Organizations

Please support these organizations that build, maintain, promote, and protect the trails we enjoy at no cost to us.

Adirondack Mountain Club, www.adk.org. Maintains trails in the High Peaks and Adirondack Park.

Finger Lakes Trail Conference, www.fltconference.org. Maintains trails in the Finger Lakes Trail System.

Foothills Trail Club, www.foothillstrailclub.org. Maintains the Conservation Trail, a component of the Finger Lakes Trail System.

New York–New Jersey Trail Conference, www.nynjtc.org. Maintains trails from the Catskills and southern Taconics, south to Harriman State Park, including the Appalachian Trail and Long Path.

North Country Trail—Central New York Chapter, www.nctacny chapter.org. Maintains the North Country Trail in central New York, between the Finger Lakes Trail System and Adirondack Park.

Taconic Hiking Club, www.taconichikingclub.org. Maintains the Taconic Crest Trail.

Trails with Waterfalls

Waterfalls are a somewhat rare feature along New York's backpacking trails, but you'll see them on these trails.

- Appalachian Trail
- Harriman State Park–South
- Shawangunk Ridge Trail
- Long Path
- South Taconic Trail
- Overlook Mountain and Kaaterskill Wild Forest
- Devil's Path
- Morgan Hill State Forest
- Connecticut Hill Wildlife Management Area and Robert H. Treman State Park
- Letchworth Trail
- Finger Lakes Trail
- Lake George Wild Forest
- Tongue Mountain Range Loop
- Cranberry Lake 50
- High Falls Loop
- Mt. Marcy–Avalanche Pass Loop
- High Peaks Loop
- Northville–Placid Trail

Trails with Lakes and Ponds

Lakes and ponds are a common feature of many trails in New York; these trails offer the best of that scenery.

- Harriman State Park–West
- Shawangunk Ridge Trail
- Morgan Hill State Forest
- Lake George Wild Forest
- Tongue Mountain Range Loop
- Pharaoh Lake Wilderness
- West Canada Lakes Wilderness Loop
- Woodhull–Bear Lake Loop
- Ha-De-Ron-Dah Wilderness
- Cranberry Lake 50
- High Peaks Loop
- Northville–Placid Trail

Looking for a Challenge?

If you have a few years of backpacking under your belt and are looking to challenge yourself, check out these trails.

- Long Path (Great Catskills Traverse)
- Devil's Path
- Algonquin Peak–Indian Pass Loop
- High Peaks Loop
- Northville–Placid Trail

Trails with Views

Almost every trail in this book offers at least a few views, but these trails have the best.

- Appalachian Trail
- Harriman State Park–South
- Harriman State Park–West
- Harriman State Park–North and Bear Mountain State Park
- Shawangunk Ridge Trail
- South Taconic Trail
- Windham High Peak and Blackhead Range Loop
- Escarpment Trail
- Devil's Path
- Wittenberg–Cornell–Slide Loop
- Southern Catskills
- Lake George Wild Forest
- Tongue Mountain Range Loop
- Pharaoh Lake Wilderness
- Algonquin Peak–Indian Pass Loop
- Mt. Marcy–Avalanche Pass Loop
- High Peaks Loop

Trails with Isolation

Need to get away? Trying to avoid crowds? Want a trail (mostly) to yourself? Go here.

- Taconic Crest Trail
- Western Catskills
- Allegany State Park
- West Canada Lakes Wilderness Loop
- Woodhull–Bear Lake Loop

- Ha-De-Ron-Dah Wilderness
- Cold River–Seward Range Loop
- Northville–Placid Trail

Trails with Rivers and Canyons

While every trail features streams and creeks, these offer something unique: hiking along rivers and canyons.

- Letchworth Trail
- Remsen Falls–Nelson Lake Loop
- Cold River–Seward Range Loop
- Northville–Placid Trail

Best Bang for Your Buck

This highly subjective list was tough to compile considering New York's range of superb trails, but for the miles hiked and the energy expended, these offer the best scenery.

- Harriman State Park–West
- Shawangunk Ridge Trail
- Taconic Crest Trail
- Escarpment Trail
- Wittenberg–Cornell–Slide Loop
- Southern Catskills
- Morgan Hill State Forest
- Letchworth Trail
- Lake George Wild Forest
- Pharaoh Lake Wilderness
- Remsen Falls–Nelson Lake Loop
- High Falls Loop
- Mt. Marcy–Avalanche Pass Loop

Map Legend

━━━━━	Trail	—(87)—	Interstate highways
━━━━━	Trail on road	—(9)—	U.S. highways
·········	Trail, other	—(17)—	State highways
━━━━━	River, stream	—[40]—	County highways
────────	Creek, brook	⊐	Shelter or lean-to
──H──	Waterfall	⌂	Campsite, campground, potential campsite
═╫╫╫═	Rapids	▲	Mountain summit or peak
v	View, vista overlook	⊔⊔⊔⊔	Cliffs
Ⓟ	Parking or trailhead from which description begins or ends	⊻ ⊻	Wetlands, bog, swampy
P	Parking area, trailhead	o—o	Gate
───────	Highway, road	o—o—o—o	Utility line or swath
────────	Rough, gutted, or seasonal road		Lake, pond
┼┼┼┼┼┼	Railroad	⌐ ¯ ¯ ⌐	State park, preserve, state forest, campground, or other public land
◄───	Direction of description		

Hudson Valley

Do not be fooled by this region's proximity to the New York City metropolitan area: It offers some fantastic backpacking with rugged terrain, excellent views, beautiful lakes, and surprising isolation.

It was here that people began to realize the importance of land conservation for the purpose of natural beauty and recreation on a significant scale. Much of this land was donated for the benefit of the public, resulting in the creation of Harriman, Bear Mountain, and Fahnestock state parks, among many other parks and preserves. From these public lands, the iconic Appalachian Trail was born, to become the world-famous destination it is today.

The Hudson Valley offers extensive long-distance backpacking opportunities that will only grow and improve over time. Besides the Appalachian Trail, the Long Path makes a presently incomplete journey north to the Adirondacks, and the sublime Shawangunk Ridge Trail presents countless views, pristine lakes, beautiful waterfalls, massive boulders, and tiers of dramatic cliffs.

While many people have started backpacking in the Hudson Valley, they can't stay away. The valley's superb trails and stunning scenery keep them coming back.

Trails maintained by: New York–New Jersey Trail Conference, www.nynjtc.org. Volunteers build and maintain these trails.

1. Appalachian Trail

Length: 88.4 miles in New York.

Direction of description: South to north.

Duration: 5 to 10 days.

Difficulty: Moderate to difficult.

Trail conditions: The trail is generally well-blazed and established. Boardwalks are frequently used in lower elevations and near streams or wetlands. The trail often follows old grades and crosses many roads.

Blazes: White.

Water: Generally sufficient, but can become rare in summer.

Vegetation: Mostly hardwoods with some pine and hemlock, swamps, meadows, and fields. Mountain laurel is common.

Highlights: Numerous views, lakes, ponds, rock outcrops, Fitzgerald Falls, Lemon Squeezer, Bear Mountain, Trailside Museum and Zoo, Hudson River, Bear Mountain Bridge, and historical features. Old mines, rock walls, and foundations exist along the trail.

Issues: Sections of the trail, particularly in Harriman and Bear Mountain State Parks, can be very crowded. Camping is limited to shelters and other designated campsites. Be very careful crossing the Palisades Interstate Parkway, as there are no traffic lights where the trail crosses the highway.

Location: The trail crosses southern New York, from New Jersey to Connecticut. Towns close to the trail include Greenwood Lake, Peekskill, and Pawling.

The Appalachian Trail, commonly known as the "AT," is the most famous hiking trail in the United States. This iconic footpath is one of the few that transcends the hiking community, as it is well known to even non-hikers. Not surprisingly, it is the most popular backpacking trail in New York. Because the AT has been described countless times in numerous publications, this description is somewhat abbreviated.

New York is a special place for the AT, for it was here that an idea first became a reality. The first section of the trail was built in Harriman and Bear Mountain State Parks. New York also has the lowest point of the entire trail, in the Trailside Zoo and Museum, and nowhere in the state does the AT exceed 1,500 feet in elevation. Don't let these modest elevations fool you: The AT in New York is challenging, with hilly, if not mountainous, terrain. The trail is known for its ups and downs,

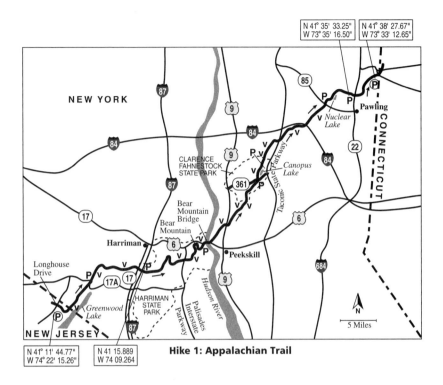

N 41° 35' 33.25"
W 73° 35' 16.50"

N 41° 38' 27.67"
W 73° 33' 12.65"

N 41° 11' 44.77"
W 74° 22' 15.26"

N 41 15.889
W 74 09.264

Hike 1: Appalachian Trail

rock slabs, outcrops, and views. The trail is also surprisingly natural and isolated, considering its close proximity to the New York City metro area. This is thanks to several generous benefactors who donated vast amounts of land to the state to create parks, which in turn hosted the trail. It may be ironic that on the outskirts of a vast, polluted, and industrial city, these people were among the first to undertake action to protect land for the purpose of natural beauty and recreation. Decades later, the AT would be born from that heritage.

Since there is no road access at the New Jersey/New York border, begin at Longhouse Road in New Jersey and head north on the trail. The terrain is hilly as the trail crosses a stream and gradually ascends a ridge. Turn left and cross the boundary into New York. Follow the top of the ridge of Bellvale Mountain, with views of Greenwood Lake from exposed bedrock. Descend along the top of the ridge. The trail becomes rolling and crosses Route 17A with a parking area. The AT continues on the ridge, passing views to the east from Cat Rocks. Wildcat Shelter is on the left before the trail drops steeply to Lakes

Road. Climb and pass scenic Fitzgerald Falls that tumbles down a crevice in the rock. For the next 7 miles, the terrain becomes more challenging and hilly as the trail meanders up and down with some nice views. In the lower elevations, hike along wetlands, streams, and ponds. Be careful of the steep descent to Route 17 and I-87.

Follow the road to the Elk Pen trailhead. For the next 10 miles, the AT crosses beautiful Harriman State Park. The hilly terrain continues along with exposed bedrock, cliffs, big rocks, numerous views, and the famous Lemon Squeezer. From Elk Pen, hike across a meadow and then make a long, and at times steep, 500-foot vertical ascent. Descend to beautiful Island Pond with great views across the water. Climb again and reach Lemon Squeezer, where the trail enters a narrow, slanted crevice in the rock that requires some scrambling. (There is a bypass trail.) Climb to an intersection with the Long Path in a scenic forest.

Hills continue to the Fingerboard Shelter, off to the right, and follow a ridge with some partial views. Descend steeply to Seven Lakes Drive, followed by a long, gradual climb. After a descent, reach the Brien Memorial Shelter on the left. Continue to follow the crest of hills. The next highlight is the steep climb up Black Mountain with several superb views from south-facing cliffs. Enjoy views of Silvermine Lake and even the Manhattan skyline. Descend to the Palisades Interstate Parkway, which you must cross without a traffic light. The cars drive fast, so watch the traffic carefully.

Cross a stream and ascend to West Mountain, featuring a dramatic ridge with several views to the west. The trail can be crowded starting at West Mountain, and can remain so until the Bear Mountain Bridge. Enter Bear Mountain State Park and drop to Seven Lakes Drive. A long, gradual climb up to Bear Mountain follows, with more excellent vistas from bedrock slabs and cliffs. Hike the crest of Bear Mountain to Perkins Tower and more fine views. All of the trails on and around Bear Mountain can be very popular and are often crowded.

Now begins the long, 1,200-foot vertical descent off Bear Mountain. Keep in mind a section of the AT descending the mountain will be rerouted in the future and trail work was ongoing when I did this hike. After a quick descent from the tower, the trail is level and rolling as it crosses some park roads. Descend more steeply and reach a park road, which the AT follows to the right; this road ends at a cul-de-sac. The rerouted AT will be from Perkins Tower down to this cul-de-sac. A long, winding descent follows over an incredibly well-built trail involving steps, grades, and stone retaining walls across the rocky and steep slope of Bear Mountain. Pass a seasonal stream and falls off to your left. The trail meanders down through boulders before leveling off and reaching playing fields, playgrounds, and Hessian Lake. The AT follows the shore of the lake, passes Bear Mountain Inn, and then turns into a picnic area. The AT goes under U.S. 9W and U.S. 202. Enter the Trailside Zoo; if the zoo is closed, follow the side trail. The AT goes through the small zoo, passing various animals and exhibits. The most popular spot is the bear pen, which is also the lowest place along the entire AT, at 124 feet in elevation. Leave the zoo and reach U.S. 6 and the Bear Mountain Bridge. Cross U.S. 6.

Turn right and cross the bridge over the Hudson River, which is also a fjord carved by glaciers. Turn left onto NY 9D and then enter the woods of Hudson Highlands State Park. From here to Connecticut, the nature of the trail changes a little. While still very hilly, the trail is not quite as rugged, there are not as many views, and it is more wooded. The AT also becomes more pastoral, with fields, meadows, and stiles as it nears Connecticut.

Climb up stone steps and reach the top of the ridge. A trail to the right leads to Anthony's Nose and its incredible view over the Hudson River and Bear Mountain Bridge. Descend 300 vertical feet to the Hemlock Springs campsite, and ascend again to a rolling ridge. Other state park trails intersect the AT. Enjoy the fine views from a side trail at White Rock, overlooking the Hudson River. Descend from the ridge, cross boardwalks at a pasture, and reach NY 403/ U.S. 9.

Ascend slightly, crossing a few roads, one of which leads .4 mile to the Graymoor Spiritual Life Center, a place where the friars and sisters allow long-distance hikers to camp. It is popular among thru-hikers. The AT continues along the rolling, wooded ridge with a fine view from Denning Hill that looks south and includes the Manhattan skyline. Cross a road and ascend to Canopus Hill with another nice view. Soon thereafter, enter Fahnestock State Park with its hilly, rocky, wooded terrain, old mines, wetlands, ponds, and streams. Several other state park trails intersect the AT. Cross NY 301 and hike above scenic Canopus Lake, culminating with a view down the lake. A side trail leads to a campground. Continue along the ridge and enjoy the excellent views to the east from Shenandoah Mountain. An American flag is painted on the bedrock, commonly known as Flag Rock. Cross a power line and road before descending to a camping area off the trail. The descent continues to the RPH Shelter (or Ralph's Peak Hikers' Cabin). Hike near some homes, cross and follow a road, pass under the Taconic State Parkway, and climb up the ridge of Hosner Mountain, where there are some views to the west.

Roller-coaster terrain follows above I-84, including one nice view to the west. Cross NY 52 with a parking area, and soon after cross I-84. The trail proceeds along a rolling ridge with a view and the Morgan Stewart Shelter. Descend to NY 55 before a gradual climb to beautiful Nuclear Lake, a highlight of the AT in New York. Hike along the shore, and then continue the gradual climb. Reach the crest of the ridge and descend; a side trail leads to nice views over Pawling. Another side trail goes to Telephone Pioneers Shelter and a small, tumbling stream. The steep, rocky descent continues until the trail crosses fields and reaches Route 20 at the massive and impressive Dover Oak, one of the largest trees on the entire AT. Climb along some fields with nice pastoral views and reach the top of a ridge. Descend to a large wetland. Hike around the wetland on boardwalks, but expect wet conditions. Cross train tracks at the famous Appalachian Trail stop, and then cross NY 22 followed by Hurds Corner Road.

Hike along a field and enjoy views of a circular, wooden water tower, another popular landmark on the trail. Continue through fields as the AT enters the Pawling Nature Preserve. Climb steeply up to Hammersly Ridge, and then descend gradually along the ridge as various side trails in the preserve intersect the AT. Descend more steeply to the Wiley Shelter. The parking area at Hoyt Road is a mile ahead, and the Connecticut border is just beyond the road.

• • •

Like all things, the Appalachian Trail began as an idea. And it was an idea unlike any other before it. In 1921, Benton MacKaye proposed a trail to run through the Appalachian Mountains. MacKaye's initial vision was not simply one trail, but a network of trails that would link farms and wilderness camps for city residents. By 1923, the first section of the trail was built in Bear Mountain and Harriman State Parks. Eventually, the AT would stretch almost 2,200 miles, from Springer Mountain in Georgia to Katahdin in Maine. Thousands of people volunteer about 200,000 hours every year to maintain, promote, and protect the trail. About 4 million people hike a section of it each year.

This footpath represents the true power of an idea. How a thought, like a benevolent virus, in one person's brain, can transmit and grow in the minds of countless others. No one could have predicted that a benign footpath would grow to become what it is today—a premier tourism destination, an economic engine with its own culture, traditions, and community. It is a trail so powerful that it has become iconic, reaching beyond the realm of hiking to be known by people who would never set foot on any trail. The AT has become an institution unto itself and represents the power of imagination, whether it be Benton MacKaye's or our own.

In my opinion, there is no other place in America like the AT; it is utterly unique. The trail does what no other landmark, destination, or park does: It explores the beautiful, genuine, gracious, and generous soul of the United States. The trail's magnetic attraction is not necessarily its scenery, but its people. The Appalachian Trail does not show how good we can be to each other—it shows how good we are. It illustrates the best of both our country and ourselves.

An idea also does something else: It changes and mutates, never staying the same, never perfectly preserved. Ideas expand, touch, influence, and trigger repercussions. They undermine our resistance to change and create the freedom of possibility. Benton MacKaye could have never known the influence his trail would have. He could have never known his idea would also come full circle. MacKaye's vision of a network of trails has long been a reality. The Long Trail, Long Path, Tuscarora Trail, Allegheny Trail, Great Eastern Trail, and even the Benton MacKaye Trail all connect to the AT. These footpaths link to trails even farther away. The Great Eastern Trail, stretching from Alabama to New York west of the AT, is already over half completed. These trails pass near organic farms, food co-ops, and intentional communities that are similar to MacKaye's vision.

Despite living in close proximity to the AT for much of my life in Pennsylvania, I never stepped foot on it until I found myself in Newfound Gap on the Tennessee–North Carolina border in the Great Smoky Mountains National Park. I wasn't there to go hiking, but to go to the bathroom. I walked north a few steps and saw a sign for the AT. As my eyes looked over the sign, a thought hatched from the back corridors of my mind and floated to the surface—I realized I could walk this trail all the way back home.

I had been given a key to a whole new world. A world, my mind presumed, that would be more beautiful, magical, and rewarding than I could ever imagine. Where I once saw a road and a car, I now knew of the existence of something even more. I was infected.

I walked from the bathroom and returned to my old, tan Ford Escort. I haven't been the same since.

2. Harriman State Park–South

Length: Approx. 18-mile loop.

Direction of description: Counterclockwise from Reeves Meadow Visitor Center.

Duration: $1^1/_2$ to 2 days.

Difficulty: Easy to moderate. Climbs and descents are usually gradual with rolling terrain. Vertical ascents reach up to 500 feet. Some sections are steep and rocky with scrambling. Several stream crossings do not have bridges.

Trail conditions: Trails are well established and usually well blazed, but do not have signs.

Blazes: The state park has an extensive web of trails with several colors for blazes.

Water: There are generally sufficient water sources along the trail, with many streams and springs. Warm and dry weather may reduce the number of running streams significantly.

Vegetation: Mostly hardwoods with some hemlock along the drainages. Several areas have mountain laurel.

Highlights: Many views, cliffs, outcrops, Pine Meadow Brook, Pine Meadow Lake, Cascade of Slid; Seven Hills Trail has the finest views of this circuit.

Issues: Legal camping is limited to the Stone Memorial Shelter. Some trails are very popular and crowded; parking areas also fill quickly on weekends.

Location: This circuit is located at the southern end of Harriman State Park and begins at the Reeves Meadow Visitor Center along Seven Lakes Drive, 2 miles from NY 17 at Sloatsburg.

This figure-eight loop explores the southern section of the large Harriman State Park. This hike features many views, nice streams, extensive exposed ledges and cliffs, boulders, meadows, wetlands, and a lake. Keep in mind that there is an extensive web of trails, with many interconnecting paths, and many unofficial trails. The trails are not signed. You will need to navigate the system based on the colors of the blazes.

From the Reeves Meadow Visitor Center, follow the red Pine Meadow Trail in a southwesterly direction and turn left onto the blue Seven Hills Trail. This trail climbs under hemlocks and crosses a small stream. A gradual climb follows as the trail enters a series of rock-

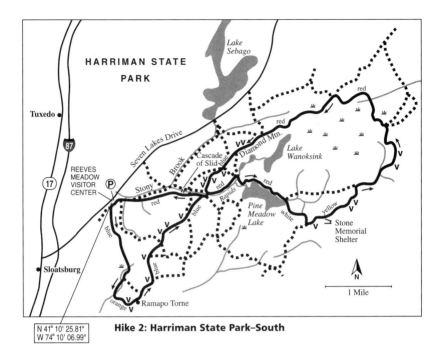

N 41° 10' 25.81"
W 74° 10' 06.99"

Hike 2: Harriman State Park–South

strewn mini-valleys that almost appear to be old excavations. The trail skirts around a wetland and crosses a small tumbling creek in a small ravine. Enter a larger, wider stream valley; the blue trail ascends to the left. Follow the orange Hillburn–Torne–Sebago Trail to the right. Cross a stream without a bridge. The trail follows the stream and crosses it again without a bridge. An increasingly steep 500-foot vertical climb follows, the largest on this hike. As you ascend, cliffs and ledges surround the trail, and the trail steepens. The terrain is rocky, although the trail itself is not that rocky. Enter what appears to have been a brush fire at the base of some cliffs. The trail steeply scrambles up ledges with pine and mountain laurel. Reach the first view overlooking rounded hills and development, and from which you can see the New York City skyline.

Another steep climb follows over boulders and ledges to the top of Ramapo Torne, where there are more fine views. The trail then traces the rolling ridge with grassy glades and more views. The blue Seven Hills Trail joins from the left, and both trails follow the same route along the rolling ridge. Make a short climb to another knob along the ridge. The blue trail leaves to the left; follow it. This juncture may be easy to miss. You are treated to more views, looking over less development. A very steep, rocky descent follows into a small, rocky valley. A gradual ascent follows to a ridge with more exposed ledges and several views, including Torne View. Descend gradually into another valley where the white Reeves Brook Trail crosses, but stay on the blue trail. A very steep climb follows with some scrambling. The trail attains the ridge again, with more views. Descend to a small stream and cross a pipeline swath. The blue trail easily ascends another ridge, Chipmunk Mountain, where my favorite view of the hike looks out from a glade of stunted trees and exposed bedrock. There is a beautiful 180-degree panorama of the Shawangunks and Catskill foothills.

Descend and pass a juncture with the orange trail. The descent continues to the red Pine Meadow Trail, a popular path in the park. Follow the red trail on a bridge across the creek and continue upstream as the scenery becomes impressive, with huge boulders, cascades, and pools. The trail moves away from the brook, passes some ruins, and meets a yellow trail. Bear right on the red trail and cross a culvert over the brook; a cascade is just upstream. The red trail soon takes you to beautiful Pine Meadow Lake.

Take some time to explore this lake, which is often bordered by cliffs and large rocks. The trail follows the north shore, offering many fine views of the lake. The trail also follows an old water line with square footers along the way. Pass the stone walls of an old building. The trail passes about four well-used campsites, the finest on this hike. However, camping here may not be permitted. Reach the end of the lake and bear right onto the white Conklins Crossing Trail, leaving the red Pine Meadow Trail. The white trail crosses a stream and begins a gradual climb through thickets of mountain laurel. The white trail ends at the yellow Suffern–Bear Mountain Trail, where you turn left. Follow the escarpment of Ramapo Mountain as the trail passes the Egg, a rounded rock outcrop with a view. Descend into a small stream valley, and then climb quickly up to the Stone Memorial Shelter, the only legal campsite on this hike. The shelter is dingy and made of stone. There are some places to pitch a tent nearby.

The trail continues along the rolling ridge, with some views to the east from ledges and meadows. Reach the red Pine Meadow Trail again at a stream and bear right; the trail is now blazed both red and yellow. Descend steeply into a glen; before reaching the cascading stream, the red trail leaves to the right. Continue on the yellow trail across the stream, followed by a steep climb up Panther Mountain with some views. The trail descends to a valley and becomes increasingly rocky before meeting the red Tuxedo–Mt. Ivy Trail at a four-way intersection. Turn left onto the red trail. Follow this trail for about 2.5–3 miles as it meanders along wetlands, crosses streams, and climbs over small hills and knobs with ledges and mountain laurel. Various old forest roads intersect the trail.

Return to the blue Seven Hills Trail and turn left. The blue trail does not disappoint as it ascends Diamond Mountain with several nice views to the northwest, where you can see Lake Sebago and the Catskills. Follow the bedrock spine of this mountain, where there are even views to the south and east. You can see the New York skyline. Along the way, you'll pass orange and yellow trails, but stay on the blue trail. As you proceed south, there are some fine views to the southwest, but the terrain becomes much steeper and more rugged. Carefully descend over a series of ledges and along the top of cliffs. Reach the white Kakiat Trail at the bottom of the valley, along Pine Meadow Brook.

To complete the loop, you have some options. You can proceed right down the white trail to the yellow Stony Brook Trail, and then to the red Pine Meadow Trail back to the parking area. These trails are closer to the creek and are probably more scenic. These trails are also closer to the Cascade of Slid, a long series of cascades over jumbled boulders where the valley narrows. Be careful hiking these trails when the creeks are high, or in icy conditions. Or, you can turn left onto the white trail, and then turn right onto the red trail where it crosses the bridge. Follow the red trail as it stays above the creek on an old grade. You can still see the Cascade of Slid via a short side hike on the orange trail. The yellow trail joins the red trail where there are some nice rapids and scenic boulders along the creek. Reach the Reeves Meadow Visitor Center to complete your hike.

•   •   •

My alarm tore through the warm solace of night, shredding my slumber with each incessant beep. I slowly got out of bed, fighting its gravitational pull. I drove away from home as the first light of dawn began to spread across the horizon.

A few hours later I was in Harriman State Park, walking along a trail that meandered through small stream valleys with slopes covered with angular rocks and ledges. The hardwood forests were bare and almost forlorn, waiting to wake from a long, hard winter.

I began the steep climb up to Ramapo Torne. My thighs burned as my breath deepened. I finally reached the crest of the ridge and turned to my right. There was the skyline of New York City, floating in the haze. It took my breath away for a second. I had not been to the city in about twenty years, and I thought this may have been the first time I had seen the skyline since 9/11. My memory tried to recreate the Twin Towers, but in their place rose the Freedom Tower.

I stood still as the chilled wind buffeted me. The city almost seemed like an alien world with its massive phalanx of towers and buildings. I thought about all the wealth and celebrity that was in that city at that very second, and just below that flawless veneer, all the poverty, decay, and hopelessness. I turned away and continued my hike. That contradiction cannot live on the trail, for all things are equal in the vast cathedral of nature.

 # 3. Harriman State Park–West

Length: 22-mile loop.

Direction of description: Counterclockwise from Elk Pen/Arden Valley Road trailhead.

Duration: 1 1/2 to 2 days.

Difficulty: Moderate. There is some brief scrambling and steep, rocky ascents and descents. Most climbs are between 100 and 300 vertical feet.

Trail conditions: Good. Trails are generally well established but do not have signs. There are many intersections, which can be confusing.

Blazes: Various colors.

Water: Generally sufficient. Trails pass several lakes and streams.

Vegetation: Mostly open hardwoods with understory of lowbush blueberry or mountain laurel; some hemlock and pine.

Highlights: Cascades on Stahahe Brook, Green Pond, views, large boulders, old mines, lakes, Lemon Squeezer, and Island Pond.

Issues: Camping is limited to the shelter areas; some trails are crowded on weekends. Trails do not have signs, and there are many intersections.

Location: This hike begins at Arden Valley Road, near Arden, New York.

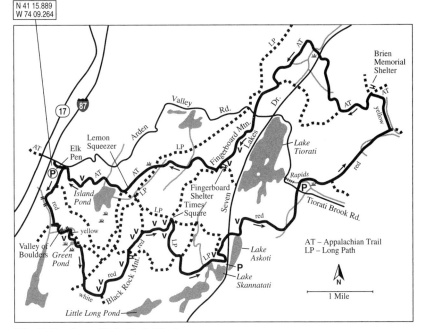

N 41 15.889
W 74 09.264

Brien
Memorial
Shelter

Valley Rd.

Lemon
Squeezer

Elk
Pen

Island
Pond

Lake
Tiorati

Rapids

Fingerboard
Shelter
Times
Square

Tiorati Brook Rd.

Valley of
Boulders

Green
Pond

AT – Appalachian Trail
LP – Long Path

Lake
Askoti

Lake
Skannatati

N

1 Mile

Little Long Pond

Hike 3: Harriman State Park–West

This loop is probably my favorite in Harriman State Park since it affords the most isolation, but also has the scenic features that make the park famous. Of course, isolation is a relative term considering the proximity of the park to a metropolitan area. Expect some trails to have traffic, particularly at Island Pond, Lemon Squeezer, Black Rock Mountain, and along the Appalachian Trail. Most backpackers utilize the Appalachian and Ramapo–Dunderberg Trails. There may also be competition for campsites in the warmer months.

From the parking area along Arden Valley Road, follow the Appalachian Trail (AT) in an easterly direction across a meadow. Enter the woods, and the AT turns to the left to begin an ascent; this will be your return. Proceed straight on a trail marked with red triangles. This level trail follows an old grade, with views of the meadow and mountain. A tall, rusted fence lines the trail. Traffic can be heard from I-87. The red triangle trail turns to the left; continue straight on Stahahe Brook Trail, marked with red stripes. This trail is also level until it reaches scenic Stahahe Brook with its many cascades and small falls. The forest is mostly hardwoods; many of the large hemlocks are dying.

The trail climbs above the cascading brook—you never really get close to it—and enters an interesting forest carpeted with moss. Meet the white Nurian Trail, on which you will turn left. The Nurian Trail begins a steeper climb and passes through a windblown forest. Enter a beautiful glen covered with massive boulders; there is a small stream with a cascading falls. Cross the creek and climb under cliffs and ledges up into a glen; there is a seasonal 30-foot falls off to your left. Enter the Valley of Boulders, a level area surrounded by massive boulders, and you'll see the small stream that creates the seasonal falls. The trail begins a steeper climb up between large boulders. Make a sharp right and hike up a bedrock ridge with views and some hemlock and pine trees. Keep a close eye on the trail in this area, as there are several turns that are easy to miss. Reach a juncture with the yellow Dunning Trail; you can take this trail to see Green Pond, but you can also see it from the white trail. The pond is small and surrounded by reeds, but very scenic. The yellow trail briefly intersects the white trail, then separates and descends into a small valley, only to soon meet the white trail once again. Follow the white Nurian Trail to the right as it tunnels through a beautiful forest of pine, hemlock, and laurel.

The forest opens up to hardwoods, and the trail enters a rocky valley. The White Bar Trail, also marked white, enters from the left and joins the white Nurian Trail for a short distance; keep an eye out for where the Nurian Trail leaves the White Bar Trail and descends to a small stream. The Nurian Trail climbs up rocks and ledges to the ridge of Black Rock Mountain, where it meets the red Ramapo–Dunderberg Trail (RDT), on which you turn left. The RDT is one of the premier trails in Harriman, extending the length of the park, and is popular with backpackers. Follow the RDT for about 2 miles along the crest of Black Rock and Hogencamp Mountains, passing many excellent views, grassy savannahs, and exposed bedrock. Along the way, pass Bald Rocks Shelter; there are several places to pitch a tent nearby. The terrain here is rolling, and the scenery is beautiful. The RDT descends steeply to Times Square, a five-way trail intersection marked with a large boulder.

Turn right and follow the green Long Path, one of New York's longest trails. The trail meanders through a scenic forest, and then drops into a small stream valley framed by large boulders. Cross beneath Cape Horn, a prominent rock outcrop, and descend to an intersection with the yellow Dunning Trail. Stay on the Long Path across rolling terrain before making a gradual descent to a scenic stream. Beautiful Lake Skannatati soon comes into view, and the trail passes a large parking area off Seven Lakes Drive. The easily accessible trails close to this parking area are popular with dayhikers. Leave the Long Path and turn left onto a red trail that makes a gradual climb up a rocky slope with a mild scramble. Follow the ridge to a nice view of the lakes below. The red-blazed Red Cross Trail intersects just before the view and is easy to miss; turn right onto it. Although you'll find that this trail is not as well established and the blazing is infrequent, follow it as it enters a hardwood forest. Descend gradually and cross Seven Lakes Drive.

Continue descending and cross the inlet to the picturesque Lake Askoti. The trail ascends up along ledges; again, the trail can be a little hard to follow, but you'll enjoy some nice views from the ridge. The trail levels and crosses a power line before descending into laurel and crossing a small stream. Turn left onto an old woods road; a quarter mile later, the old Hasenclever Road joins from the right. The trail soon reaches some old mines with water-filled pits. Follow the old woods road, and you'll see some potential campsites. Cross a small stream and reach Tiorati Brook Road. After crossing the road and a field, you'll enter some woods. The trail hops across rocks over a stream; look upstream to your left for a view of the cascades. The trail is level and can be wet in places as it crosses the streams. Begin a mild ascent as the trail enters thick mountain laurel that nearly crowds the trail. Descend into another rock-strewn valley, where you'll cross another stream as you continue your descent. Reach a yellow trail and turn left onto it. You went too far if you cross a footbridge over a creek.

The yellow trail ascends to a scenic glen ringed with ledges and big rocks. The yellow trail levels off, passes campsites, and reaches the AT and Brien Memorial Shelter. The remainder of this hike follows the AT to the left, back to the parking area, winding up Letterock Mountain before descending over ledges. The RDT branches off to the left; stay on the AT as it descends into another valley with an open hardwood forest. Cross Seven Lakes Drive; the trail skirts a pine plantation and crosses a footbridge over a creek. An ascent follows as it becomes increasingly steep up Stockbridge Mountain; the AT turns left and follows sidehill for a more gradual ascent. Reach the ridge and cross an outlet stream from a swamp. Descend into a rocky valley with a small stream before another climb. The AT crosses a paved park road at a blind curve, and then passes some water tanks as it climbs more steeply up to the ridge of Fingerboard Mountain, passing grassy meadows and some partial views. A blue side trail to the left leads to Fingerboard Shelter. The trail descends into the valley of Surebridge Brook, where you'll see evidence of old mine pits, culm piles, a stream, and a wetland. The valley is framed with ledges. Despite the mining history, it is scenic and interesting. Climb away from the brook and cross a minor ridge. The trail descends into a beautiful mini-valley with cliffs and some large trees. Reach the intersection with the Long Path in a scenic forest. The AT meanders across interesting terrain with bedrock depressions filled with wetlands and bogs.

Ascend Island Pond Mountain, with more partial views and grassy meadows. Exposed cliffs and a chasm loom on the left as you descend steeply toward the famous Lemon Squeezer; a short side trail bypasses a difficult scramble. The "squeeze" itself is not that tight, but it is slanted, so it is awkward to pass through. Huge boulders mark the entrance of the Lemon Squeezer. After the Squeezer, descend into another valley, and then ascend a slope of gorgeous Island Pond. The AT stays away from the shore, but obvious side trails lead to beautiful views. Cross over the sluice and stonework at the pond's outlet. The trail makes a quick climb and then a short descent to cross an access road. Turn left onto an old woods road; the trail climbs again to the top of Green Pond Mountain, where you will find more lovely views. A long descent follows with a 500-foot elevation change, the most dramatic of the entire circuit. Watch your step on this descent, but it is not particularly difficult. The trail reaches the meadow at which you began; your car is just ahead.

• • •

The early spring sun felt intensified through a magnifying glass as it pierced the bare forest canopy. The leaves on the mountain laurel thickets reflected like ripples on a pond. Even the gray trunks of the trees seemed to reflect light. My sunburned skin welcomed the warmth, as my eyes squinted to try to protect themselves. To my surprise, I had most of this hike to myself. I walked along the famous Appalachian Trail, alone. I passed through shaded valleys as towering ash and poplar trees tried to compete with cliffs and ledges. Wild turkeys scampered along a stream and disappeared into the forest. I contorted and bent my body through the Lemon Squeezer. I had been there once many years before, but I remembered nothing else from that hike.

I reached Island Pond at twilight, as ribbons of clouds and a horizon of orange reflected off the mirrored surface. The reflection slowly lost color and light. I sat there, welcoming the darkness and wanting to see what else it revealed. When I continued down the trail, I intentionally walked without my headlight, the white blazes becoming apparitions on the skin of trees. I made my way along the trail, watching for any rock or root, squinting for any last sliver of light. The lights of a town blinked through the trees; it felt like a vision from a thousand miles away.

I finally pulled out my headlight as I made my way across a meadow. My car was the last in a once-filled parking lot. Nearby was the low growl of the interstate as infinite columns of cars and trucks swept along in a current of red and white. I was surrounded by everyone, but felt as if I had this entire park to myself.

4. Harriman State Park–North and Bear Mountain State Park

Length: 21-mile loop.

Direction of description: Counterclockwise from the Long Path trailhead on U.S. 6.

Duration: 1½ to 2 days.

Difficulty: Moderate.

Trail conditions: Trails generally are well marked and established, although they do not usually have signs. Expect many trail intersections.

Blazes: Various. Long Path is blazed green/aqua; the Appalachian Trail is blazed white.

Water: Generally plentiful.

Vegetation: Forests are mostly hardwoods with occasional understory of mountain laurel. There are some areas with pine.

Highlights: Several lakes and ponds, excellent views, Bear Mountain, Trailside Museum and Zoo, Popolopen Gorge, historical features, Turkey Hill Lake.

Issues: Camping is limited to shelter areas and the trails around Bear Mountain are very popular and often crowded. Numerous trail intersections can lead to confusion. Hikers will have to navigate by following the various trail markers and blazes. There is noise from roads and highways along this loop. Backpackers must cross the Palisades Interstate Parkway without any traffic lights.

Location: This hike can be accessed off U.S. 6 in Harriman State Park.

This enjoyable loop contains the standard scenery of Harriman State Park, with views from bedrock ledges, rocky valleys, and several lakes. Added bonuses are impressive Bear Mountain and Popolopen Gorge.

From the parking area, follow the green Long Path in a southerly direction across U.S. 6 and onto an old woods road. The trail descends, leaves the old road, and bears right to cross a small stream in a rock-strewn valley. A gradual ascent follows to the ridge with a campsite and the impressive Cave Shelter, a rock outcrop with overhanging ledges and a stone fireplace. A steep rocky climb follows, to the top of the ridge with a view to the west. Reach the Stockbridge Shelter, one of the nicest in the park, near the bedrock summit of the ridge. Descend over ledges and reach a small valley. Turn onto the yellow Menomine Trail, which joins from the left. The yellow trail descends into the valley, reaching a pine plantation and views of beautiful Lake Nawahunta. The trail leaves the lake and soon reaches Seven Lakes Drive. As you cross the drive and pass some gravestones, to your right is a large, abandoned parking area. Cross an old road and

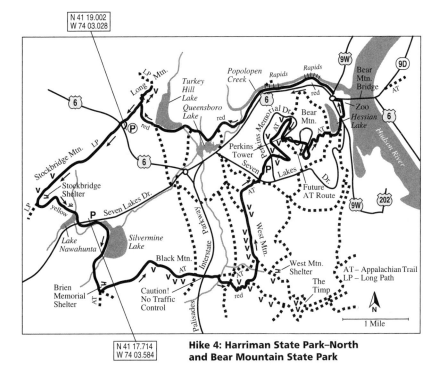

N 41 19.002
W 74 03.028

N 41 17.714
W 74 03.584

Hike 4: Harriman State Park–North and Bear Mountain State Park

enter a picnic area. The trail reaches a parking area, crosses a stream at the inlet of Silvermine Lake, and passes some buildings and old ski slopes. The trail meanders above the shore of the lake (as you hike, you'll get better views), and then moves away from the lake and enters a valley with some wet areas. Reach an unmarked trail; bear left and continue on the yellow trail. A steady ascent over loose rock follows, and the trail is surrounded by mountain laurel. Reach the top of the ridge and the William Brien Memorial Shelter.

Turn left onto the Appalachian Trail (AT) and red Ramapo–Dunderberg Trail (RDT), and make a steep, rocky ascent up to a forested ridge. Descend into a small valley and cross the old Silvermine Road, an interesting historic feature now paved with moss and still supported with stone retaining walls. Cliffs loom overhead as you cross a small stream. The AT/RDT makes another short, rocky ascent to the crest of Black Mountain, where each view is grander than the last: Silvermine Lake, rolling hills to the south, the Hudson River, and the New York City skyline. Descend steeply from the ridge, cross a small stream, and pass the blue 1779 Trail. These numerical trails are the historic routes the British and Americans took in the Revolutionary War in the attacks on Fort Clinton and Fort Montgomery. The AT descends to the Palisades Interstate Parkway. There is no bridge, so you must cross all four lanes of traffic. Thankfully, there is a forested median to provide a respite from dodging traffic.

Here the AT and RDT separate; follow the RDT to the right as it descends and crosses a new footbridge over a creek. Bear left onto a wider grade, which also serves as a bike trail. Continue to follow the RDT as it leaves the bike trail to the right for a steep ascent via stone steps. Cross another bike path and continue the steep climb through mountain laurel. The trail levels off in an open forest, allowing you to catch your breath before beginning a steeper, rockier climb over ledges. You'll be rewarded with a series of nice views from the exposed ledges.

Bear left onto the yellow Suffern–Bear Mountain Trail. If you want more miles—and more views—continue on the RDT, and then turn left on the blue Timp–Torne Trail (although most of the views are similar to what you have already seen). The blue Timp–Torne Trail will take you back to the Suffern–Bear Mountain Trail. This will add about 2.5 more miles onto your hike.

Otherwise, continue on the yellow Suffern–Bear Mountain Trail as it follows a grassy ridge with stunted trees; parts of the trail are brushy, but the trail is obvious. Descend into a small valley with a stream, and then climb back out to meet up with the blue Timp–Torne Trail, onto which you turn left. The blue trail crosses near glades before reaching the AT at a nice view, where you turn right. You will be following the AT all the way to the Bear Mountain Bridge. The AT follows the ridge of West Mountain for about a mile with many fine views to the west. Descend from the ridge with superb views of Bear Mountain and Anthony's Nose before beginning a winding descent, with some steep sections, to the 1777 Trail and Seven Lakes Drive.

Cross the drive and begin a steep, 200-foot vertical ascent to a rocky ridge with some partial views; then descend and cross Perkins Memorial Drive. The AT follows an old paved road, and then makes a sharp left up a staircase around boulders and ledges. As you ascend, great views become more common from the exposed ledges, culminating in a wide panorama to the west, where you can see U.S. 6 winding through the mountains. The AT ascends slightly through the woods, following a wider gravel path, and then reaches nice views of the Hudson River to the north. Hike the crest of Bear Mountain to Perkins Tower and more fine views. All of the trails around and on Bear Mountain can be very popular and are often crowded.

Now begins the long, 1,200-foot vertical descent off Bear Mountain. Keep in mind a section of the AT descending the mountain will be rerouted in the future; trail work was ongoing when I did this hike. After a quick descent from the tower, the trail is level and rolling as it crosses some park roads. Descend more steeply and reach a park road, which the AT follows to the right; this road ends at a cul-de-sac. (The rerouted AT will be from Perkins Tower down to this cul-de-sac.) A long, winding descent follows over an incredibly well-built trail involving steps, grades, and stone retaining walls across the rocky and steep slope of Bear Mountain. Pass a seasonal stream and falls off to your left. The trail meanders down through boulders before leveling off and reaching playing fields, playgrounds, and Hessian Lake. The AT follows the shore of the lake, passes Bear Mountain Inn, and then turns into a picnic area. The AT goes under U.S. 9W and U.S. 202, and then through the small Trailside Zoo, passing various animals and exhibits. The most popular spot is the bear pen, which is also the lowest spot along the entire AT, at 124 feet in elevation. (If the zoo is closed, follow the side trail.) Leave the zoo and reach U.S. 6 and the Bear Mountain Bridge. Cross U.S. 6.

Here, leave the AT and turn left, following U.S. 6 to a traffic circle. Bear right at the circle and continue along U.S. 9W. Before reaching the bridge, look for a red trail across the road and cross carefully. This red trail is the Popolopen Gorge Trail. Hike along old grades down to views of Popolopen Creek, where you'll reach a nice falls and impressive rapids. The trail never gets very close to the creek, but you can see it when the leaves are off the trees. Popolopen Creek is a beautiful place, with big boulders, rapids, and pools. In high water, it is a favorite of whitewater kayakers. It is well worth your time to hike down to the creek to take a break and enjoy the scenery. When you're ready to continue, climb steeply away from the creek and follow a series of wood roads high above the creek and just below U.S. 6. Keep an eye on the blazes. When you reach one "Y," the trail bears right. Enter a hemlock forest and you'll see a juncture with a blue trail, which goes down to a footbridge over the creek, another nice place to take a break. Otherwise continue straight on the red trail; a blue trail, and the 1779 and 1777 Trails also follow the same route. Even though many other named trails follow the same route, your return hike back to the Long Path is along the Popolopen Gorge Trail.

The trail passes along the West Point boundary and descends to Queensboro Brook, where there is an island. Cross over the brook via a water pipe encased in cement. Old concrete walls surround the creek and appear to be part of an old water supply project. Hike across level terrain through a scenic forest of pine and hemlock, which eventually becomes dominated by hardwoods. Turn left on an old woods road and then bear right off the old road; the blue Timp–Torne Trail leaves to the left. Here the path follows a route of the Continental Army during the Revolutionary War; there are several signs describing its historical significance. The trail passes near a firing range and soon reaches beautiful Queensboro Lake. Cross a small stream (with potential camping) and begin a mild ascent. The 1779 Trail leaves to the left, and the red trail climbs higher, above a glen with cascades. Cross a creek and hike below an earthen dam. Climb up along the dam and reach scenic Turkey Hill Lake, probably the most picturesque of all the lakes on this hike. Mountains rise over the lake, which has a sense of isolation the others lack. The trail follows the shore fairly closely, with many views over the water.

Pass a white trail to the left, and the red trail begins to move away from the lake, crossing small streams with potential camping. A steady, gradual, 250-foot vertical climb follows up to the ridge of Long Mountain. Meet the green Long Path in a mini-valley, where the red Popolopen Gorge Trail comes to an end. To see the views from the crest of Long Mountain, turn right. This is a 200-foot vertical climb over some steep, rocky slopes, but the view is worth it: You can see to the west, south, and east. Turkey Hill Lake lies below as Bear Mountain rises in the distance; Black Mountain is to the south. You can see many of the places where you hiked on this loop. At the view is the Torrey Memorial, etched in the bedrock; Raymond H. Torrey was a hiking and outdoors advocate in the 1920s and '30s who supported the Long Path. Retrace your steps and follow the green Long Path back to the parking area where you began.

• • •

We backpack to experience isolation, scenery, and wildlife. Sometimes we are critical of the masses of people on popular trails, likening it to an invasion of places we would otherwise hold dear. Regardless of whether a trail is packed with people or only caters to one, we are all strangers to those who call it home. And with a change of perspective, the stories of those you pass on the trail can be as rewarding as any wildlife sighting. Besides, is it better for all these people to be on the trail or in the mall? That crying kid you passed a few minutes ago could be an Appalachian Trail thru-hiker in fifteen years, or an advocate for the environment and our public lands. The popular trails are where most of us begin, introducing countless people to the sacredness of nature. Hiking is as much a journey through humanity as it is through landscapes.

I began this hike alone until I reached the Stockbridge Shelter, where several friendly college-age men were just getting up. I hiked along Silvermine Lake and began my descent as several women flew by me, trail running down the rocky slope with the sure and measured steps of a deer. Black Mountain brought views and a man and woman who did not seem to know each other well but were hiking together as part of a hiking club. The man's parents were professors who were originally from Israel and moved to America in the late 1950s for better opportunities; he was born soon after, but visits Israel every year. The man marveled at the antiquity that exists in Israel as compared to America and spoke at length about the Wailing Wall. I tried to listen as best I could while watching for rocks. The woman seemed more interested in hearing his parents' story and why they came to America.

A short while later I passed several groups of Asians. Each looked at me and said an accented "Hi," with a nod and smile. As sweat glazed my skin and stained my clothes, I briefly wondered how they could look so fresh and unaffected by the conditions.

I followed a man and two women on the steep climb up West Mountain. As we reached a series of views, the man suddenly said to one of the women, "Is this the spot?" She thought for a second, and said, "Yeah, it is." This view was the place where they had taken a picture of a friend who had since died of cancer. Even to a stranger, that few feet of trail where their friend once stood felt more sacred.

At the top of Bear Mountain, several young men stretched out on a ledge, shirtless and carefree in the sun. A mother held a toddler, and another fed a baby. I made my way to Perkins Tower, where bikers with their Harleys mixed with hikers in their Merrells and hipsters in their flip-flops and skinny jeans. The descent off Bear Mountain featured a man playing a banjo, and at Hessian Lake, Muslim women in headscarves and Indian women in saris played in the field, but not with each other.

I continued on, alone again as I hiked up the Popolopen Gorge, followed the shore of Queensboro and Turkey Hill Lakes, and climbed up Long Mountain. The sun was setting and the shadows cooled the air. Although tired, I decided to hike up to the view on Long Mountain. I made it to the top as a vast panorama of pink, red, and orange spread across the sky. The colors deepened to blue and purple, and began to fade to black as the sun dissolved into the horizon.

I will never know the people I passed. They came from different continents, cultures, religions, and backgrounds. They've had experiences that are both wildly different and exactly the same as mine. But it was a simple dirt footpath that brought us together, even if for a moment, and therein lies the incredible power of the trail.

5. Shawangunk Ridge Trail

Length: 27.5-mile linear trail.

Direction of description: North to south.

Duration: 2 days.

Difficulty: Moderate.

Trail conditions: Trails are generally well established.

Blazes: The trail is blazed blue, but the trail is also blazed orange, lilac, or teal in Minnewaska State Park. Part of this route also follows the Long Path, which is blazed aqua or green.

Water: Conditions can be dry depending on the season.

Vegetation: Hardwoods, some hemlock, stunted pine and blueberry meadows at Sam's Point.

Highlights: Extensive vistas, Awosting Lake, Mud Pond, Ice Caves (via side trail), cliffs, overhangs, Rainbow Falls, Verkeerderkill Falls, Sam's Point Preserve.

Issues: Camping is very limited and prohibited in Minnewaska State Park and Sam's Point Preserve, requiring an 18-mile day. The trail can be dry, and be prepared for sun exposure. Minnewaska State Park has an extensive web of trails and various colored blazes, which can make it hard to follow this route. Some turns are easy to miss, and the trail meanders a lot through the park. It will take time to backpack through Minnewaska.

Location: Between Wurtsboro and Minnewaska State Park.

The Shawangunk Ridge Trail (SRT) is a 70-mile side trail of the Long Path. The "Gunks" are famous for their scenery, with tiers of white cliffs, towering waterfalls, sky lakes, beautiful streams, boulders, outcrops, fantastic views, and world-class rock climbing. This trail offers some of the finest scenery in all of the Gunks. The SRT begins at High Point in New Jersey, at the Appalachian Trail, and ends at the Rosendale Trestle in Rosendale, New York. The section described here is the most scenic and feasible for a backpacker, since the other sections have more roadwalking and cross more private land.

Begin at the Jenny Lane parking area off Routes 55/44 in Minnewaska State Park. Cross the road and follow the trail on a steady, gradual ascent into a hardwood forest with an understory of mountain laurel. As you climb, the trail crosses many bedrock slabs, a common feature. There are some partial views to the north. Reach a ridge and a blue state park trail; continue straight on the SRT. Follow the crest of a ridge with some views into the valley below. Cross a power line, continue along the ridge, and then descend to a carriage road. Turn right at the next intersection and cross Peters Kill Creek on a carriage road. Keep an eye to your left since the next turn is easy to miss. The SRT turns left onto an orange trail (also marked with cairns); the path is curvy as it crosses and climbs up along a series of bedrock slabs with excellent views of the Catskills to the north. Reach a ridge above Huntington Ravine and descend as a series of cliffs provide fine views. The descent steepens and you'll have to scramble some before entering a ravine and meandering along a stream lined with large hemlocks. The trail goes by the base of 50-foot-tall Rainbow Falls as they tumble from a cliff. Cross a small stream and begin to hike out of the ravine along a gradual ascent, large hemlocks towering overhead.

After crossing a carriage road, the SRT climbs to a ridge with more superb views to the north. The trail climbs under pine and hemlock before leveling off at a dramatic series of cliffs with excellent views over Awosting Lake, the Shawangunk Plateau, and the Catskills. Continue along the rim of cliffs with more fine views. The SRT reaches another carriage road and turns left (a shortcut is to the right); follow it up along the rim of cliffs, although in places the trail jumps off the road briefly. Enjoy nonstop views from the white cliffs. Pass Blueberry

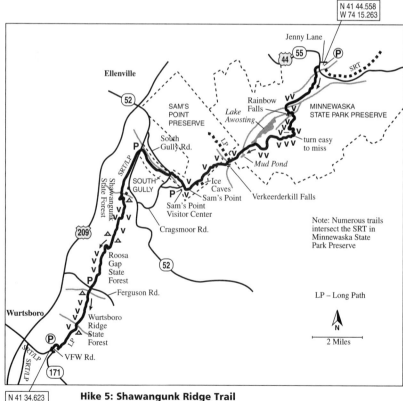

Hike 5: Shawangunk Ridge Trail

Run Trail on the left and reach Castle Point, with breathtaking views in nearly all directions. Here, the SRT makes a subtle turn to the right, heading down a series of ledges along the cliff on a trail blazed lilac or lavender; this is also known as the Scenic Trail. The scramble down is easier than it looks, although it is a little exposed. Reenter the woods and drop down to a carriage road, where the SRT turns right. Follow the road for a few hundred yards until you reach a four-way intersection. The Scenic Trail/SRT turns left and enters the woods, soon encountering a series of cliffs and an impressive over-hang where a short side trail goes through a very narrow cave. Hike across large boulders, go straight across another trail, and then over more ledges. Reach Margaret Cliff with more fine views to the south, showing the escarpment of the Shawangunks. Descend into a small valley to a trail intersection. The SRT goes right and then turns left; the trail that goes straight leads to beautiful Awosting Lake, a worth-while side trip with clear water and fine views of the cliffs and wooded hills that surround the shore. The SRT climbs to Murray Hill with more views, and then descends to another trail intersection, where it goes left while the trail straight ahead again leads a short dis-tance to Awosting Lake.

Climb up the ridge with more bedrock slabs and views, and then descend to Mud Pond and cross the outlet stream. The trail keeps its distance from the water, although you can see the pond through the trees; climb a ridge with some nice views over the shallow pond. Con-tinue the climb up the hill and enter a stunted pine forest with more views as the trail crosses into private property. The Long Path joins from the right and will follow the remainder of this route on the SRT south to Wurtsboro. Descend to the rim of impressive Verkeerderkill Falls and cross the creek above it. In high water, these falls are stun-ning. Begin a long, rocky, gradual ascent up to Sam's Point. The forest slowly changes to stunted pine and blueberry meadows with more views. Reach a gravel road; to the left is a side trail to the famous Ice Caves, formed by the separation of massive rocks, where ice lingers into the summer. It is well worth the trip if you have the time. The trail follows the road to the right and then turns left onto another gravel road where it continues through a stunted pine forest. You will come to a road to the right that leads to excellent views of the escarpment from Sam's Point, but the SRT goes straight and descends on another road, passing more views along the way. Enjoy the views of the mas-sive cliffs from the bottom. The trail winds down to the visitor center (parking is available for a fee); however, the SRT makes a sharp right onto another forest road before reaching the center.

The trail climbs gradually and soon leaves the road, entering the forest. Begin a long descent with some steep sections along a trail that is not always well established. Reach Gully Road and turn left onto it for a very short distance. Turn right off the road and enter the woods as the trail meanders in and out, up and down a series of ravines with seasonal streams. Begin the descent of South Gully, at times following an old grade. The trail crosses some side streams, although the South Gully stream remains well below the trail. Be careful, as the SRT follows eroded sidehill and the gully, or gorge, drops steeply to your right. After a short ascent, the trail continues its descent until it reaches Route 52; turn left onto the road and cross it. The trail now follows an old forest road through private land on a slight ascent. Enter state forest land and continue on the old grade, crossing over seasonal side streams. The old road begins to switchback up the mountain and reaches a yellow trail to the left, where there is some potential camping. The SRT turns right off the old road and begins to climb. The climb is not very steep, but it will make your legs burn. Hike along more bedrock slabs with fine views to the north before reaching the crest of the ridge where larger slabs provide excellent views, especially to the northeast. The trail continues along the eastern edge of the ridge as it follows the top of a series of cliffs with crevices and even some separated boulders that almost look like pedestals in the forest. Meander back and forth over the crest of the ridge, entering forests of stunted pine and birch with meadows of blueberries. This section is a pleasure to hike since it is almost rock free and has stunted forests with views.

Descend and enter mature forests interspersed with pine. The trail continues to be rock free as it crosses a level area traversed with old rock walls. This is another good option for dry camping. The trail turns right along a series of cliffs and boulders before climbing above them and reaching the top of the ridge, where you'll find more meadows, stunted forests, and views. A large warehouse dominates the valley below; a small airport is next to it. Descend from the ridge along steep and rocky terrain before reaching Ferguson Road; cross the road and continue the descent. At the bottom is a reliable stream and potential camping. A climb follows back to the ridge, and then the trail drops gradually as it goes through a spooky, burned-out forest. Reach the bottom of the valley, where a small stream and some large pine trees create an inviting campsite. The trail climbs again to the wooded ridgetop, where you'll find a fine view to the south of the valley and the Basha Kill Wildlife Management Area, its waters glistening in the distance. The trail begins a long, gradual descent, which includes a long switchback. Cross a small stream and reach a white trail to the right. Take the white trail down to the VFW and the parking area.

• • •

This was my final backpacking trip for this book. After driving for thousands of miles and hiking for hundreds, I had finally reached the end. My friends Matt, Bryan, and Ian joined me for this hike. As we got our gear together in the parking area, a young park ranger drove up to us and asked where we were hiking. We said the Shawangunk Ridge Trail to Wurtsboro, and the ranger excitedly replied that was a hike he had always wanted to do. Looking at the ranger as we spoke, I felt like I was seeing myself fifteen years ago. Even where we live and work every day there are places we don't see, things we don't do.

The sun blazed through the brisk, chilled sky. A thin layer of snow powdered the forest. We hiked quickly through the laurel and bedrock slabs that gradually revealed views to the north. Slide Mountain, one of the first hikes I did for this book, rose on the horizon, draped with frost. The trail meandered along rims of cliffs and tiers of ledges, exposing countless views from the white rocks of the Shawangunks. The Catskills rose to the north with serrated peaks and ridges. The Hudson Valley, clothed in haze, was to the east. The Taconics, dusted white, rose on the far side of the valley. The rolling Shawangunk Plateau spread out to the south, defined by a sheer escarpment of cliffs. I could see why this place has attracted people for generations.

It took much longer to hike through Minnewaska State Park than I anticipated. The trail meandered incessantly and we had to pay close attention to avoid missing a turn. By the time we reached Sam's Point, the sun was quickly setting. The questions soon came: How much farther to camp? How many miles have we done? Are we going to have to hike in the dark? I grunted my answers.

An arctic wind buffeted Sam's Point, a place that always seems colder than its surroundings. We reached the view as the sun burned out on the horizon into swirls of red and orange. New Jersey's High Point was on the southern horizon. Below us, a lone porcupine clung to a branch at the top of a tree, chewing contentedly. I wondered how it kept warm.

By the time we descended into the South Gully, it was dark and our headlamps ricocheted light off each other. There was discontent among the ranks; morale was low. It was cold, and we didn't know where we would camp. Some of us were low on water, and we were exhausted. In times like these, lying works—I said Route 52 was only a half mile away. The thought of the beer we had stashed there provided some temporary solace and the group was placated, for now.

We crossed Route 52 and Ian retrieved the hidden beer. The trail followed an old forest road, which offered some easy hiking, and we took turns hauling the beer. My eyes scanned for a place to camp, but the terrain was rocky, and we preferred to camp a little farther from the road. Finally, we came to a place where the road made a bend and there was enough space for all of us to camp. The ground was rocky, but at least it was level. I set up my tent, got a quick bite to eat, and crawled into my bag to sleep. No one stayed up. The beer sat next to a tree, forgotten.

The next morning was overcast, but warmer. We packed up and divided the beer among us. I didn't feel like carrying my ration, so I quickly drank it. My body was so hungry for calories, I didn't even feel buzzed. I had never started a day backpacking by chugging a couple of beers. Some routines are better kept.

Today's fewer miles ensured that there would not be a revolt. However, at the next road crossing, the path of least resistance proved to be too sweet. Ian and Matt decided to follow a road and rail-trail to the car. Bryan chose to stick with me and continue on the trail. Again, I saw the value in lying, telling him the two climbs on this section of the trail wouldn't be too long or steep. Bryan sighed in resignation and asked what time we'd be done; I said 2 P.M.

We reached the ridge and looked down to see an airport in the valley. As we descended again, I kept conversation to a minimum, not wanting to remind Bryan of how tired and aching he felt. The trail descended gently, as if to apologize. We reached the car at 2 P.M., proving that it is OK to tell a lie that doesn't matter, as long as you also tell a truth that does.

We convened at the Gilded Otter brewpub in New Paltz for our traditional after-hike meal. After ordering some beers, I left to go to the bathroom. When I returned, Bryan informed me there had been an intervention, and the group had decided they would have to first approve our next hiking destination. I was given clear guidelines as to mileage and expected natural features. The mutiny was complete. I accepted my place, overthrown. All good things must come to an end.

6. Long Path

Length: 356 miles from Fort Lee Historical Park in New Jersey to John Boyd Thacher State Park east of Albany. The trail is being extended farther north to Northville in the Adirondacks, where it will connect to the Northville–Placid Trail.

Direction of description: South to north.

Duration: 3 to 5 weeks.

Difficulty: Moderate to very difficult.

Trail conditions: On public lands, the trail is generally well established and blazed, although the blazes can be in a variety of colors. Extensive road walking exists between public lands. The trail occasionally follows old grades and forest roads. On private land, the trail is often harder to follow and is less established, with more briars and brush.

Blazes: Aqua or green. Signs and blazes for the Long Path can be infrequent through the Catskills since the trail follows local trails blazed red, yellow, or blue.

Water: Generally sufficient. Higher elevation ridges are usually dry.

Vegetation: Hardwoods, fields, wetlands, pine, hemlock, spruce, and fir at the higher elevations in the Catskills. Reforestation plantations are common on the northern sections of the trail.

Highlights: Palisades, Harriman State Park, Shawangunks, Catskills, John Boyd Thacher State Park. Numerous views, streams, waterfalls, ponds, excellent camping, isolation.

Issues: Extensive road walking, limited camping outside of Harriman State Park, Shawangunks, or the Catskills. The trail has been relocated over the years, particularly off of roads, so it has been difficult to keep a definitive and accurate guidebook for the trail.

Location: The trail goes through or near the following towns: Fort Lee, New Jersey; Piermont, Nyack, Mt. Ivy, Woodbury, Goshen, Wurtsboro, Wawarsing, Phoenicia, Palenville, and Middleburgh, New York.

Vincent Joseph Schaefer first imagined the Long Path (LP) in the early 1930s. He named the trail after Walt Whitman's poem, "Song of the Open Road," which contains the line, "the long brown path that leads wherever I choose." However, Schaefer imagined a very different "trail"—one that was not marked or even maintained—where hikers found their own way, with only landmarks to guide them. Raymond H. Torrey, an outdoors columnist for the *New York Post*, and W. W. Cady also assisted in the initial creation of the trail where they scouted a route to the Catskills. They hoped the trail would someday end at Whiteface Mountain in the Adirondacks.

However, the concept of an open, or undefined, trail did not prove to be viable, and the LP faded away until it was revived in the 1960s, this time with the intention to make it a traditional trail. Work began on finding routes through parks and public lands from the Palisades, through the Catskills, and north to Albany. As the years passed, trails were cleared and more sections of the trail were taken off the roads and into the woods. The process continues to this day.

Like the Finger Lakes Trail, the LP demonstrates the incredible commitment and hard work of volunteers to create a footpath over so much private land. Despite the challenges, the LP has survived and is even growing. This trail includes a truly diverse and impressive assortment of natural and scenic features. While I have not hiked the entire LP, I have hiked several sections of it. An abbreviated description is included in this guide so that hikers can be aware of this beautiful and challenging trail.

One hiking opportunity that has not received the attention it deserves is the "Great Catskills Traverse" along the LP. The LP is continuous, with little road walking, from Upper Cherrytown Road at the Sundown Wild Forest to NY 23 at the Windham High Peak Wild Forest, a distance of 94 miles. This long-distance hiking extravaganza is unlike any single trail in the state as it explores the Catskills from south to north, revealing a wonderland of summits, views, cliffs, big rocks, streams, waterfalls, spruce and fir forests, and wilderness. An added benefit for the long-distance hiker on the traverse is that services can be had in the scenic villages of Phoenicia and Palenville, and in the North/South Lake State Campground in season.

The LP begins in New Jersey's Fort Lee Historic Park, just south of the George Washington Bridge. The trail proceeds north along the impressive Palisades, with great views of New York City. Highways and urban areas surround the wooded trail corridor as it passes old foundations and roads. Entering New York, the trail follows roads between parks that feature ridges offering views over wetlands and the Hudson River. The LP continues north along this hilly ridge, which is a part of the Palisades Escarpment, culminating at High Tor State Park, with vistas in all directions. Descend to Mt. Ivy and walk the roads through town. Soon after, the LP enters Harriman State

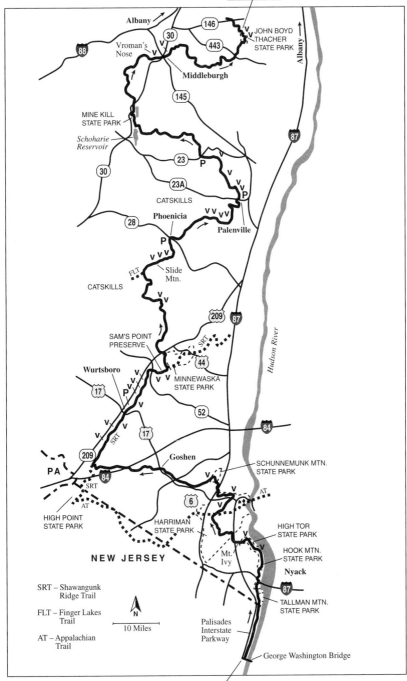

N 42° 39' 18.40"
W 74° 01' 05.62"

Albany

146

443

JOHN BOYD
THACHER
STATE PARK

30

Vroman's
Nose

Middleburgh

Albany

88

145

87

MINE KILL
STATE PARK

*Schoharie
Reservoir*

30

23

P

23A

CATSKILLS

P

28

Phoenicia

P

Palenville

FLT

Slide
Mtn.

CATSKILLS

209

87

Hudson River

SAM'S POINT
PRESERVE

SRT

44

Wurtsboro

P

MINNEWASKA
STATE PARK

17

52

84

17

SRT

Goshen

209

SCHUNNEMUNK MTN.
STATE PARK

PA

84

AT

SRT

6

AT

HIGH POINT
STATE PARK

HARRIMAN
STATE PARK

HIGH TOR
STATE PARK

HOOK MTN.
STATE PARK

NEW JERSEY

Mt.
Ivy

Nyack

87

SRT – Shawangunk
Ridge Trail

FLT – Finger Lakes
Trail

AT – Appalachian
Trail

N

10 Miles

TALLMAN MTN.
STATE PARK

Palisades
Interstate
Parkway

George Washington Bridge

Hike 6: Long Path

N 40° 51' 05.38"
W 73° 57' 47.09 "

Park, a popular area that features rugged, rocky terrain with hardwood forests and mountain laurel.

The LP passes rock outcrops, several views, lakes, and even an intersection with the Appalachian Trail. The trail continues north along Stockbridge Mountain with some views and one shelter. Cross U.S. 6 and climb Long Mountain to see the Torrey Memorial and superb views to the east and south. The LP then turns west, with rugged and steep terrain in and out of stream valleys until it leaves Harriman State Park. Continue mostly on roads to Woodbury; from there the trail heads west to the Shawangunk Ridge, between Port Jervis and the Basha Kill Wildlife Management Area.

Leave Woodbury and begin the climb into Schunnemunk Mountain State Park. This is the first significant climb on the trail, ascending over 1,000 vertical feet as the state park trails intersect. Head west along the ridge, enjoying the superb views, and enter private land as the trail descends to a scenic lake. Walk along the lake and turn onto the Heritage Trail, a rail-trail north of Monroe. Follow the Heritage Trail 11 miles to the west, through the scenic town of Goshen, and past some wetlands and ponds. Thereafter, the LP follows roads for about 14 miles through pastoral countryside.

Reach the Shawangunk Ridge and climb before descending along a valley with ponds and a stream. The Shawangunk Ridge Trail joins from the left at the bottom, and both trails head north along old grades and roads. After a short ascent, descend to the Basha Kill Wildlife Management Area, with views across this vast wetland that is home to an impressive diversity of birds. The LP is close to the wetland and can be flooded. Walk through Wurtsboro on roads and follow Route 171 to the ridge. North of Wurtsboro to Route 52 the LP follows the rugged ridge, with descents and ascents in and out of stream valleys. There are numerous views from bedrock slabs, stunted forests, and rock outcrops. The ridge is dry, but the valleys usually have some water. An old forest road leads to Route 52. Begin a climb along the South Gully Trail, above a deep gorge, as the trail enters Sam's Point Preserve. Traverse a series of ravines and reach the Sam's Point Conservation Center; the trail continues across the plateau, passing superb views from cliffs and more stunted forests. The white side trail to the Ice Caves is a worthwhile detour. Descend to the top of impressive Verkeerderkill Falls. Soon thereafter, the LP leaves the Shawangunk Ridge Trail and heads north through stunted forests of pine and blueberry meadows. Enjoy great views to the north on a long descent that steepens as the trail nears the bottom.

Follow roads for 12 miles, through Wawarsing and north to the Sundown Wild Forest at Upper Cherrytown Road. In the future, this section may be rerouted off roads and into the Vernooy Kill Wild Forest. As you reach Sundown Wild Forest, leave the road and enter Catskill Park. For the next 94 miles, the LP will traverse this beautiful area with little road walking. Keep in mind that the LP follows the various blazes of other trails, whether they be red, blue, or yellow. Signs and blazes for the LP can be infrequent. Watch for turns and carefully follow the trail maps.

Make a steady climb to Vernooy Kill Falls, where a stream tumbles over a series of ledges. The LP continues across rolling, mountainous terrain, passing small streams, before reaching a steep, 1,000-foot vertical descent to Peekamoose Road. Turn right onto the road and walk along it in the beautiful, isolated valley for three-quarters of a mile to a parking area on the left. A long, 2,600-foot vertical ascent follows to Peekamoose and Table Mountains with deep spruce forests and some great views. Descend to the East Branch Neversink River, where you will find great camping. A gradual 1,800-foot vertical climb brings you to the forested summit of Slide Mountain. The trail traverses the spectacular and rugged ridge of the Burroughs Range, with views from Cornell and Wittenberg Mountains. A new trail takes the LP along the ridge of Cross Mountain, Mount Pleasant, and Romer Mountain with occasional views. Descend via switchbacks to a small parking area on Lane Street. Follow roads through the scenic village of Phoenicia where there is a post office, restaurants, and a campground.

Now begins an isolated, rugged, and beautiful stretch of trail. From Phoenicia to Palenville is a distance of 40 miles, and there are no services close due to the few road crossings. Climb nearly 2,000 vertical feet to the summit of Tremper Mountain, passing two shelters and a fire tower at the summit with some views. Follow a ridge until a steep 1,000-foot descent to scenic Warner Creek with its cascades and slides. Be careful crossing the creek in high water. Ascend the ridge again, and then descend to Silver Hollow Notch where the LP has been rerouted on a new trail that climbs 1,500 vertical feet to Plateau Mountain. Here, the LP turns right onto the famous Devil's Path with its steep, rugged, and rocky terrain that separates a series of mountains with superb views. The trail unmercifully climbs up and over each mountain. Descend from Indian Head Mountain—the last on the Devil's Path—and drop to Platte Clove Mountain Road above an impressive falls, which can be reached by a side trail.

Rolling, and at times wet, terrain continues to the rim of Kaaterskill Clove where the trail crosses several streams with waterfalls below. The LP makes a long descent to Palenville and goes through the village via roads. A long, gradual ascent on an old grade follows out of Kaaterskill Clove. Meet the blue Escarpment Trail near the top; the LP follows this trail to NY 23 and the north boundary of Catskill Park. Hike along the escarpment of the Catskills, with many spectacular views from cliffs over the Hudson Valley. The LP passes the site of the Catskill Mountain House and goes behind the North/South Lake State Campground, where there are camping, water, restrooms, and a beach in season. Climb gradually to North Point, passing more impressive cliffs, views, rock outcrops, and ledges. It is a gorgeous trail—North Point has epic views to the south. The rolling ridge to Blackhead Mountain has occasional views, limited camping, and limited water sources. Blackhead is beautiful, but the summit is covered with spruce.

Descend steeply from Blackhead and continue along a ridge with spruce and hardwoods. There are several fine views from Acra Point and Burnt Knob. Climb to Windham High Peak with more good views, and then begin a long, mostly gradual descent to NY 23 and the limit of Catskill Park.

From this point to the end of the trail, the LP crosses more private land, there is more road walking, and camping is limited. Some sections of private land may be closed during hunting season. The trail links state forests, parks, and other public lands, but roads are often required to make the connection. Briars and brush also impact the trail.

Follow a rolling, wooded ridge on private land and descend to Route 10, and then make a steep climb into Mt. Pisgah State Forest, with some nice views to the south. Descend steeply from the ridge, cross a few small streams, and then ascend into the Ashland Pinnacle State Forest. The LP descends along a small stream to a road; walk for 3 miles along the road to a trail in private woodlands. Descend to see views of beautiful Manor Kill Falls, and then follow a road above the Schoharie Reservoir. Follow a combination of roads and trails down the valley of the Schoharie River to Mine Kill State Park, where you will find views of impressive Mine Kill Falls in a narrow chasm. Enjoy views of the reservoir below and hike past a visitor's center. Continue down the valley, and then climb into a state forest, which is an elevated plateau with steep glens and forest roads that cross the top of the plateau. The sides of the plateau are steep. The LP continues its hilly and rugged ways through Patria State Forest as it winds in and out of glens. A steep, 1,400-foot descent takes the trail out of the state forest and onto a road in the valley. Leave the road and climb up a seemingly minor ridge until you reach Vroman's Nose, a natural landmark with stunning views across a level valley surrounded by rolling mountains. Descend again, this time to the small town of Middleburgh.

Leaving Middleburgh, enter the woods as the trail makes a long 800-foot vertical ascent over hilly, if not rugged, terrain. The LP is above cliffs on the climb, with many fine views over Middleburgh. Pass small streams and drainages, and climb the ridges that separate them. The trail is mostly wooded, but there is some road walking; as the trail heads east, the terrain becomes more moderate. The trail continues to link small state forests and public lands, with roads and paths allowed on private land. The setting becomes increasingly pastoral, with some ponds and several fields in the beautiful countryside. Follow roads into John Boyd Thacher State Park, a gem along the trail. The LP explores the scenic wonders of this gorgeous park: its escarpment of cliffs, stunning views, falls, and the Indian Ladder Trail. Hike across a parking area and park road, and soon after a meadow. The trail meanders through the woods, but keep an eye out for deep crevices in the limestone bedrock, which is slowly being dissolved. Enjoy another view to the east, follow some old forest roads, cross a field, and reach a parking area at Old Stage Road. This marks the end of the formal LP. The remainder of the trail is mostly on roads to the Adirondacks.

Taconic Mountains

Lying in the shadows of the Adirondacks and Catskills, the beautiful Taconic Mountains have received little attention from backpackers. Here, trails explore vistas, cliffs, ponds, glens, and extensive forests. The most notable feature of these mountains may be the grassy balds that cover a couple of the summits, creating a setting like those found in the Southern Appalachians. Not even the Catskills feature such gorgeous open summits. If you are looking for a challenging backpack off the beaten path, this is the place to go.

The Taconic Crest Trail is maintained by the Taconic Hiking Club, www.taconichikingclub.org. The South Taconic Trail is maintained by the New York–New Jersey Trail Conference, www.nyn jtc.org. These trails are built and maintained by volunteers.

⚇ 7. South Taconic Trail

Length: 15.7-mile linear trail.

Direction of description: South to north.

Duration: 1¹/₂ to 2 days.

Difficulty: Moderate to difficult. This hike requires some steep climbs and some scrambling over ledges.

Trail conditions: Trails are well established.

Blazes: White.

Water: There are generally sufficient water sources along the trail; however, in dry periods water may be limited to Bash Bish Brook.

Vegetation: Mostly hardwoods with some pine and hemlock often along streams. There are grassy balds at the summits.

Highlights: Superb views, scenic streams, grassy balds at the summits, Bash Bish Falls.

Issues: Camping opportunities are limited on this trail; sections of it, particularly Bash Bish Falls and Alander Mountain, can be crowded with dayhikers on weekends from the spring to fall.

Location: The trail goes from Catamount Ski Area to north of Millerton, New York.

The South Taconic Trail (STT) is a wonderful trail offering several scenic features over its modest number of miles. The trail meanders back and forth over the New York–Massachusetts border. Sections of this trail are very popular with dayhikers; however, for some reason there is not a lot of traffic from backpackers. As a result, you will have some sections of this trail to yourself.

The STT is being extended south about 6 miles to the Taconic State Park–Rudd Pond Area in Millerton, New York. The new trail being built by the New York–New Jersey Trail Conference promises some beautiful scenery and should be complete in 2016. This new extension should make the STT a superb backpacking destination.

From the trailhead along Quarry Hill Road (in a spacious housing development), the trail makes a gradual climb that steepens as it ascends. Hike above a ravine under hardwoods and some pine; you can hear waterfalls when the creek is running. The trail meets the small stream at some huge boulders as cascades plummet over ledges and cliffs. The stream is small and usually just a trickle, but after a heavy rain it would be a sight to behold. Turn left, away from the stream at the highest cascade, and begin a series of scrambles over steep, exposed ledges. The terrain is very difficult and potentially dangerous in winter with ice. The terrain moderates a little as the trail climbs over a series of sloping ledges with many nice views of the valley and ridges. Reach the top of the glen as the small stream babbles off to your right. Up to this point, this was a 900-foot vertical climb.

The STT bends left and continues to ascend, but more moderately along the edge of the ridge. The trail bears right and a steep climb resumes; this one is about 400 vertical feet. The forest continues to be mostly hardwoods, and the trail crosses several exposed ledges. As you ascend, the trees become more stunted, and the trail passes grassy glades. Reach some nice views to the west, east, and over Riga Lake to the south. The trail is marked with cairns. The ascent continues to a knob with views to the east and more exposed ledges. A gradual descent into a col is promptly followed by a climb up to Mt. Brace, a highlight of the trail. The trail follows a ridge with glades, stunted oak trees, and several nice views. This culminates at the dramatic summit of Mt. Brace, where there is a huge rock pile and windsock. The exposed, grassy summit offers views in all directions, including Mt. Frissell and Round Mountain to the east, the Berkshires and Mt. Greylock to the north, and the Hudson Valley and Catskills to the west. This is a beautiful place to camp, but it is both dry and exposed. This is also a popular spot for paragliders.

The STT descends from the summit along a wide trail, following a ridge with more glades and stunted trees. In the col, reach a four-way intersection with a jeep trail to the right; continue straight on the trail, passing the Mt. Frissell Trail to the right. The STT keeps to the right of the more exposed ridge, where there are some impressive views via a side trail. The trail appears to follow an old woods road as it descends slightly through the woods for a mile to the Loop Trail on the right. This section of the trail can be wet from several springs. After a short climb, another gradual descent follows to a small seasonal stream with potential camping. Pass the Robert Brook Trail to the left and continue a descent, passing small streams along the way to Gentz's Corner, where the Loop Trail meets to the right. The STT goes left and descends toward the Alander Brook Trail along an old forest grade, only to turn right again and make a steep, eroded climb back up to Alander Mountain. The trail follows an exposed ridge to the summit with nonstop views.

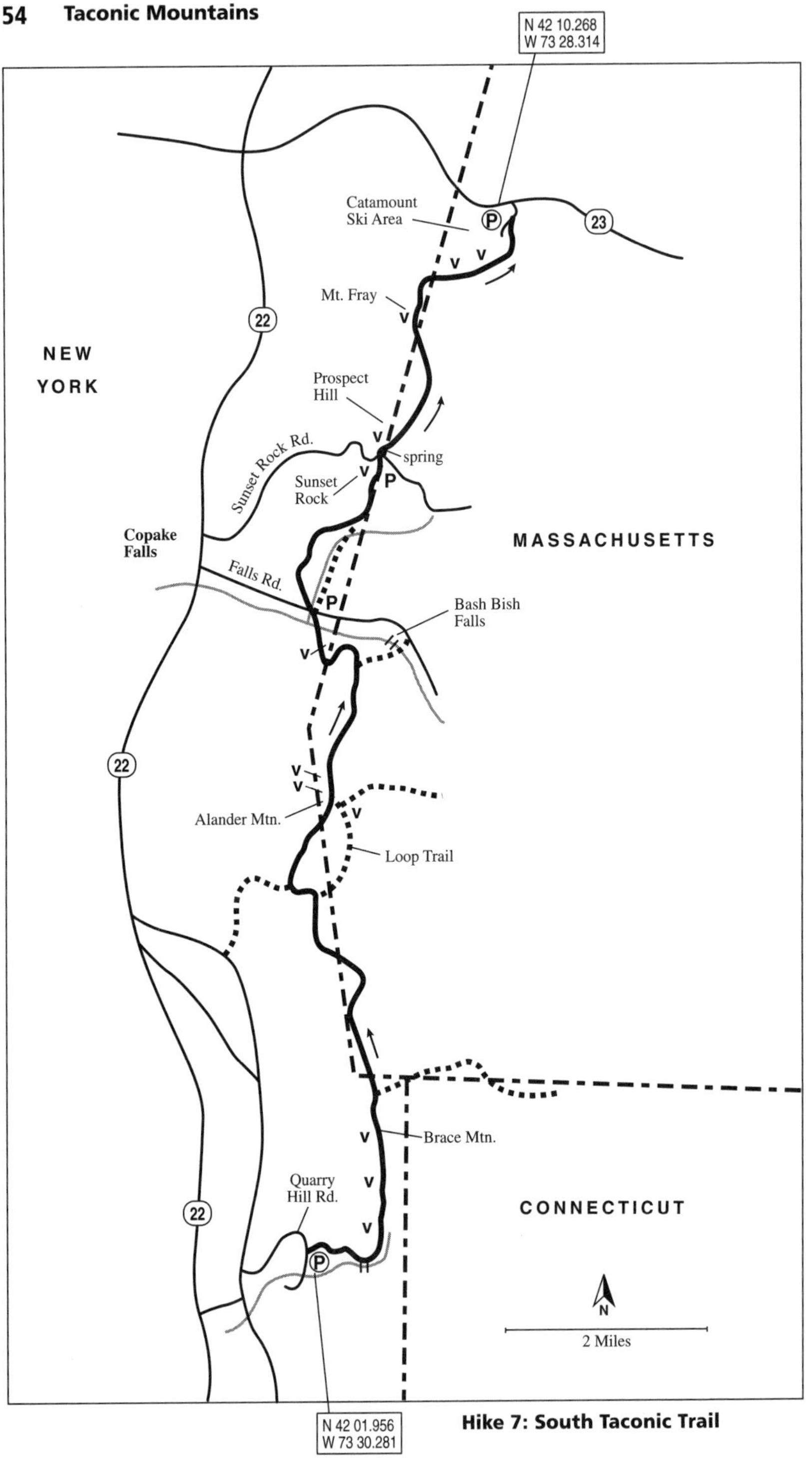

N 42 10.268
W 73 28.314

Catamount
Ski Area

P

23

V
V

Mt. Fray
V

NEW
YORK

22

Prospect
Hill

V

Sunset Rock Rd.

V
P

spring

Sunset
Rock

MASSACHUSETTS

Copake
Falls

Falls Rd.

P

V

Bash Bish
Falls

V
V
T

Alander Mtn.

V

Loop Trail

22

V
Brace Mtn.

Quarry
Hill Rd.

V

CONNECTICUT

22

V

V

P

N

2 Miles

N 42 01.956
W 73 30.281

Hike 7: South Taconic Trail

The Loop Trail is another option to reach the summit of Alander Mountain. While it avoids the needless loss of elevation, it is not that much easier. The Loop Trail is not as well established but can still be followed fairly easily as it climbs steadily under a hardwood forest. The climb steepens as you approach a ridge, with stunted oak and views from ledges; at times the oaks narrow the trail, even creating tunnels in some places. The trail meanders over a series of false ridge summits, offering more views to the south. The terrain through here is interesting, with false summits separated by small cols. Reach a col between the ridges where there is an intersection with the Alander Mountain Trail and the Loop Trail ends. The Alander Mountain Cabin, a camping option, is a short distance down the trail to the right. However, it is rather spooky and generally has no water source. Turn left onto the Alander Mountain Trail and climb to a juncture with the white STT, where you must turn left to see the spectacular summit and its stunning views to the south and west. The ridge is exposed, with grassy meadows and stunted trees. It is a beautiful place, but popular with dayhikers. Retrace your steps on the STT and head north.

Descend the exposed ridge with more nonstop views to the west, north, and east. Dip into a small valley under a hardwood forest, and then climb along the bedrock ridge of the mountain, in a series of small ascents and descents. The trail steepens as it leaves the ridge and heads into a hemlock forest, where it meets the blue trail that goes down to Bash Bish Falls.

This blue trail is an optional route but very steep and difficult. It crosses Bash Bish Brook above the falls without a bridge. Do not attempt this crossing in high water, as it is very dangerous. The blue trail leads to a parking area where you can follow trails down to the base of the falls. From there, follow a wide, level path that leads to a parking area in Taconic State Park, where the trail rejoins the STT.

While the blue trail to Bash Bish Falls enables you to include the falls directly along your hike without backtracking, I feel it is best to follow the STT. Leaving the hemlock forest, descend over ledges and reach a side trail that leads to a ledge with views of a small, bucolic valley with fields surrounded by mountain; the Catskills rise in the distance to the right. A very steep section of trail follows with some short scrambles and loose rock, but then the STT levels off into a beautiful hemlock and pine forest. The level respite is short-lived as the trail descends again—although not as steeply—along a ravine with a stream where you can hear the waterfalls. The trail moves away from the ravine and continues its descent until it follows some old grades that bring the trail back to the ravine; from here you can see some cascades. Drop down to the park road that goes to the cabin area. Follow the park road to the left and cross over Bash Bish Brook with its rapids, pools, and slides. A large parking area is to the right. From here, a level trail goes up the creek for three-quarters of a mile to the base of the falls. I highly recommend you take this side trip. The falls are impressive and are located in a stunning gorge. The water plummets from the crevices of a sculpted fin of a boulder into a deep, clear pool. The falls are very popular and you can expect crowds.

Retrace your steps to the STT and cross the road to begin the climb up to Sunset Rocks. Again, you have a choice: The STT goes left, while the red Cedar Brook Trail follows a gated grade straight ahead. The Cedar Brook Trail is more difficult, but is considered more scenic as it goes up along a gorge with cascades and slides; it leaves the small stream and steeply climbs back to the STT.

Continue on the STT from the road. The trail climbs along an old forest grade that soon levels off. Turn right and climb into a spruce plantation before following an old forest road through a scenic pine forest. Blue and yellow side trails join from the left. The climb steepens a little as the trail enters a hardwood forest, but then levels. The red Cedar Brook Trail joins from the right. The STT begins a steeper climb along the eroded, rocky old forest road. Reach the top of the ridge where a side trail to the left goes to Sunset Rock, known for its wide panorama of valleys, farms, and the Catskills in the distance. From here you can see almost the entire profile of the Catskills, from Windham High Peak to Slide Mountain. The STT enters a tunnel of mountain laurel and stunted oak trees along another old grade before reaching Sunset Rock Road where there is a small parking area.

Cross the road and drop down to a small stream and crumbling concrete spring house. Climb gradually to the top of Prospect Hill with another fine view to the west. The STT descends as it heads north along the ridge, entering forests of stunted oak, lowbush blueberry, and laurel. In places the vegetation forms a tunnel, and the trail can be brushy. Descend from the ridge and the trail meanders through a mature hardwood forest. Ascend to Mt. Fray, where a small clearing offers views to the south. The trail again tunnels through stunted oak trees, laurel, and blueberry bushes.

Reach a ski slope at Catamount Ski Area, turn right and hike down the slope. (If hiking south, this turn off the ski slope is easy to miss.)

The blazes are infrequent, but they are usually on the trees to the left of the ski slope. There are some nice views to the north. The STT briefly enters the woods, then reemerges at another slope. Enter the woods again along a forest road, passing more views to the north; this road goes behind the slopes, staying in the woods. Leave the forest road and follow a trail up a hill, and then begin a long descent in a hardwood forest. Pass a meadow (full of wildflowers in the summer) and reenter the woods. Reach a dirt road, follow it to the left, and then descend to a small parking area off Nicholson Road. The STT ends at Route 23.

●   ●   ●

Bryan, Matt, Ian, and I followed the grassy trail up to Brace Mountain; as we reached the ridge, the clouds broke and we were treated to sunshine. The breathtaking view revealed valleys and glistening ponds far below. The atmosphere was alive; you could feel the moisture as distant clouds slowly gathered across the sky. The sunlight and soft breeze hinted at the possibility of a serene evening. I thought we were safe. We weren't.

We pitched our tents, mine with views of the Taconics and Berkshires. Mt. Greylock and the Catskills were hidden by distant clouds. This was the first time I had camped on top of a mountain, but my hopes for a great sunset were dashed when a stream of fast-moving clouds flowed in a single line to the west. The dark clouds to the south and east expanded, covering Frissell and Bear Mountains. Soon the cloud wall reached Brace and the sun was extinguished.

After eating our meal in a steady wind, there was little point in staying up, and I crept into my small tent around 7:30 P.M. The wind twisted and shook my tent as I drifted into an uneasy sleep. I awoke to a strange flash. It happened again, but there was no noise. As rain began to splatter my tent, I realized it was lightning, but took comfort there was no thunder. The storms must be far away, I thought, as I counted the seconds. The rain intensified, boiling and hissing against my tent. My poles bent with the howling winds as the nylon flapped, and then snapped tight as the wind changed direction. The noiseless lightning continued. It was as if we were in the middle of the storm, where thunder could not be heard. When the storm eventually subsided, I looked out from my tent. The summit was covered with a veil of ghostly mist; there was just enough light to see the dwarfed, twisted trees.

We awoke the next morning to clear, cool skies and wisps of mist draped over the mountains. Fog hung in the deeper valleys and hollows. The sun rose behind low, distant clouds gathered to the east as their edges burned with translucent light. The valleys filled with sunlight as Brace Mountain cast its shadow across the lower hills. The wind was still blowing, but everyone had survived the storm. Mother Nature spared our lives as easily as she could have taken them, and she thought nothing of either.

8. Taconic Crest Trail

Length: 36-mile linear trail.

Direction of description: South to north.

Duration: 2 to 3 days.

Difficulty: Moderate to difficult.

Trail conditions: The trail is fairly well blazed, sections of the trail are overgrown, extensive ATV impacts.

Blazes: White diamond on a blue background. In New York, the trail is also blazed blue.

Water: The trail has a reputation for being dry. However, from U.S. 20 to Hancock, there are usually sufficient sources of water. North of Hancock, conditions become drier, although the trail does cross a few small streams that run most of the year. North of the Robinson Hollow Trail, the TCT becomes very dry. We were able to locate a small spring next to the TCT in the Hopkins Forest, north of Route 2.

Vegetation: Mostly hardwoods with an understory of ferns. There were some groves of hemlock and pine. Spruce becomes a little more common as the trail heads north, and at the summit of Berlin Mountain.

Highlights: Twin Pond, Berry Pond, vistas, Berlin Mountain, Hopkins Forest, Snow Hole, isolation.

Issues: Extensive ATV use impacts north of Hancock, resulting in erosion, mudholes, and ruts. Virtually no established backpack camping, dry conditions; lots of climbs and descents with few views. The trail is overgrown in several areas.

Location: New York border with Massachusetts and Vermont, between U.S. 20 and Route 346.

The Taconic Crest Trail (TCT) is a little-known trail with a long history. The Taconic Hiking Club began to develop the trail in 1948, growing it to 29 miles in length, and in 1987 it was further extended south to U.S. 20. Considering that hiking is very popular in this area of the country, I thought it odd the TCT has largely gone unnoticed by the backpacking and hiking community. After hiking the trail, it is easy to see why. While the TCT has some good qualities, it also faces some significant challenges, which make backpacking, in particular, difficult.

If backpacking the entire trail, it is generally advised that you hike south to north. This avoids the grueling ascent from Route 346. The TCT begins along a pull-off on the north side of U.S. 20 and begins a gradual ascent along the western escarpment of the Taconic Range. The trail is well graded along the contour of the land, crossing small streams and springs in groves of hemlock. Hike to the top of the rolling ridge and begin a descent to Twin Pond where the TCT intersects with the Taconic Skyline Trail, a multi-use ATV trail. Here, the TCT is not impacted by ATVs. Twin Pond is a small and scenic body of water that reflects the surrounding forest. It is a fine place to rest, and possibly camp, although backcountry camping may be restricted in the Pittsfield State Forest.

A short climb follows to a ridge; descend, cross a small stream, and make another short climb back to the ridge. Descend gradually to the Lebanon Springs Trail to the left and a small stream. This could be another place to camp, depending on state forest regulations. The trail ascends again and follows the ridge with rolling terrain. Reach an intersection with the Tower Mountain Trail. A winding climb follows to the top of Tower Mountain; there are no views, but there is an overgrown meadow. The trail gradually switchbacks down the mountain. Rolling terrain follows to Berry Pond camping area. The pond is the highest natural body of water in Massachusetts and is a scenic place to take a rest.

The trail follows a road and passes a nice view to the west that overlooks mountain ridges and farm valleys. Reenter the woods; the blazes may be a little hard to follow in this section. Descend and avoid an obvious trail that turns right—stay straight on the less established TCT. For the next 2 miles the terrain becomes increasingly hilly, with several fern meadows that are overgrown in the summer. Briars are also an issue. Descend from the ridge via long switchbacks to gated Potter Mountain Road on which the trail turns left. Hike down the

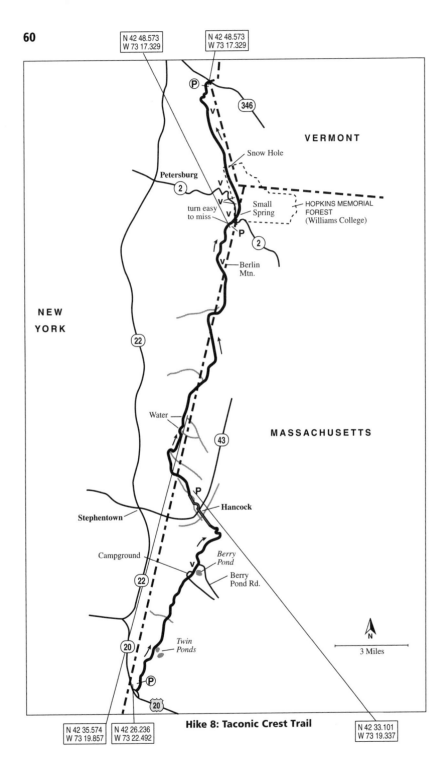

N 42 48.573
W 73 17.329

N 42 48.573
W 73 17.329

P

346

VERMONT

Snow Hole

Petersburg

2

turn easy
to miss

Small
Spring

HOPKINS MEMORIAL
FOREST
(Williams College)

P

2

Berlin
Mtn.

**NEW
YORK**

22

Water

MASSACHUSETTS

43

P

Hancock

Stephentown

Campground

*Berry
Pond*

22

Berry
Pond Rd.

20

*Twin
Ponds*

N

3 Miles

P

20

Hike 8: Taconic Crest Trail

N 42 35.574
W 73 19.857

N 42 26.236
W 73 22.492

N 42 33.101
W 73 19.337

dilapidated road and pass a gate where there is place to park. The road walk is very scenic as it passes hilly farm fields and bucolic barns. Cross straight across a highway and then make the next right. Turn left onto Madden Road and hike up to a small parking area on the left. The creek nearby is a good place to get water.

For the backpacker, the next section to Petersburg Pass can be frustrating. There are several issues. First, there are extensive ATV impacts along the trail, creating ruts, mudholes, and erosion. Second, where the TCT does not follow ATV trails, it is often overgrown and brushy, particularly with ferns. Third, water becomes scarcer as you head north. Fourth, there are about sixteen pointless ups and downs (PUDS) to reach Berlin Mountain. Fifth, there are virtually no established backpack campsites.

From Madden Road, the TCT follows an old logging road. The trail leaves the old road to the right, passes a register, and begins a steep ascent. After climbing 600 vertical feet, the trail levels off, but a steep climb soon follows to the top of Pounds Mountain. Here, the TCT encounters the first of the ATV impacts. The trail tries to avoid these impacts by following a different route that is often overgrown along narrow sidehill. The TCT eventually returns to the ATV trail. Begin to climb up and over the first in a long series of PUDS that offer no views. The descents are often steep over loose rock due to the ATVs. The vertical climbs and descents range from 100 to almost 400 vertical feet. About a mile after Pounds Mountain, cross a small stream. Sidehill follows as another climb ensues. The trail descends, levels off, and then reaches another small stream. This stream may be the last reliable water.

The TCT passes the yellow-blazed Robinson Hollow Trail to the left; the TCT features several such side trails, which are usually on the left and blazed yellow. The roller-coaster trail continues along the top of the ridge until a 400-foot vertical descent reaches Mattison Hollow Trail, on the left. Climb out of the hollow and continue the up-and-down hiking over the knobs on the ridge. As you head north, spruce trees become more common, but they never dominate. ATV impacts continue in varying degrees. In some places, the ATVs keep the brush down and seem to have little impact on the trail. In most places, there are extensive erosion and mudholes.

Another steep descent brings you to Southeast Hollow Trail to the left; dry camping is possible here. Climb out of the hollow and hike over the knobs on the trail as you begin a gradual ascent up to Berlin

Mountain, the highest point on the TCT and the highest point in New York outside of the Catskills and Adirondacks. Hike through a scenic spruce forest and reach the open, alpine-like summit. Views to the west are overgrown by spruce trees; however, there are fine views to the east as Mt. Greylock rises prominently. Berlin Mountain is the perfect place to see the sun rise. It is also the only view, or notably scenic spot, between Hancock and Petersburg Pass.

A gradual descent follows to Berlin Pass and the Green Hollow Trail. Climb gradually to the eastern flank of Mt. Raimer, the site of an old ski resort. Pay careful attention to where the TCT turns right off an ATV trail, which continues straight. The TCT descends steeply but then levels off along an old grade, which leads to a large parking area and kiosk along Route 2 in Petersburg Pass. There are views from the parking area in the pass.

Carefully cross the road since it is at a curve. Enter the scenic Hopkins Memorial Forest, which is owned by Williams College. Camping is not permitted in this forest. The trail enters a meadow with a view to the north. The trail is scenic as it explores a mature hardwood forest; keep an eye out for a small spring at the base of a ledge. Begin a gradual climb along glades and meadows with nice views to the west. This section of the TCT is popular with dayhikers going to the Snow Hole. The trail uses boardwalks over wet areas; side trails that explore the Hopkins Memorial Forest join from the right.

The trail gradually ascends along the crest of the ridge. Begin a steeper ascent that levels and then descends across an open area that had been logged, illustrating forest succession. Level hiking follows, and then the trail descends to a side trail that leads to the Snow Hole. This unique geological feature is a deep crevasse in the forest floor that holds snow and ice into early summer.

North of the Snow Hole, the ATV impacts return, as do the PUDS. Some of the climbs are along narrow ridges on precipitous forested slopes. The roller-coaster terrain continues to the Prosser Hollow Trail; I could not locate the Pownal Overlook on the trail. A final climb remains from Prosser Hollow; at the top is a nice view to the east. The descent to Route 346 is very long, and in several spots very steep. Be careful over the loose rock and gravel. As you descend, springs become more common, making the trail wet, rutted, and slippery. Cross a gravel road and follow the trail as it circumvents a meadow. The steep, wet terrain returns as the trail follows the remnants of an old forest road. Cross a small stream and reach the parking area.

The TCT is a demanding and challenging trail on a variety of levels. While sections of it can be a rewarding dayhike, it is not a trail I would recommend for backpacking. The consistently best parts for hiking are between U.S. 20 and Berry Pond, and in the Hopkins Memorial Forest from Route 2 to the Snow Hole. The rest of the trail is simply too heavily impacted by ATVs, although Berlin Mountain is worth visiting. I hope the TCT can find a future as a backpacking trail.

• • •

Hiking is not always fun. There are bugs, sweat, heat, chafing, poison ivy, snakes, bears, and dozens of other potentially pesky maladies that can ruin your day on the trail, or even your life. Being outside, at the mercy of nature's coldhearted elements, quickly makes you realize how much can go wrong. Sometimes, even the trail itself is the problem.

This trail thoroughly frustrated me. At times, my brain was so desperate for the trail to end that every step triggered a tiny explosion in my head. Curse words erupted from my mouth when I rounded a bend and failed to see my car—my sanctuary—waiting to whisk me away from this outdoorsy hell.

Maybe I wasn't being fair to the trail, or I wasn't in the mood to hike, or my expectations were too high for a trail that even the Internet knew little about. I don't consider myself a trail snob. After all, I've hiked some really boring trails, and I've learned to enjoy the "micro-scenery" of moss and fungi on a fallen log, a small brook in a shaded glen, or the shadows of trees across a green understory. Not every trail can offer vast vistas, towering waterfalls, or alpine peaks. And those that don't can be just as rewarding.

But this trail just wasn't doing it for me. I was tired of the fern-choked trail, the endless ATV mudholes, and the PUDS that revealed nothing but the magic of gravity. I was tired, I was done, and the trail wasn't getting me to the end soon enough.

We reached Petersburg Pass, unwilling to accept the miles still ahead. Blood coated the skin on my legs like a fine veneer. Dirt and grime were so deeply embedded in the creases of my skin that I could not even rub it off. Sweat stained my ball cap and leaked through my clothes. I felt like a walking petri dish. Clouds threaded over the mountains and thunder rumbled with the assurance that rain and lightning were a guarantee, not a possibility.

I was mired in the mind-cursing depths of frustration. Frustration is like an ominous storm cloud from within—it forms suddenly, fueled by the anger of lacking control. The beauty of frustration is that if you give it some space, it can offer a new perspective. If you change your expectations and accept things as they are, not as you want them to be, those same storm clouds evaporate just as easily.

I decided to accept the rain, and in essence the trail. I didn't bother with a rain jacket, continuing to hike as the clouds gathered and raked over the mountains. Thunder exploded with a sound that felt solid. I didn't care. I continued to walk. The rain began with gentle taps but soon became an aerial waterfall, flowing through the trees. I became soaked, and it felt good. Lightning flashed, but I kept walking. It was all I could do. In the real world I would be cordoned inside in a rain like this, looking at it through a window. But today I was within it. I was a part of it. I tasted my sweet salt on my lips as the rain ran down my forehead. My dirty forearms looked new again, my legs were refreshed. Renewal does have a price—my glasses kept fogging up and I found myself running into trees, rocks, and branches, or losing a foot in the mud.

We reached the end, and I apologized to my hiking partner, Ian, for taking him on this hike. Maybe he lied to me when he said it was no problem. Regardless, these are the trails we'll remember for the rest of our lives and laugh about for years to come. And that is where the trail defied all expectations.

Catskills

Famous for their beauty and extensive trails, the Catskills are a place where you can spend a lot of time. How could you not? With eye-popping vistas, ponds, waterfalls, isolation, awesome camping, pristine streams, historical ruins, and peaceful forests of spruce, fir, pine, hemlock, and hardwoods, the Catskills demand to be experienced. It is hard to believe that only a few hours from New York City lies this sublime, and significant, wilderness.

The Catskills have played a very important role in man's relationship with nature. The artists of the Hudson River School came to these mountains to paint the natural world for the sake of its beauty. The use of such imagery would become a powerful tool for future generations in creating national parks and protecting natural areas. Humans have a genetic need to experience natural beauty, and the Catskills are where we first expressed that need through paintings and imagery.

While some have used paintbrushes, you can use your feet. Go there. Now.

Trails maintained by: New York–New Jersey Trail Conference, www.nynjtc.org. Volunteers build and maintain these trails.

9. Windham High Peak and Blackhead Range Loop

Length: 18 miles.

Direction of description: Clockwise.

Duration: 1¹/₂ to 2 days.

Difficulty: Moderate to difficult. This hike requires some scrambling over ledges 5 to 15 feet in height.

Trail conditions: Trails are well established but can be brushy in summer, particularly from Windham High Peak to Blackhead.

Blazes: Blue, yellow, and red.

Water: Trails tend to be dry. Water availability is generally limited to side hikes on the Elm Ridge Trail and Batavia Kill Trail.

Vegetation: Mostly hardwoods with some pine and hemlock. Higher elevations on the Blackhead Range contain birch, fir, and spruce.

Highlights: Superb views, beautiful forests of fir and spruce.

Issues: Camping opportunities are limited on this loop and logistically limited to the Batavia Kill Trail and shelter.

Location: The loop is located near Maplecrest.

This beautiful loop explores the northern limits of the Catskills. However, few backpackers hike it as a loop due to a 3.8-mile road walk; most people shuttle cars between the parking areas on Peck Road and Barnum Road. This description is clockwise from Peck Road.

From the parking area, register and follow the yellow-blazed Elm Ridge Road along what appears to be an old forest road, often lined with ancient rock walls. Several springs and a small stream are along the trail. Gradually ascend and watch your footing on slick ledges. Reach the blue-blazed Escarpment Trail, on which you will turn right. There is a nice shelter off to your right, but other than being a place to camp for late arrivals, it is too early in the trek to serve any use.

Begin a gradual climb up Windham High Peak. The climb is not too difficult and is interspersed with level areas. Pass a massive, stunted oak tree off to your right and cross an old rock wall into a spooky spruce plantation; the treadway is a web of roots. The trail crosses other spruce plantations. The forest becomes mostly hardwoods as the trail gains elevation and can be a little overgrown in summer. Pass a

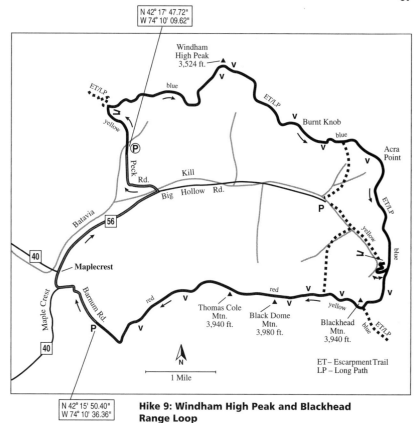

N 42° 17' 47.72"
W 74° 10' 09.62"

Windham
High Peak
3,524 ft.

blue

ET/LP

ET/LP

Burnt Knob

blue

Acra
Point

yellow

Peck

Rd.

Kill

Big Hollow Rd.

P

ET/LP

Batavia

56

yellow

blue

40

Maplecrest

Barnum Rd.

red

red

Maple Crest

P

Thomas Cole
Mtn.
3,940 ft.

Black Dome
Mtn.
3,980 ft.

yellow

Blackhead
Mtn.
3,940 ft.

blue

ET/LP

40

N

1 Mile

ET – Escarpment Trail
LP – Long Path

N 42° 15' 50.40"
W 74° 10' 36.36"

Hike 9: Windham High Peak and Blackhead Range Loop

narrow view of the Blackheads to the south. The climb continues before leveling off at the summit, where there is another view to the south and a more impressive one to the north.

Begin the descent and pass a view to the east, looking over the Hudson Valley. The descent is steep in parts and the trail is narrow. The trail levels and then climbs a knob with a view to the west. Descend again and climb Burnt Knob, with a beautiful view to the north and east from a large ledge. Another view follows, this one looking across to the Blackheads from a narrow cliff.

After a sharp descent from Burnt Knob, pass an intersection with the red-blazed Black Dome Range Trail; stay on the blue-blazed Escarpment Trail for a climb to Acra Point. This is a gorgeous spot, offering a panorama of Black Dome Valley, Burnt Knob, and the Blackheads. The spruce forest at the view makes it even more scenic. Descend gradually from Acra Point and—in typical fashion along this ridge between Windham High Peak and the Blackheads—begin a short climb over another knob. The forests are interspersed with spruce. Descend, passing some small, dry campsites, and reach the intersection with Batavia Kill Trail.

To camp for the night, turn right on the yellow-blazed Batavia Kill Trail as it gradually descends into a stream valley with several springs and reaches the shelter, which leaves a lot to be desired. It is somewhat rundown, located in a wet area, and mice are a problem. This shelter is best used in cold weather. The best alternative is to find a place to set up a tent, although there isn't much space for many tents. Batavia Kill Creek provides good water.

Retrace your steps back to the Escarpment Trail to begin the steep, 1,100-foot vertical climb up Blackhead. The trail traverses several rock outcrops and ledges and passes one nice view to the left that looks over the valley and ridges to the southeast. The forest becomes primarily spruce and fir. Leave the Escarpment Trail and turn right onto the yellow-blazed Blackhead Mountain Trail. The trail follows a gravel pathway across the forested summit. The trail descends and reveals a view to the west as Black Dome rises prominently. Descend into the col between Blackhead and Black Dome; continue straight on the red-blazed Black Dome Range Trail. A steep but short climb follows up Black Dome. Scramble up a ledge to the crest of a tremendous view on the eastern flank of the mountain. Now you have a view of Blackhead. You can also see the low ridge of Burnt Knob and Acra Point. To the south is Lake Capra and Kaaterskill High Peak. Continue the climb over Black Dome. The forests continue to be beautiful with deep, verdant spruce and fir. An easy climb brings you to Thomas Cole Mountain, where there are no views.

A somewhat gradual descent follows as the trail traverses a long ridge. Pass a meadow with aromatic spruce. The forests soon become hardwoods; enjoy a minor view from a ledge to the left. Descend over some small ledges. The trail levels and climbs to a small knoll; a nice view off the trail to the right looks north to Windham High Peak and a sea of ridges. The trail descends more steeply and reaches a large ledge with a small view from the top. Carefully descend this large ledge and cross some small streams. Reach the boundary of state lands at a kiosk and follow an old woods road over spring-slicked ledges. The eroded road crosses more small streams with some cascades. The trail passes near a home and reaches Barnum Road and the parking area.

If you didn't park here, a 3.8-mile road walk awaits you back to Peck Road. Follow Barnum Road and turn right onto NY 40; turn right onto NY 56 in the scenic village of Maplecrest; hike along NY 56, turn left onto Peck Road, and hike up to the parking area.

• • •

For me, this trail represents the change of seasons. When I first hiked the loop, it was during an October weekend with indigo blue skies and fiery fall foliage. A group of college friends joined me, and we made our way up Windham High Peak as leaves drifted to the forest floor in a kaleidoscope of colors. The bright autumn sun pierced through the thinning canopy, casting the trail in a pattern of light and shade.

We seemed to talk and joke about the same things we did years before, on campus. The years changed both everything and nothing. The trail brought us together, allowing us to reconnect and catch up, a respite from our routines.

We descended from Windham High Peak and hiked to Acra Point, the valley spreading out before us. Distant ridges rose into the blue sky. The Blackheads soared to the south, and we climbed over each, awed by the views. There were more views to the east, and we wondered if we were looking into Massachusetts or Vermont.

Eventually, the trail ran out and so did this chapter of our lives together. The trail would bring us together again, somewhere; it has become a baseline of where our lives once were, and where our lives are going.

I returned to this trail a few years later as the heat of summer baked the jungle-like foliage of the mountains. I came with Wes, a hiking friend I had met a year before. I was a lawyer with a stressful and political job; he was a boilermaker with a union, now working on an organic farm. Part of me envied him. And we drove up in his Ford Mustang—I couldn't help but smile on the ride.

We arrived at the trailhead as several trail workers—all young, college-age men—were loading boxes and tools on their huge external backpacks. One man had to prop himself against their van to stay upright under the weight. Despite the bugs they were shirtless, with sinuous, galvanized muscles from working on the trails, building steps, and cutting sidehill. Each knew what had to be done with no instruction. They were at ease with each other, themselves, and the forest. One by one they disappeared up the trail, as if walking home.

Wes and I repeated the route of my earlier hike with the long, gradual climb up Windham High Peak. We reached the top, and I walked out to a vista looking north, only to be greeted by a graceful glider skimming above the trees and riding the crest of the ridges. It was silent, effortless. It seemed more bird than plane.

The undergrowth was so thick it nearly concealed the trail as we descended. I looked below to see a black mass walking, snapping sticks with each step. It was a huge black bear. We were silenced with awe and anticipation. The bear waddled through a thicket of briars, looking for berries. It soon disappeared into the forest as we sped down the trail. We reached a large cliff with a view over the Hudson Valley, looking out over countless farms, homes, and towns. Cars and trucks moved along distant roads and highways, between towns, factories, and shopping centers. Everyone was moving, oblivious to what their world would look like from afar. Hikers escape into the woods, only to look at civilization from a different perspective.

 # 10. Escarpment Trail

Length: 23-mile linear trail.

Direction of description: North to south.

Duration: 1^1/$_2$ to 2^1/$_2$ days.

Difficulty: Moderate to difficult.

Trail conditions: Trails are generally well blazed and established. Most trail junctures have signs. The network of trails around North and South Lake can cause some confusion.

Blazes: Blue.

Water: The trail tends to be dry, although there may be seasonal springs along it. Reliable water sources can be reached by side trails. Tap water is available at the North-South Lake picnic area in season.

Vegetation: Hardwoods predominate, with many spruce/fir forests.

Highlights: Many excellent views of the Hudson Valley and Catskills, Blackhead Mountain, small plane crash on Stoppel Point, rock overhangs, cliffs, ledges, crevices, diverse forest types, North Lake, site of the Catskill Mountain House, Kaaterskill Falls (off trail).

Issues: The trail is often dry and campsites are limited. The trail does get close to the edge of cliffs and ledges.

Location: Hensonville and Haines Falls, New York.

The Escarpment Trail (ET) is one of the premier backpacking trails in the Catskills. It offers tremendous views, superb scenery, a reasonable shuttle, and terrain that is usually moderate in difficulty. Ironically, the ET does not see as many backpackers as it should. While sections of the trail are very popular with dayhikers, the dry conditions and limited camping may keep the backpackers away. Regardless, this is definitely a trail you should backpack.

From the parking area along Route 23, cross the road to begin the trail. Most of this hike also follows the Long Path. Cross a creek and several boardwalks over wet areas through overgrown meadows. Reach a register and kiosk; avoid the trail that veers off to the left, which is part of a multi-use system. Continue straight and begin a gradual climb. As you hike, the trail steepens, culminating in some switchbacks. Reach the top of the ridge where a yellow trail joins from the right. There is also nice shelter off to your right.

Begin a gradual climb up Windham High Peak. The climb is not too difficult and is interspersed with level areas. Pass a massive, stunted oak tree off to your right and cross an old rock wall into a spooky spruce plantation; the treadway is a web of roots. The trail crosses other spruce plantations. The forest becomes mostly hardwoods as the trail gains elevations and can be a little overgrown in summer. Pass a narrow view of the Blackheads to the south. The climb continues before leveling off at the summit where there is another view to the south, and a more impressive one to the north.

Begin the descent and pass a view to the east, looking over the Hudson Valley. The descent is steep in parts and the trail is narrow. The trail levels and then climbs a knob with a view to the west. Descend again and climb Burnt Knob with a beautiful view to the north and east from a large ledge. Another view follows, this one looking across to the Blackheads from a narrow cliff.

After a sharp descent from Burnt Knob, pass an intersection with the red-blazed Black Dome Range Trail; stay on the blue-blazed Escarpment Trail for a climb to Acra Point. This is a gorgeous spot as it offers a panorama of Black Dome Valley, Burnt Knob, and the Blackheads. The spruce forest at the view makes it even more scenic. Descend gradually from Acra Point and—in typical fashion along this ridge between Windham High Peak and the Blackheads—begin a short climb over another knob. The forests are interspersed with spruce. Descend, passing some small, dry campsites and reach the intersection with Batavia Kill Trail.

To camp for the night, turn right on the yellow-blazed Batavia Kill Trail as it gradually descends into a stream valley with several springs, and reach the shelter. The shelter leaves a lot to be desired. It is somewhat run-down, located in a wet area, and mice are a problem. This

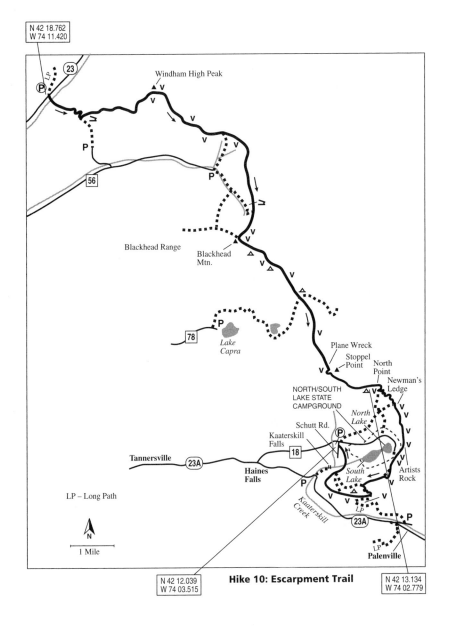

N 42 18.762
W 74 11.420

Windham High Peak

P

56

Blackhead Range

Blackhead Mtn.

78

Lake Capra

Plane Wreck

Stoppel Point

North Point

Newman's Ledge

NORTH/SOUTH LAKE STATE CAMPGROUND

North Lake

Schutt Rd.

Kaaterskill Falls

18

Tannersville

23A

Haines Falls

South Lake

Artists Rock

LP – Long Path

Kaaterskill Creek

LP

23A

LP

Palenville

1 Mile

N

N 42 12.039
W 74 03.515

Hike 10: Escarpment Trail

N 42 13.134
W 74 02.779

shelter is best used in cold weather. The best alternative is to find a place to set up a tent, although there isn't much space for it. Batavia Kill creek provides good water.

Retrace your steps back to the Escarpment Trail to begin the steep, 1,100-foot vertical climb up Blackhead. The trail traverses several rock outcrops and ledges and passes one nice view to the left that looks over the valley and ridges to the southeast. The forest becomes primarily spruce and fir, and there are some moderate scrambles over ledges. Reach the top of Blackhead Mountain with its thick, aromatic forest of spruce and fir. While there are no views at the summit, there is still a feeling of accomplishment to be on top of the fifth highest peak in the Catskills.

Turn left to continue on the blue ET. The trail descends, passing a partial view to the left from a ledge; a small winter campsite is nearby. Continue the descent, which becomes steeper over ledges. The hardwood forest soon returns. The trail levels along the ridge with rolling terrain and groves of spruce trees. A potential—and dry—campsite is off to the right. Pass a view to your right, looking over Lake Capra and a forested valley. Stoppel Point rises to the south. This view can be another dry campsite. Descend steeply from the ridge as the trail goes down over tiers of ledges with some unique overhangs, crevices, and outcrops. Reach the bottom of the gap and a yellow trail. There is a small campsite at this intersection. Continue straight on the blue ET.

Begin a gradual climb that levels off along a ridge. The climb steepens and enters a spruce and fir forest. Reach a dramatic view from a cliff looking east over the Hudson Valley. The trail continues the climb up to Stoppel Point as the terrain steepens. Just before the top you'll pass the crash site of a small twin seat, single-engine plane. The engine is gone and the inside is gutted, but much of the twisted, broken frame remains. Hike away from the crash site and enjoy a narrow view of the Blackheads to the north. The trail curves around and then climbs gradually to the summit, where there are "No Camping" signs. Reach a ledge with a fine view to the east. A short, steep descent follows before the trail levels off. It is hard to notice, but there is a good campsite in a spruce forest off to your right. The trail descends, curves to the left and reaches the edge of the escarpment at a ledge with more good views to the east. The cliffs of North Point are below. Descend to North Point, with superb views to the south of North Lake and Kaaterskill High Peak. The trail continues to drop steeply over ledges until it levels off. A red trail is to the right; turn left on the blue trail and descend more gradually as the trail proceeds to the edge of the escarpment. Reach a bedrock bald area where the trail turns left and descends steeply over ledges and crevices. Continue to descend past Badman's Cave and a modest-size rock overhang, and reach a juncture with a yellow trail. Continue left on the blue trail as it circumvents a swampy area.

Descend gradually along the meandering trail across cracked bedrock. The surrounding forest is beautiful, with hemlock and spruce. The eastern exposure makes it an ideal hike in the morning. Reach a dramatic cliff at Newman's Ledge with awesome views to the east over the Hudson Valley. Continue along the edge before the trail moves higher in the forest. Pass a yellow side trail to the left that leads to Lookout and Sunset Rocks. The blue trail enters a beautiful grotto surrounded by cliffs and ledges. Hike along the base of a conglomerate outcrop with overhangs. Descend toward the forested edge of the escarpment with occasional minor views. Reach Artists Rock along a towering cliff with superb views to the east. The ET enters the North-South Lake Campground and picnic area as a fence lines the cliff. Hike behind a picnic area; the lake can be seen off to your right and is worth a visit. In season, there are bathrooms where you can get water.

The trail crosses an old railroad grade and turns left onto a gravel road that ascends to the former site of the Catskills Mountain House. All that remains is a field and some informational signs, but the view is nice. Ascend up the hill and pass a unique, sloping boulder with carvings from the 1800s; another fine view is nearby. The trail climbs more steeply to a red trail; follow the blue trail to the left as it descends to Boulder Rock where a large boulder sits on a ledge with a narrow view across Kaaterskill Clove. The blue trail bends back around and passes the other end of the red trail. Follow an old, rocky forest road along the contour of the mountain as several unofficial trails intersect. Reach another red trail, but follow the blue ET as it makes a winding descent through mountain laurel down to the edge of the plateau. A red trail on an old grade joins from the left, but continue on the blue trail to the right. The Long Path now leaves the ET and follows the red trail down to the bottom of Kaaterskill Clove.

The ET now follows the edge of the clove, traversing ledges and cliffs. Exercise caution along this terrain. Inspiration Point and Sunset Rock are two of the many spots with superb views of the clove, including the side streams that cascade down the other side. The trail also passes some dry campsites. Reach a yellow trail to the right, which is a shortcut for those wishing to end the trail sooner. The blue ET descends steeply to the rim with more views before becoming more wooded. Reach Layman Monument, dedicated to a local man who died fighting a forest fire. The trail ascends through the forest, and then descends to Spruce Creek at the site of an old, breached dam and the site of the Laurel House. Cascades fill the creek. An unofficial side trail to the left may follow the creek down to the top of Kaaterskill Falls, but this is not advisable since it is dangerous, and the better view is from the bottom of the falls.

Follow Spruce Creek along a gradual incline as the red trail joins from the right. Cross the creek and continue to climb, crossing two old railroad grades, remnants of the grand mountain resort era when tourists would come here via trains. The trail gradually climbs through a scenic pine forest before ending at the parking area on Schutt Road.

While here, you should make the side trip to see dramatic Kaaterskill Falls, the highest in New York at 260 feet. Parking is very limited along Route 23A, and you must walk along the road to reach the yellow Kaaterskill Falls Trail. The popular trail is a half-mile long and rugged, but the rapids, cascades, and boulders along the way make for a beautiful hike. The trail ends at the bottom of the spectacular falls as it plummets over a stunning amphitheater of overhanging cliffs.

• • •

It is easy for every generation to think it was the first. It is convenient to think we are innovative, groundbreaking, forward thinking, and can correct the sins of the past. We may judge how prior generations destroyed the environment, polluted with impunity, and were devoid of appreciation for the natural world. But, really, we are no different. The fundamentals of human nature change little over the centuries.

On this trail alone, I descended from the ice-frosted summit of Blackhead Mountain to a ridge with sweeping views of the Hudson Valley bathed in a weak autumn light. As twilight encroached, I passed another stunning view to the east. Just before everything faded to black, I found a nice campsite hidden in a grove of spruce trees.

Clear skies welcomed the morning, and the air was light and invigorating. The trail reached a series of cliffs at North Point in the morning light as mist lifted above Kaaterskill High Peak and Roundtop Mountain. Clouds rose to the south, their undersides illuminated white and gold. The calm waters of North and South Lakes sparkled in the valley below. I had to stop and take it all in, feeling I was one of thousands who have come here over the generations. We did not come for just the view, but to learn a lesson: The world is far larger and more beautiful than we can even imagine. This place had the same effect on me as it might have on a man standing here 170 years ago.

The trail followed rims of cliffs and ledges that slanted through forests of spruce and hemlock in the golden morning light. I hiked along the escarpment above the Hudson River, views unraveling through the trees and revealing themselves at towering cliffs. I felt like I was in a Hudson River School painting. I hiked by a level meadow on the edge of the escarpment, the former site of Catskill Mountain House, once a gleaming white resort with columns and porticos. This resort attracted the wealthy and elite, who were as focused on materialism as our generation is accused of being today. But the resort also proved something else: humanity's inherent need to experience natural beauty, to be in awe of something far larger than ourselves. In some sense, these resorts and paintings laid the foundation for the parks and public lands we so love today. Their appreciation is now our appreciation. Prior generations were the first to get it right, and their foresight was a gift to all succeeding generations. We need to do the same. Our need for beauty, awe, and wonder has always been a part of us and will never change.

Several weeks after completing this hike, I saw Thomas Cole's painting "A View of the Two Lakes and Mountain House, Catskill Mountains, Morning," on a computer screen. It was almost the identical view I saw from North Point, 170 years later.

11. Overlook Mountain and Kaaterskill Wild Forest

Length: 21-mile linear trail.

Direction of description: South to north.

Duration: 1¹/₂ to 2 days.

Difficulty: Moderate. This hike features gradual terrain with the exception of the descent into Kaaterskill Clove. The climb up Kaaterskill High Peak is difficult.

Trail conditions: Trails are well established and most junctures have signs.

Blazes: Red, blue.

Water: There are generally sufficient water sources along the trail.

Vegetation: Mostly hardwoods with some pine and hemlock. Higher elevations contain birch, fir, and spruce.

Highlights: Superb views, scenic streams, Echo Lake, beautiful forests of fir and spruce, Overlook Mountain House ruins, old quarries, waterfalls.

Issues: Camping opportunities are limited, and sections of the trail can be crowded on weekends from spring to fall. The trail through the Kaaterskill Wild Forest is wet in several areas.

Location: The trail is between Meads and Palenville.

This is a great weekend trip, offering a tremendous diversity of scenery and historical features. This trail has it all: expansive views, towering waterfalls, a backcountry pond, and historical ruins. Two negatives: You should expect company, and you'll find that camping options are somewhat limited.

This route heads south to north, from Meads to Palenville. This leaves the sublime scenery—and the long, punishing descent—of Kaaterskill Clove for the end. Begin from the trailhead along Meads Mountain Road, across the road from a Buddhist temple or monastery. The trail is marked red and follows a gated forest road up Overlook Mountain. The forest is mostly hardwoods with some hemlocks, and the climb is long and gradual, but never steep. Several springs flow across the road. Reach the crest of the ridge and the trail levels off as it approaches the impressive, spooky ruins of the Overlook Mountain House. This was to be one of the Catskills' mountain resorts, but it was never completed; all that is left is the massive concrete shell towering several stories high.

Reach a trail juncture and turn right to see the summit of Overlook Mountain and its fire tower. There are superb views from the fire tower; a trail goes by the hut and down to a large ledge with great views of the Hudson Valley. Retrace your steps to the trail juncture and turn right onto the blue-blazed Overlook Trail. This trail descends gradually through a hardwood forest, with massive ledges looming off to the right. The trail traverses the side of the mountain, passing a huge boulder balanced on the edge of a ledge. Descend to the trail juncture with the Echo Lake Trail, blazed yellow. Follow the trail down to Echo Lake, a beautiful pond about 15 acres in size. There is a lean-to on the north

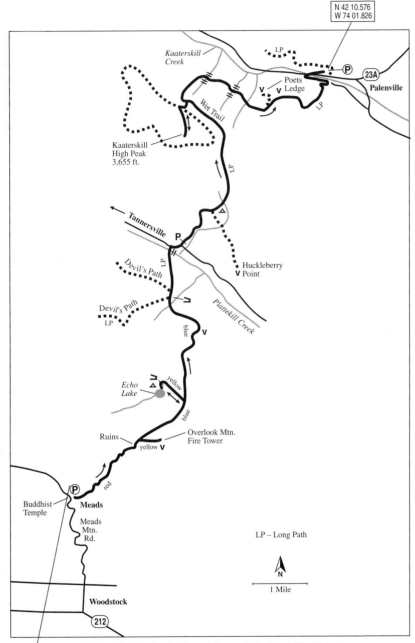

N 42 10.576
W 74 01.826

Kaaterskill Creek

LP

Poets
Ledge

Palenville

23A

Wet Trail

V V

Kaaterskill
High Peak
3,655 ft.

LP

Tannersville

P

Huckleberry
V Point

Devil's Path

LP

Devil's Path
LP

blue

V

Plattekill Creek

Echo
Lake

yellow

blue

Ruins

yellow V

Overlook Mtn.
Fire Tower

red

P

Buddhist
Temple

Meads

Meads
Mtn.
Rd.

LP – Long Path

N

1 Mile

Woodstock

212

N 42 04.274
W 74 07.360

Hike 11: Overlook Mountain and Kaaterskill Wild Forest

shore and seven other designated campsites around the lake. Beavers have a dam at the outlet, raising the water level, and hemlocks grow along the south shore nearby. The lake is untouched and can only be reached by hiking, but it is a popular place, so expect company. For weekend backpackers, it is an ideal Friday night campsite.

Climb back up to the Overlook Trail and proceed north. The trail levels out under a hardwood forest with an understory of mountain laurel and follows an old grade along the contour of Plattekill Mountain; note the old stone retaining walls supporting the level grade. Pass above an old quarry and reach a short yellow trail to the right that leads to Codfish Point and its view of the Hudson River valley. Rest a moment on the stone furniture at the lookout spot.

Continue north on the Overlook Trail as it descends gradually to a stream and another lean-to. Pass the famed Devil's Path to the left; here, the Long Path joins the route, blazed aqua or green and comprising the remainder of this hike. The trail gradually descends and enters a private preserve, crossing some small streams. The forest becomes increasingly scenic, with hemlocks and some spruce; you will find a far greater diversity of forest types along the trail for the remainder of this hike.

The trail reaches Plattekill Creek; its beautiful waterfalls are just downstream. Turn right onto Platte Cove Mountain Road. Side trails lead to the bottom of the falls, almost 100 feet high. Turn left off the road at a large parking area and continue to follow the Long Path. Palenville is about 9 miles farther at this point. The trail follows an old woods road and climbs steadily through a scenic forest of hemlock and pine. A creek is off to your right. Enter a hardwood forest and pass a juncture with the yellow Huckleberry Point Trail to the right; this 1.4-mile trail leads to its namesake, a large cliff with great views of Plattekill Clove and the Hudson Valley. The trail climbs gradually and enters a nice hemlock forest. Potential camping is found off the trail, to the right, before the footbridge over the creek.

Cross the creek and enter a boggy area with some narrow boardwalks. Climb away from the stream as the hemlock forests continue. The trail continues to climb gradually and the hardwood forest returns. Reach the top of the ridge as the trail levels off and enters an extensive, and very beautiful, spruce forest. The only drawback is that this section of trail is notoriously wet. Pass a side trail to the left marked with small cairns that lead to a campsite. (I believe this unmarked side trail continues on to the snowmobile trail and enables hikers to climb Kaaterskill High Peak from the south.)

The Long Path is rolling or level as it continues through the scenic spruce forest. The hardwoods return and the trail reaches a juncture with the snowmobile trail. If you want to include Kaaterskill High Peak in your hike, turn left and climb to the snowmobile trail loop. Turn right onto the loop and follow for a few hundred yards to a small stream and an unmarked side trail to the left that climbs up the mountain. The climb is steep with some scrambling, but is clearly established. As you near the top of the high peak, enter a sublime spruce and moss forest. Reach the forested summit near the remnant of a plane and bear left at the "Y." This trail leads down to Hurricane Ledge, offering a dramatic view of the Devil's Path Range to the south. When I hiked here, I did not go far enough to see the view. (The side trip to the peak will add at least an hour and a half to your hike.) Retrace your steps back to the Long Path; be careful with the steep descent off the high peak.

The Long Path begins its descent into Kaaterskill Clove, traversing a series of ledges often capped with hemlocks. You will hear the sound of Buttermilk Falls leaping from a cliff before you see it. The trail traverses close to the edge of the gorge under hemlocks and soon reaches the top of the falls. From the trail over the top of the falls it is hard to see the water below, but there is an awesome view from the top. Another falls is upstream. Rolling terrain follows as the trail ascends slightly, passing a few more streams and ledges. The beautiful forest continues, with pine, hemlock, and some spruce. The trail climbs gradually and then levels off before reaching a yellow side trail to Poet's Ledge. This half-mile trail descends to a cliff and an impressive view looking up Kaaterskill Clove.

The long descent begins in earnest as the trail drops down from the mountain. There are a few steep sections, but the descent is separated by level stretches. Pass Maeli's View to the left, hike along private property, and pick up a gravel jeep road. The trail follows this road all the way down and behind some houses to Malden Avenue. Turn left onto the avenue, which is really a side street. Impressive Kaaterskill Creek is off to your right, with rapids, cascades, smooth bluestone, and deep pools; however, there are a lot of "no trespassing" signs. Malden Avenue ends where it is closed, but the trail continues on the abandoned avenue. Impressive overhanging ledges are to the left. Reach NY 23A and turn right; watch for traffic. Follow this road for about two-thirds of a mile to the parking area on the left.

• • •

The bare, gray trees paled into a monochromatic forest under milky clouds. Brown, wet leaves carpeted the forest, dusted with snow. This trail threaded its way from ruins to abandoned quarries and homesteads. I wondered how many others had come this way. What were their stories? Did they come here to appreciate the beauty and solitude, or to struggle for a livelihood eked from rock and bare soil? We passed the usual squirrels, chipmunks, and deer, but were surprised to encounter thousands of tiny tan moths that fluttered with utter silence in the bare, wet woods. They looked like fallen leaves suddenly come alive and seemed to be going nowhere in particular, as if they had missed their season to live and were biding their time in the chilled air. Maybe these moths had a reason, a purpose, to be there on that gray autumn day. But even for a moth, time brings change to the reason and purpose of where we find ourselves.

12. Devil's Path

Length: 24.8-mile linear trail.

Direction of description: East to west.

Duration: $1^1/_2$ to $2^1/_2$ days.

Difficulty: Very difficult. Climbs and descents are steep and rocky; scrambling over ledges is often required. The tops of the mountains tend to be level and rolling. Vertical ascents reach up to 1,500 feet at Stony Clove; however, most are between 500 and 1,000 vertical feet.

Trail conditions: Trails are well established and usually well blazed. There is very rocky and steep terrain.

Blazes: Red.

Water: Sources are limited, particularly on the eastern section of the trail. Bring additional containers in warm, dry weather. The western section has more water sources.

Vegetation: Mostly hardwoods and hemlock with fir and spruce at the summits.

Highlights: Incredible vistas, beautiful forests, scenic streams, caves, waterfall, Stony Clove.

Issues: Camping options are limited; there are three lean-tos on or near the trail. The trail is very difficult, but popular on summer weekends. There is a long shuttle to hike the entire trail; it takes about 1$^1/_2$ hours to complete the shuttle.

Location: The trail is located near Tannersville and Hunter; it is north of Phoenicia.

The Devil's Path (DP), considered by many to be the premier trail of the Catskills, is not only the single most famous trail in the Catskills, but also one of New York's most well-known trails. This linear trail is famous for its incredibly rugged and rocky terrain as it traverses the peaks of six mountains and the steep notches that separate them. Logistically, the trail is divided by Stony Clove Road (NY 214). The eastern Devil's Path is more rugged, longer, and usually considered more scenic than the west. (Most people tend to hike east to west, so that is the direction of this description.) Many hikers attempt to cover the entire DP in one day.

From Prediger Road, ascend gradually and enter the Indian Head Wilderness Area, where you'll reach a juncture to the right with the blue Jimmy Dolan Trail. A small stream is nearby. Stay on the red DP as it bends left and follows level and rolling terrain for almost a mile. Reach the Long Path in a beautiful hemlock forest; the DP promptly leaves the Long Path to the right. Straight ahead to the south is a lean-to near a scenic stream. This is a popular place for backpackers to camp on Friday night for those trying to do a weekend backpack of the DP.

Ahead is a 1,200-foot vertical climb of Indian Head Mountain. At first the climb is gradual, but it becomes increasingly steep, and you will soon be scrambling up ledges with the help of roots as handholds. Some of these scrambles can be a little intimidating. Reach the crest of Indian Head in an aromatic and scenic forest of spruce and fir, a feature found on all the mountains. The trail offers some superb views to the east and then continues along the rolling ridge for a half mile before descending into Jimmy Dolan Notch; the trail of the same name joins from the right. A steep, 500-foot vertical climb follows up to Twin Mountain, which has some of the most breathtaking views in the Catskills; panoramas reveal themselves to the south where you can see Slide Mountain. Another steep and rocky descent follows into Pecoy Notch; the blue Pecoy Notch Trail joins from the right.

The climb up Sugarloaf Mountain requires some scrambles and meanders along and between ledges. There are some views of Twin Mountain, and a side trail near the summit leads to a fine view to the south. The descent from Sugarloaf into Mink Hollow is absolutely heinous, as you must traverse boulders and ledges across steep terrain. This descent will take time, since your legs will already be burning. In the hollow, reach an intersection with the blue Mink Hollow Trail. A lean-to is to the left.

The ensuing climb up Plateau Mountain is steep and relentless, but not nearly as rocky as the descent off Sugarloaf. Hikers love Plateau for the level 2-mile walk along its top through a boreal forest of fir and spruce, although some sections are wet. While there are no views on this section, it is a pleasure to hike, and a welcome respite. There are fine views from Plateau before the descent into Stony Clove Notch. The descent is long and punishing on your knees. Watch for loose rock along the trail. A stream can be heard in a steep glen to your left. Reach a parking area at NY 214 and Notch Lake in Stony Clove Notch. A fee is required to park here. The setting is absolutely beautiful and rugged as the mountains tower overhead. Just down the road to the left is Devil's Tombstone State

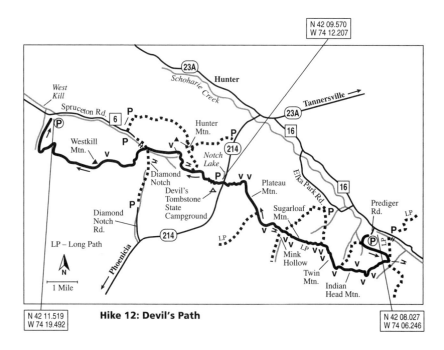

Hike 12: Devil's Path

Campground, a small and scenic place to basecamp for those not wanting to backpack the DP.

The western section of the DP is not as popular as the eastern, since there are fewer side trails for dayhikers and fewer vistas. As you head west, the trail becomes increasingly less used, but it is still established. The western section is also easier and has more water and better camping opportunities. Follow an old forest grade up the mountain, passing large rocks. The trail leaves the grade and begins a steeper climb that moderates at 3,000 feet with a more gradual ascent. The trail levels off at 3,500 feet as it explores a beautiful forest of spruce and birch. The yellow Hunter Mountain Trail joins from the right. The summit of the second highest mountain in the Catskills is a gradual climb of about 1.3 miles up this trail.

Continue on the DP and reach Devil's Acre lean-to and spring. Level terrain follows for .7 mile where you will reach a side trail to the left that leads to a nice view. A long, gradual descent follows to beautiful West Kill Creek and Diamond Notch Falls. The blue Diamond Notch Trail leaves to the left and climbs gradually for .4 mile to Diamond Notch lean-to. The DP continues with a long climb up Westkill Mountain with springs and some rock overhangs. Before reaching the summit of Westkill, there are great views to the north, south, and east. Begin a gradual descent, passing another spring, and hike along the long forested ridge. The trail makes a short climb up a summit on the western ridge of Westkill and then begins a descent that grows increasingly steeper down to a wetland in Mink Hollow (not the same Mink Hollow as on the eastern section). The trail turns right and descends to a small parking area along Route 6.

•   •   •

I first hiked the Devil's Path about ten years ago. It would be the trail that marked a change, a beginning. Prior to my first hike on this trail I had spent most of my time in Pennsylvania, but some friends decided to organize a hike on the Devil's Path with the goal of completing the entire length in one day. I was naïve enough to think I could do it.

On the morning of the hike I awoke early, leaving my tent as the sun lifted over the mountains, casting the summits in a golden glow. Deep spruce forests covered the ridges as cliffs adorned the notches. I couldn't believe this entire world had always been so close to home. I realized that there was so much more to see, to experience. This is how I need to spend more of my life, I thought. And the great thing about mountains is that they are incredibly patient.

We began our hike in the cool of the morning. At first, I was able to keep up with the group, but as we climbed Indian Head Mountain, I began to fall behind. I was amazed by the endless serrated ridges that faded toward the horizon of the mist-shrouded Hudson Valley. I climbed up Twin and Sugarloaf Mountains and rested at the views that looked to the south. Slide, Wittenberg, and Cornell mountains rose across a forested wilderness. My mind began to map out all the places I needed to visit. I tried to imagine what the view was like from the top of Slide Mountain. From the Catskills, my thoughts spread to the Whites, Adirondacks, Shenandoahs, and Great Smokies.

My muscles strained on the climb up Plateau Mountain as my lungs imploded. The rolling 2 miles across the top of the mountain in a deep spruce forest felt like heaven. I reached the western edge of Plateau and had to stop to absorb the view. The mountain fell into rugged Stony Clove Notch as the sun glistened across a cobalt sky. The trail began a long, steep descent off the mountain. My legs ached and cramped with exhaustion. As I hobbled down the mountain, I glanced at my watch. Both time and sunlight were fading.

I wasn't going to finish the Devil's Path in a day, but a far greater journey was just beginning.

13. Wittenberg–Cornell–Slide Loop

Length: 16 miles.

Direction of description: Clockwise.

Duration: 1¹/₂ to 2 days.

Difficulty: Moderate to difficult. This hike requires some scrambling over ledges 5 to 15 feet in height.

Trail conditions: Trails are well established and most junctures have signs.

Blazes: Red, yellow, blue.

Water: There are generally sufficient water sources along the trail, but the trail from Wittenberg to Slide Mountain can be dry in the summer months.

Vegetation: Mostly hardwoods with some pine and hemlock. Higher elevations contain birch, fir, and spruce.

Highlights: Superb views, scenic streams, Giant Ledge, beautiful forests of fir and spruce, Slide Mountain, the highest peak in the Catskills.

Issues: Camping opportunities are limited on this loop, and it can be crowded on weekends from the spring to fall.

Location: The loop passes through Woodland Valley Campground, near Phoenicia.

This is the classic hike, and finest loop, in the Catskills. With a wide array of scenic features, beautiful forests, isolation, and views, this is widely considered a "must hike" in the area. Expect company on the weekends, where sections of the loop receive a lot of traffic, particularly from dayhikers going to Wittenberg, Slide, or the Giant Ledge.

You can start from either Woodland Valley or Slide Mountain parking area. This description begins from Woodland Valley because it seems to be the more common place to begin this hike. Many hikers shuttle cars between the two trailheads and only hike the Burroughs Range, or Wittenberg, Cornell, and Slide. However, it is a long shuttle for a relatively short section of the trail. While some hikers dismiss the northern half of this loop because it doesn't feature the elevations of the Burroughs Range, I feel it is scenic, isolated, and worth hiking, particularly if you include the Giant Ledge.

The easier way to hike the loop is to go counterclockwise; this would avoid the climb up Wittenberg. However, this description is clockwise from Woodland Valley.

The parking area at Woodland Valley has information kiosks. A small fee is required to park here. Follow the red-marked Wittenberg–Cornell–Slide Trail to the left along the park road, enter a campground to the right, and cross a bridge over flood-torn Woodland Creek. You are immediately faced with the biggest climb of the hike, the 2,400-foot vertical ascent of Wittenberg Mountain. However, it is manageable and very scenic. Initially, the climb is gradual and broken up by level sections. Pass large ledges and boulders with white lichens and carpets of moss. There are many seasonal springs and small streams. The trail passes along cliffs to the left with partial views. The forests are mostly hardwoods with several groves of hemlocks.

The trail levels off for a while, passing ledges and more seasonal streams. Reach a trail intersection with the Terrace Mountain Trail on the left. About .3 mile farther, pass the new, blue-blazed, Phoenicia–

East Branch Trail on the left, which is also the route for the Long Path. (The Phoenicia–East Branch Trail traverses the rolling ridge of Cross Mountain, Mount Pleasant, and Romer Mountain before descending to the end of Lane Street in Phoenicia. It avoids the prior 7-mile road walk out of Woodland Valley to Phoenicia. A fine view to the north from a large, exposed ledge is about a mile down this blue trail.)

The nature of the trail begins to change as it becomes steeper and the forests change to more birch. Negotiate a couple of scrambles, one with a small, overhanging ledge. Above the scrambles, the forest promptly changes to fir and spruce, with a carpet of moss, and is very beautiful. Continue the climb over many ledges and small scrambles. The terrain levels off as you near the summit and the trail soon brings you to one of the best views in the Catskills: a spectacular view to the southeast from an exposed ledge overlooking the Ashokan Reservoir. This is the finest view of the hike and a popular dayhiking destination.

The trail reenters the scenic spruce and fir forests and descends to the col before Cornell Mountain. It isn't a big climb up to Cornell, but there are some challenging scrambles, including one with a narrow crevasse that you must use to wedge yourself to climb up the ledge.

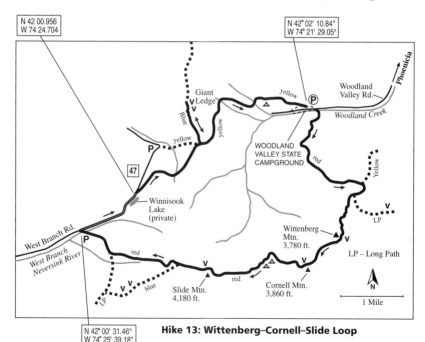

Hike 13: Wittenberg–Cornell–Slide Loop

You will notice the trails over the summits are often gravelly and retain water. A short trail to the left on the top of Cornell leads to a minor view, but the best views from Cornell come as you descend the west slope toward Slide, where two small ledges offer nice views over a forest of stunted spruce and fir. Descend into the col between Cornell and Slide and pass the first of about five campsites, most to the left of the trail. The forests are beautiful, but water is not reliable and often dries up in the summer.

Next comes a steady but manageable climb up Slide. A short side trail to the right leads to a seasonal spring. Soon thereafter are a couple of ladders that bring the trail into the spruce and fir forest. Negotiate more scrambles over mossy ledges and reach the Burroughs Plaque, embedded into a large ledge below the summit of Slide. There are only partial views from the top of Slide. Continue on the level gravel trail and pass a nice view to the right, looking north. The trail begins a gradual descent and passes the blue Curtis–Ormsbee Trail to the left. This is an alternate way down from Slide and offers some nice views. If you go this way, turn right onto the yellow Phoenicia–East Branch Trail to return to your car. This will add about a mile to your hike.

Otherwise, continue on the red Wittenberg–Cornell–Slide Trail to descend from Slide. The descent continues to be gradual, but then steepens before following an old, eroded woods road through a forest of hardwoods. Turn right onto the Phoenicia–East Branch Trail as it follows its own old forest grade over some small streams. Descend steeply from the grade and cross the West Branch Neversink River without a bridge. The Slide Mountain parking area is just ahead.

Turn right onto Slide Mountain Road and climb gradually. There are occasional yellow blazes along the road. The road passes a private club and Winnisook Lake, guarded by a fence. After the lake, there is an important trail to take. Look for a sign and an old forest road to the right. The sign indicates there is an easement for public hiking, but you must remain on the unblazed trail. It is clearly established. This route avoids both the extended road walk and an unnecessary descent and climb totaling 800 vertical feet. The unblazed trail is level and crosses several small springs under a forest of stately hardwoods; stinging nettle may be a problem in the summer. The trail crosses back into public land where several large, flat rocks cross the trail. The trail remains unblazed and unsigned. Cross a small stream and gradually climb to a trail juncture with the yellow Phoenicia–East Branch Trail.

Turn right, and then turn left onto the trail to the Giant Ledge, a side hike off the loop that is worth doing. This blue-blazed trail is level and follows a causeway of rocks over wet areas. The climb begins gradually, but becomes increasingly steeper over rocks and ledges. Pass a short trail to the left that leads to a spring. The climb steepens and then levels over ledges. Pass a few dry campsites and reach the first view from the Giant Ledge, a phenomenal panorama looking over Woodland Valley, the Burroughs Range, Panther Mountains, and the Devil's Path range in the distance. Additional views are up the trail. Retrace your steps back down to the Phoenicia–East Branch Trail on which you'll turn left back to Woodland Valley.

The descent is gradual under hardwoods as it passes small springs. The hardwood forest is scenic, and there is one grove of hemlocks. Cross a stream as the trail becomes rockier and the descent steepens to a larger stream with potential campsites, although there may be no established sites. Cross the boulder-filled creek, which may be difficult in high water, or dry in summer. A climb promptly follows up a series of stone steps into exposed ledges. Turn right and the trail levels with some interesting cross-bedded sandstone ledges to the left. A dry campsite is on a level bench below the trail to the right. The trail descends down to the parking area at Woodland Valley, bringing an end to the hike.

•   •   •

I reached the trailhead as a May storm slowly approached from the west, casting the blue morning sky with a veil of high clouds that gradually dimmed the sun. Shadows in the forest were replaced with the glow of the fresh green foliage. Everything seemed alive. The ground gave birth to countless springs and small streams that tumbled down the slope and collected on the trail.

By the time I reached Giant Ledge, the veneer of clouds had extended to the east and the sun offered only a faint glow. The view was still breathtaking, and I had it to myself. Woodland Valley was a carpet of green that extended almost to the tops of the mountains, which were still bare of leaves, capped by the deep green forests of spruce and fir on the summits.

By the time I reached Woodland Valley, the clouds made good on their promise, and a soft rain began to fall. Drops tapped the leaves of the trees and painted the forest with deeper, richer hues of green, brown, and gray. The rain was a relief instead of an annoyance. The cool drops traced my skin and eased the sweat and heat of the day as the percussion of rain danced in the canopy.

I made my way up Wittenberg into a bare forest of birch with leaves just beginning to bloom. Continuing my climb, I soon entered a spruce and fir forest that dripped with moisture from the clouds. Rich green moss covered the forest floor as florescent lichens caked the ledges and rocks. I reached the view from Wittenberg. The rounded summits to the south seemed to defy gravity as they floated in a sea of mist and clouds. The Ashokan Reservoir had disappeared. Wisps of mist sailed between the mountains and hung in the cols. The clouds had become the landscape as I stood within it, alone.

14. Southern Catskills

Length: 17.7 miles from Woodland Valley Campground to Peekamoose Road. From Lane Street in Phoenicia to Peekamoose Road, the trail is 24.3 miles.

Direction of description: North to south.

Duration: 1^1/$_2$ to 2^1/$_2$ days.

Difficulty: Moderate to difficult.

Trail conditions: Trails are generally well blazed and signed.

Blazes: Blue, red, yellow.

Water: Generally sufficient but can be limited in dry summers.

Vegetation: Hardwoods, while the mountain summits have deep spruce/fir forests.

Highlights: Superb vistas, Slide Mountain, Neversink River, isolation, good camping.

Issues: The trails on Cornell, Wittenberg, and Slide Mountains can be crowded on the weekends with competition for camping.

Location: The trail is between Woodland Valley or Phoenicia and Peekamoose Road.

This linear trail explores five Catskills peaks with excellent views and great camping along the Neversink River. While the Neversink is a popular place to camp, and the trail on Cornell, Wittenberg, and Slide can be crowded, you can expect fewer people on Table and

Peekamoose Mountains. This route is also isolated, as it does not cross a single road.

If you want a longer trek, you can begin at the small parking area at the end of Lane Street in Phoenicia. A total of 9.5 miles of new trail was finished in 2014, representing the work of over 100 volunteers and almost 10,000 hours of labor. The trail is blazed blue. It is known as the Phoenicia–East Branch Trail and is also the route of the Long Path. It avoids a 7-mile road walk of the former route. The trail meanders through a small stream valley and ascends via old forest grades and newly dug sidehill across small streams and springs. Some of the rock work and stone steps are impressive. The grade is gradual as the trail follows many switchbacks under pine and hemlock dying from the woolly adelgid. Reach the ridge of Romer Mountain in a hardwood forest. Follow the rolling ridge with ledges, boulders, and one narrow crevice through which the trail passes. The trail follows near the edge of some cliffs on Mount Pleasant with a partial view of Wittenberg Mountain. Continue along the cliffs and descend into a col before climbing gradually up the rolling ridge of Cross Mountain. Enjoy beautiful views to the north from a large, exposed ledge. Continue to climb to the intersection with the red Wittenberg–Cornell–Slide Trail, where you will turn left to continue this hike.

For a shorter hike, begin at Woodland Valley. The parking area at Woodland Valley has information kiosks. A small fee is required to park here. Follow the red-marked Wittenberg–Cornell–Slide Trail to the left along the park road, enter a campground to the right and cross a bridge over flood-torn Woodland Creek. You are immediately faced with the biggest climb of the hike, the 2,400-foot vertical ascent of Wittenberg Mountain. However, it is manageable and very scenic. Initially, the climb is gradual and broken up by level sections. Pass large ledges and boulders with white lichens and carpets of moss. There are many seasonal springs and small streams. The trail passes along cliffs to the left with partial views. The forests are mostly hardwoods with several groves of hemlocks.

The trail levels off for a while, passing ledges and more seasonal streams. Reach a trail intersection with the Terrace Mountain Trail and turn right on the red trail. About .3 mile farther, pass the new, blue-blazed, Phoenicia–East Branch Trail on the left, which is also the route for the Long Path.

The nature of the trail begins to change as it becomes steeper and the forests change to more birch. Negotiate a couple of scrambles, one with

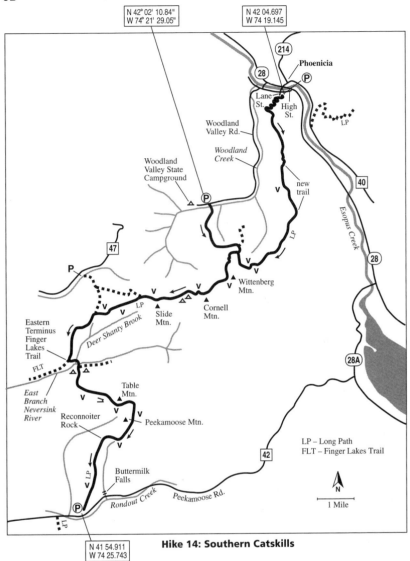

N 42° 02' 10.84"
W 74° 21' 29.05"

N 42 04.697
W 74 19.145

Phoenicia

Lane St.

High St.

Woodland Valley Rd.

Woodland Creek

Woodland Valley State Campground

new trail

Esopus Creek

Wittenberg Mtn.

Cornell Mtn.

Slide Mtn.

Deer Shanty Brook

Eastern Terminus Finger Lakes Trail

FLT

East Branch Neversink River

Table Mtn.

Reconnoiter Rock

Peekamoose Mtn.

LP – Long Path
FLT – Finger Lakes Trail

Buttermilk Falls

Rondout Creek

Peekamoose Rd.

N
1 Mile

N 41 54.911
W 74 25.743

Hike 14: Southern Catskills

a small, overhanging ledge. Above the scrambles, the forest promptly changes to fir and spruce, with a carpet of moss, and is very beautiful. Continue the climb over many ledges and small scrambles. The terrain levels off as you near the summit, and the trail soon brings you to one of the best views in the Catskills, a spectacular view to the southeast from an exposed ledge overlooking the Ashokan Reservoir. This is one of the finest views of the hike and a popular dayhiking destination.

The trail reenters the scenic spruce and fir forests and descends to the col before Cornell Mountain. It isn't a big climb up to Cornell, but there are some challenging scrambles, including one with a narrow crevasse that you must use to wedge yourself to climb up the ledge. You will notice the trails over the summits are often gravelly and retain water. A short trail to the left on the top of Cornell leads to a minor view, but the best views from Cornell come as you descend the west slope toward Slide, where two small ledges offer nice views over a forest of stunted spruce and fir. Descend into the col between Cornell and Slide and pass the first of about five campsites, most to the left of the trail. The forests are beautiful but water is not reliable and often dries up in the summer.

Next comes a steady but manageable climb up Slide. A short side trail to the right leads to a seasonal spring. Soon thereafter are a couple of ladders that bring the trail into the spruce and fir forest. Negotiate more scrambles over mossy ledges and reach the Burroughs Plaque, embedded into a large ledge below the summit of Slide. There are only partial views from the top of Slide. Continue on the level gravel trail and pass a nice view to the right, looking north. The trail begins a gradual descent through a gorgeous spruce and fir forest with carpets of moss; the treadway is comprised of white gravel. Reach the blue Curtis–Ormsbee Trail, where you turn left.

The Curtis–Ormsbee Trail descends via well-graded switchbacks under a thick spruce and fir forest. Descend over some small ledges as the trail becomes steeper; the hiking levels off as the forests change to more hardwoods. Extensive trout lilies bloom in this area in May; trilliums are also common. Reach a side trail to the left that leads to a minor view of Table Mountain to the south, which you will climb later. Continue a descent over small ledges and reach another vista, just to the right of the trail where you can see the valley and lower hills to the west. Both views are gradually being grown over. A steeper scramble follows as the trail descends between tiers of ledges. The terrain levels off before reaching a unique chasm, or crevasse, where a huge boulder separated from the cliff. When it is wet, springs tumble down into this crevasse, and the trail scrambles down steeply to its bottom. The terrain moderates and soon the blue trail ends at the yellow Phoenicia–East Branch Trail, where you turn left.

This trail follows an old forest road as it gradually descends off the mountain. The old, narrow road is somewhat eroded and follows the contours of the mountain. When it is wet, this trail tends to collect water, and streams flow down it. At one point, the grade hugs the steep slope of the mountain as it is surrounded by boulders. The descent steepens a little as it nears the stream valley. While the forest is mostly hardwoods, you will also pass some large, old-growth hemlocks. Reach the blue Peekamoose–Table Trail, where you turn left. This trail juncture is also the rather diminutive eastern terminus of the Finger Lakes Trail, which stretches all the way across New York to Allegany State Park at the western end of the state. The yellow Phoenicia–East Branch Trail continues straight and ends at the Denning Road parking area.

The blue trail descends and enters a hemlock forest before crossing two bridges, one on each side of what appears to be an island over the East Branch Neversink River. The bridges are high and well constructed, although it is advised you do not use the bridges in high water as the river is very dangerous. The second bridge is a more exposed log bridge. There are nice campsites near the river, and this is a popular camping area for people coming in from Denning Road. Climb away from the river and pass an unofficial trail to the left that goes up along the river. This is known as the Fisherman's Trail and is a popular place for camping.

The blue trail makes a steady climb, going up small ledges and scrambles. The trail levels off, passing a view now grown over. The trail descends into a wet area and makes another climb up through ledges. Pass a side trail to the right that leads to a fine view of Van Wyck Mountain, but be careful—the view is from a narrow fin of rock. Descend into another small col and begin a steadier climb. Pass a spring to the left, and shortly thereafter a side trail to the right that leads to a shelter. At just under 3,500 feet it is one of the highest in the Catskills. The shelter has a western exposure, so there are sunsets when the leaves are off the trees. If you want to see a sunset while camping here, however, I recommend hiking up to the view on Table Mountain. A privy and small campsite are up the hill behind the shelter.

The blue trail makes a steeper climb under birch trees and soon enters a spruce/fir forest. As the trail levels off, look for a side trail to the right that leads to a narrow ledge with a superb view of the western foothills with Doubletop Mountain rising in the distance. This is the sunset view you should take advantage of if camping at the shelter. The trail across Table Mountain is level, but offers no other views. The spruce/fir forests with carpets of moss are very scenic.

Descend steeply into the col on Peekamoose Mountain; this col is deeper and larger than what is shown on most maps. A gradual climb up Peekamoose follows to a large, random boulder at the summit. Look for a side trail to the left just after the boulder; it leads to an amazing view to the east, including Ashokan Reservoir and Ashokan High Point.

The blue trail begins the long descent off Peekamoose, following a ridge and descending over series of ledges. The forests gradually change from spruce/fir to hardwoods. Reach a fine view just to the left of the trail looking west. A steep scramble follows, and in typical fashion, level hiking is divided by tiers of ledges and some scrambles. Reach Reconnoiter Rock, a large boulder perched on a ledge. The trail steadily descends under a scenic and mature hardwood forest. Pick up an old forest grade and reach a trail register. Descend to the parking area along Peekamoose Road and the scenic, isolated Rondout Creek valley. This is a beautiful area, with swimming holes and primitive car camping. While here, be sure to check out gorgeous Buttermilk Falls, about a mile up the road, on the left.

• • •

The trail was a brown thread through a bare, early spring tapestry. The naked forest clawed the blue sky and divided the bright sun with grids of shadows. Countless yellow trout lilies provided a splash of color and a hint of the season to come. We took a break along the East Branch Neversink River, snacking on granola bars and soaking our tired feet in the frigid water. The light of the sun twinkled across the current, and then angled to the streambed below.

A group marched across the bridge with massive packs for one night. They were camping off the trail, up the river, and their dogs barked and circled around us. A second group soon arrived, college students who belonged to an outdoors club. They carried with them a fresh, crisp energy in contrast to our more weathered experience. When I went to college, it seemed to be the limit of my tiny, self-contained universe. Now I see how deluded I was, and how much time could have been better spent as I sat in this isolated valley, deep in the Catskills—a realm I never even knew existed back then.

The long climb up Table Mountain brought us to a lean-to, dedicated to the memory of someone who had put much time and energy into the very place we would call home for only one night. The rusted sun sat bloated and decayed on the horizon until it dissolved into the clouds. The red light coated everything it touched. The woods were silent until a massive 747 roared above, appearing too close before turning south toward the city. A weak fire glimmered between the rocks as I shivered in the cold night, despite my sleeping bag.

Blue skies returned the next morning as we hiked quickly up Table and then Peekamoose Mountains. We followed a trail to the left on the summit of Peekamoose to a breathtaking vista that rose over the morning mist; the Ashokan Reservoir shimmered like polished metal. From the rugged Devil's Path range to the Hudson Valley, a whole world was spread before us.

 # 15. Western Catskills

Length: 36.5 miles.

Direction of description: West to east.

Duration: $2^1/_2$ to $3^1/_2$ days.

Difficulty: Moderate to difficult.

Trail conditions: Trails are generally well blazed and most junctures have signs. Some areas are brushy and have briars. Steep ascents and descents frequently have loose rock. Trails often follow old forest roads, grades, or snowmobile trails. Much of this route also follows the Finger Lakes Trail.

Blazes: Blue, red, yellow.

Water: Variable. Trail can be dry in summer or periods of low precipitation, particularly between Cat Hollow Road (Route 206/7) and Big Pond.

Vegetation: Hardwoods with some plantations of spruce and pine. There is a spruce/fir forest on the summit of Balsam Lake Mountain.

Highlights: Trout Pond, Big Pond, Alder Lake, waterfall, ledges, boulders, crevices, some views, Balsam Lake Mountain, isolation.

Issues: These trails are isolated and do not see a lot of backpackers. The shuttle is long and can take almost an hour, one way. The views that do exist tend to be narrow in scope or partially overgrown.

Location: The trails are north of Roscoe, south of Downsville.

This trail is for those looking for a lonely, woodland hike in a fairly isolated setting. Do not be fooled by the relatively modest elevations—this is a challenging hike as the trail crosses roller-coaster terrain with many, sometimes steep, climbs and descents. These climbs reach 800 vertical feet and feature loose rock and narrow side-hill. The trail often winds its way up through tiers of ledges and boulders where there are some interesting overhangs, crevices, and formations. The elevation profile is probably easier if you hike east to west, but this description goes from west to east, saving Balsam Lake Mountain for the end. You can also easily shorten this hike since most road crossings have a parking area. The most scenic and interesting areas are in the western half of this hike; shortening this backpack from Beech Hill Road to Balsam Lake Mountain is a good option.

From the parking area on Russell Brook Road, follow the gated road down to the brook and cross a bridge. Enter a small, overgrown meadow where unmarked trails to the right go a short distance to a beautiful waterfall in a scenic glen. Back on the main trail, pass a campsite on the bank to the right and reach a trail juncture in short order. Follow the blue trail to the right to Trout Pond. A different blue trail to the left goes to Mud Pond. If you have the time, visiting Mud Pond is worth your while since it is very scenic. Trout and Mud Ponds are part of a popular dayhike loop, or can be a quick overnight, with lean-tos and campsites at Trout Pond.

The blue trail to Trout Pond gradually climbs along an old forest grade, passing a side trail to the left that goes to some campsites. The trail soon reaches the beautiful, undeveloped pond surrounded by rolling mountains. Hike along the eastern shore with fine views across the water. Reach the northern end of the pond where you'll find a spring and a campsite to the right, and a lean-to and trail juncture just beyond. The blue trail to the left goes to another lean-to farther up the hill and continues on to Mud Pond. Take the blue trail to the right to Campbell Mountain.

The roller-coaster terrain on this hike now begins. Hike along an old forest road that doubles as a snowmobile trail. There is a gradual 400-foot vertical ascent, followed by a much steeper 450-foot vertical descent to a stream. Cross the stream over a bridge and climb gradually to Campbell Brook Road. Follow the road to the left for a short distance and enter the woods, again on an old forest grade. There is a 300-foot vertical ascent, and then a winding 450-foot vertical descent; at the bottom, cross Campbell Brook over a bridge. Climb gradually to Campbell Mountain Road where there is a parking area. Climb again up to Campbell Mountain, crest over the ridge, and descend more steeply. The Finger Lakes Trail joins from the left and follows the same

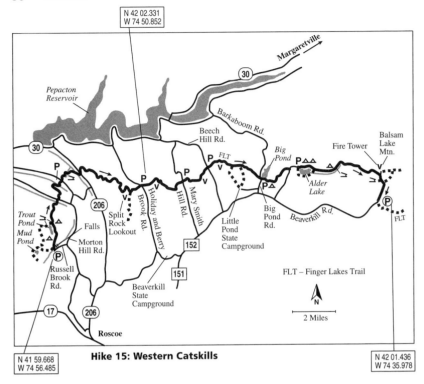

N 42 02.331
W 74 50.852

N 41 59.668
W 74 56.485

N 42 01.436
W 74 35.978

Hike 15: Western Catskills

route to the end of the hike. Watch for loose rock on the winding descent into a small drainage. A side trail to the right goes to the Campbell Mountain lean-to and a small stream that flows behind it. Continue the descent to Cat Hollow where there are spruce plantations and several stone foundations of old homesteads, now long gone. Climb to, and cross, Route 206/7.

A 600-foot vertical climb follows, with some steep slopes. Reach the top of the ridge, where you'll find rolling terrain and some interesting piles of moss-covered stone, possibly the remnants of a quarry. Climb again for 300 vertical feet to the top of Brock Mountain and then descend, passing a small campsite. The descent becomes steeper. When the leaves are off the trees it is possible to see the Pepacton Reservoir, which is often shrouded in mist in the morning. Reach the bottom of the valley, and then make a slight ascent followed by a long, winding ascent around some spruce plantations. Reach the bottom again in a spruce forest with old stone walls. Reach an eroded, old forest road surrounded by rock walls, where the trail turns right. Reach a juncture with a yellow trail, but turn left onto the blue trail; an increasingly steep climb follows. Enter an area full of briars before the trail levels off above some ledges. Reach beautiful Split Rock Overlook—the view to the west is one of the finest on the trail. There is a boulder at the view; be careful, a deep crevice divides the ledge on which the boulder sits. A very steep climb follows. Reach a trail juncture and turn left on the red Mary Smith Trail.

Descend to a meadow and power line before reaching Holiday and Berry Brook Road, where there is a trailhead and register. A very steep 500-foot vertical ascent follows. The top features rolling terrain and a narrow view to the south. (I could be wrong, but I thought I saw New Jersey's High Point monument almost 50 miles to the south.) Climb gradually to the top of Mary Smith Hill and then descend to another narrow view to the southeast. The trail is then very steep down to Mary Smith Road where there is parking and a register. The climb up to Middle Mountain is about 700 vertical feet, which becomes steeper as you ascend. Descend into a col and climb over Beech Hill before descending 500 vertical feet to Beech Hill Road. Follow the road to the right and then turn left, off the road, at a parking area and register. Cross a wet area between private land and begin another steep 500-foot vertical ascent to a rolling ridge and then another short ascent to the top of Cabot Hill. Reach a ledge with an overgrown view to the east. A steep descent follows to a col. Pass a yellow trail to the right that goes down to the Little Pond Campground. Climb a 300-foot vertical ascent up Touch-Me-Not Mountain and pass a blue trail to the right; continue on the red trail. A long descent begins to beautiful Big Pond where rolling mountains rise in the distance. Hike along the road a short distance and then turn left onto another road to a parking area. The trail goes through meadows and along pine forests where there is camping allowed.

A climb follows, but this one features more gradual switchbacks. Pass through some spruce forests and round the side of the mountain with brush and briars. Descend gradually, passing small springs, and reach a small stream. Cross the stream and turn left onto an old forest road, continuing a gradual climb. A meadow is off to your left as the slight climb continues. The trail turns right and climbs over a ridge, only to then descend between ledges. Cross a small stream at the bottom and reach Alder Lake Road. Cross the road and then follow a gated gravel road to Alder Lake; there are few blazes and no trail signs here. The road ascends and then levels off to a parking area, register, and kiosk. Continue straight, passing the massive stone remains of a mansion. Reach the beautiful lake where water cascades over the dam. There are picnic tables and a number of campsites are on the north and south shores of the lake. Bear left on the red trail along the north shore. The trail is brushy and it is hard to see the lake at first. Cross a few small streams over bridges and then wrap around the east end of the lake. Ascend gradually along an old grade and reach the yellow trail, where you turn left.

The yellow trail climbs gradually up a stream valley along an old, eroded forest road. There are some steeper slopes and small side streams, and the grade narrows down to a trail as you hike. Reach the scenic Beaver Meadows lean-to on the right where it overlooks its namesake. The climb steepens up to the ridge as it meanders around and over ledges. Reach the ridge and climb up and down two hills where there is a minor view from an overgrown ledge. The trail now begins the climb up to Balsam Lake Mountain, the sixteenth highest, and westernmost, of the Catskill's high peaks. The climb is mostly gradual along ledges and boulders on the side of the mountain, but there are some steep slopes. The trail follows some long switchbacks and enters a spruce forest. Level terrain follows, through birch and spruce, until it reaches a red trail. To go to the summit, turn left and climb gradually through a beautiful spruce/fir forest. Reach the top where there is a picnic table, small cabin, and fire tower, which you can climb to see the superb views. The summit is otherwise forested. Retrace your steps and continue the descent on the red trail. The descent is much steeper than the climb as it entails some stone steps and ledges. Pass a good, piped spring and a side trail to a lean-to. Reach the bottom, and a trail juncture. Bear right on the blue trail as it descends gradually along an old forest road. Pass some meadows to the right and continue the easy descent along a private property line. The trail soon reaches the parking area.

• • •

Once again I found myself alone on the trail, slowly engulfed by darkness. I hiked up to Trout Pond and took a moment to look over the still water, perfectly reflecting the metallic shades of twilight. Some geese honked on the far shore. As I pushed on, I was soon hiking in darkness. Not even the moon was in the sky as thousands of stars shone through the bare trees. The trail took me up and over hills and down through stream valleys. I felt lonely, knowing I'd probably see no one else on my trip.

I reached a desolate country road, almost hoping to see a car drive by. My headlamp seemed to be losing power and I had to pay close attention to find the trail. Finally, I arrived at the top of a ridge, surrounded by a vast, invisible forest. In this dark, cool, bare world I felt utterly inconsequential.

I descended off the ridge and found the side trail to the Campbell Mountain lean-to. It was strangely comforting to hear some traffic in the valley below. The lean-to had seen better days, but I laid out my sleeping bag, a mouse sniffing for crumbs my only company.

When the morning light began to glow through the crevices of the lean-to, I welcomed the noise of traffic from the valley. I headed down the trail as the sun's orange glow painted the tops of the hills and ridges. The trail went by abandoned stone foundations, cloaked in moss and sunk in the ground, and along an old road broken by the roots of trees. There were once homes and barns in this place, where people were born, lived, and died. But the forest is very patient, and it has returned. There is incredible power in patience and the slowest persistence.

I hiked by houses and farms and along roads, but I saw no one. Few people lived here, and even fewer stayed. Farms were grown over, subdivided into lonely vacation homes. I looked down to see fresh footprints in the mud on the trail and wondered if I would catch up to this person. Who was he and where was he going? I would never know.

I hiked into the night again on the second day and made my home in another lean-to as the wind surged through the trees like a tide. The moonlight tore through wisps of fast-moving clouds. The next morning was cool and gray as low clouds concealed the sun. I hiked the trail up the ridge and into the clouds, driven by a powerful wind. The trees dripped with moisture condensed from the clouds.

I descended from the mountain and reached the trailhead, one of the most isolated in the state. Another car was in the parking area, waiting for its owner to return from the trail. It was all the company I got—or needed.

Central and Western New York: Finger Lakes Trail System and North Country Trail

This region of New York provides a backpacking experience unlike any other. Alpine peaks and wilderness are traded for friendly towns, farms, and pastoral views. Central and western New York were once the playground for glaciers, which dug massive trenches that filled to create the Finger Lakes, rearranged rivers and streams, and morphed the topography to allow the formation of the state's most stunning waterfalls. You will find the trails here to be diverse and worthwhile, with gorges, glens, and waterfalls surreal in their beauty.

All the backpacking opportunities in this area of New York are along the vast Finger Lakes Trail System. The North Country Trail overlays the route of the Finger Lakes Trail from the Pennsylvania border to the village of Cuyler. These trails showcase man's relationship, utility, and dependence on the environment. The choice is not between development and preservation; we can accomplish both, as these trails illustrate.

Trails maintained by: Finger Lakes Trail Conference, www.flt conference.org. The Conservation Trail is maintained by the Foothills Trail Club, www.foothillstrailclub.org. Volunteers build and maintain these trails.

16. Morgan Hill State Forest

Length: 14-mile loop.

Direction of description: Counterclockwise.

Duration: 1¹/₂ to 2 days.

Difficulty: Moderate. Terrain tends to be gradual with a few steep sections.

Trail conditions: Trails are well established.

Blazes: The North Country Trail/Onondaga Trail is blazed blue; trail to Tinker Falls is orange.

Water: There are generally sufficient water sources along the trail.

Vegetation: Hardwoods with some pine and hemlock, as well as extensive spruce plantations.

Highlights: Jones Hill view, Spruce Pond, Shackham Pond, Tinker Falls, Hemlock Ravine, spruce forests, scenic streams.

Issues: Road walking is required to complete the loop. Some areas of the trail are wet and muddy.

Location: The trails are north of Truxton.

Morgan Hill State Forest is home to the North Country Trail (NCT) and offers some of the finest backpacking in central New York. Here, you will find ponds, scenic streams, waterfalls, deep ravines, and spruce forests. This loop is an ideal overnight trip and includes almost all the highlights in the forest. It is more convenient than hiking the 17 miles of the NCT through the state forest, as that is a linear trail and requires a shuttle. Expect to see the most people around Tinker Falls, Jones Hill vista, and the ponds.

Begin at the Tinker Falls parking area along NY 91 and follow the wide, graded trail up along the creek and into a glen. This trail ends at beautiful Tinker Falls as it drops about 50 feet from an overhanging ledge. Retrace your steps back toward the road and turn right onto an orange-blazed trail that ascends the north edge of the Tinker Falls glen. The climb is steep in parts. The trail levels off and meets the blue-blazed NCT; to the left, the NCT goes uphill; instead, go straight (or slightly right) on the NCT. The NCT drops down to the creek and passes above Tinker Falls where there is a neat waterslide eroded into the bedrock. Climb up a series of wooden steps before the trail makes a gradual incline, followed by a series of switchbacks up the slope.

Reach the edge of the plateau with a spruce forest off to your left. The trail follows the precipitous edge of the plateau, offering a unique and striking topographic perspective. When the leaves are off the trees, you can see a large wetland down in the valley. The trail begins a descent that is steep in sections. The descent eases a little as the trail enters a spruce forest, one of many along this trail. Pass a register and reach Shackham Road.

Cross the road and drop down to a scenic creek with a footbridge and campsite. A side stream cascades down a small waterslide. Cross the bridge and turn right, heading downstream through a scenic spruce and hemlock forest. The NCT traverses the bank above the creek. Turn left and reach Hemlock Ravine, a highlight of the trail. The NCT climbs up along the ravine, passing one falls about 10 feet high and many other cascades. As you climb, the ravine becomes much steeper and narrower; the trail follows the rim of the ravine. True to its name, there are many hemlocks; some are quite large. The scenery is superb. The climb is steady, but never very steep. Reach the Hemlock Lean-to, which is in a beautiful location. The trail drops down to the creek and crosses it. Begin a steeper climb as the trail leaves the hemlocks. The gradient eases before the trail descends into a unique mini-glen; do not miss the falls off to your right as you cross the creek. Climb out of the mini-glen and follow the trail up through a pine forest. Pass a register and reach Morgan Hill Road.

The NCT crosses the road and continues south, or right, where it enters a resplendent spruce forest. However, this route turns left onto Morgan Hill Road. A three-mile road walk follows; while not ideal, it isn't bad for a road walk. The road is single lane, dirt, and rarely traveled outside of hunting season. It passes through many deep spruce forests. The road descends and meets Herlihy Road to the left; continue straight on a narrower, gated forest road. This road descends to a small stream. Turn left onto the blue-blazed NCT. You will follow the NCT all the way back to Tinker Falls.

These miles of trail are a pleasure to hike as the NCT meanders and climbs gradually through more spruce forests, crossing some small streams and drainages. Hike along a forested ridge before descending to a nice stream with potential camping. The trail crosses the stream and meanders through a beautiful spruce forest. Pass a register and cross Herlihy Road. Begin a slight ascent that follows the contour of the hill, and then descend into more spruce. You can see Shackham Pond glistening through the woods. The trail crosses the grassy embankment of the beautiful pond, which is undeveloped and surrounded by pine and spruce. This is the perfect place to take a break. Reach a small peninsula with a huge pine tree and small cemetery. There is also a campsite, and it would be hard to find a nicer place to camp. The trail crosses the other outlet of the pond and climbs to Shackham Road.

The NCT switchbacks up the hill and then begins to descend toward a creek. This section of the hike has many wet and muddy spots. Cross the creek and hike up along it through hemlocks. There is good potential camping in this area. Reach a wetland and cross a logging road. The trail traverses the side of a hill and drops down to beautiful

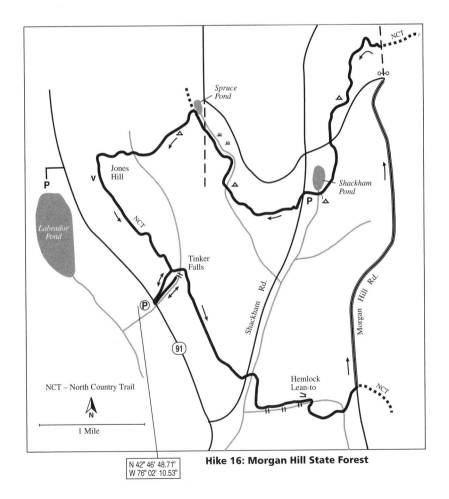

N 42° 46' 48.71"
W 76° 02' 10.53"

Hike 16: Morgan Hill State Forest

Spruce Pond, a small body of water surrounded by its namesake trees. This is a popular place for car campers. The trail leaves the pond and makes a steep climb up the hill, and then levels off (with some muddy sections) and passes a nice dry campsite to your left. The forest becomes hardwoods as the trail descends and enters private property. This section of trail has many wet areas. Reach a small creek and cross it. A steady climb follows up to Jones Hill. The NCT turns left along the crest of the mountain and reaches a dramatic view at a hang glider launch area. The view overlooks Labrador Pond and the rolling farmlands to the northwest. The pond is the most dramatic aspect of this view, as it is so large and lies so close to the foot of Jones Hill. To the right of the pond is a hilly field that seems out of place—maybe it is the glacial moraine. Begin a long, gradual descent from Jones Hill, crossing a forest road that is the more popular route taken to the vista. The NCT switchbacks and descends to where you began the loop, near the top of Tinker Falls. Turn right onto the orange trail and descend steeply down to your car.

While here, check out the Labrador Hollow Unique Area, only a mile or two north of the parking area along NY 91. A long boardwalk offers views of beautiful Labrador Pond and wetlands that are home to plants usually found in the Adirondacks.

• • •

The trail meandered through a cathedral of spruce trees with a mosaic of deep green across the canopy. The setting sun sent shafts of amber light between the trees and across the forest floor of ferns and mosses, casting them with colors as if being lit by stained glass windows. The forest was serene and peaceful, except for the loud hoot of a great horned owl that echoed across the columns of trees. I stood still for just a few minutes. I had to keep moving; in a few hours it would be dark and I still had miles to go.

This was one of the first hikes I did for this book. I was on the cusp of a great journey and it was hard to imagine what awaited me on all the miles of trails I had yet to hike. The scope of this journey felt vast, as if it could harbor a life of its own. My instincts hinted from deep within—I wouldn't be the same when I reached the end.

17. Connecticut Hill Wildlife Management Area and Robert H. Treman State Park

Length: 21-mile linear trail.

Direction of description: West to east.

Duration: 1¹/₂ to 2 days.

Difficulty: Easy to moderate.

Trail conditions: Trail is well established and blazed. There may be a few easy-to-miss turns; a few sections of the trail are wet along the meadows. This trail is virtually rock free.

Blazes: White.

Water: Generally sufficient.

Vegetation: The trail goes through scenic and diverse forests of spruce, pine, hemlock, and hardwoods. The trail passes along and through some meadows.

Highlights: Cayuta Creek and its gorge and tributaries, scenic forests of Connecticut Hill Wildlife Management Area, pastoral views, and the dramatic falls and gorge in Robert H. Treman State Park, which is just off this trail.

Issues: There are approximately 2 miles (total) of road walking. Some areas of the trail are very wet and muddy. Camping is officially restricted in the wildlife management area.

Location: The trail is between Cayuta Lake and Robert H. Treman State Park, south of Ithaca, New York.

This relatively easy linear backpack is ideal for beginners as it explores scenic woodlands, meadows, and streams with cascades. The hike culminates at the impressive Robert H. Treman State Park with its incredible shale gorge and waterfalls. This description is from west to east, saving the state park for the end. If you intend to hike a longer distance on your first day, there are more camping options if you go east to west.

From the small parking area along Gulf Road, follow the white-blazed trail down along Cayuta Creek, passing a memorial. The trail follows an old forest road along the placid creek and into a deep gorge. There are hemlocks, and trilliums in the spring. Considering the deep gorge, the creek resembles a long, narrow pool. As you continue, the current of the creek picks up and you'll notice some riffles. Cross a side stream with cascades over a footbridge, and then a second, larger side stream. A gradual climb follows along old forest roads into a scenic hemlock forest. Descend through a spruce plantation and reach the edge of a glen. The trail eventually makes its way down to the cascading creek. The scenery improves, with larger cascades, slides, and hemlock forests with good potential camping. Leave the creek with a gentle climb, pass a register, and cross Todd Road.

The trail to Ridge Road is a long and very gradual climb with diverse forests of pine and hardwoods. Reenter the woods and the trail turns left, passing small streams and meadows before Cabin Road. The trail is mostly level as it follows an old woods road through more scenic forests. Reach Boylan Road, where the trail turns right, and then cross the road to enter a neat red pine plantation with perfect rows of trees. Enter a hardwood forest as the trail makes a descent; watch the blazes here as it is easy to follow an unblazed trail to the left. Descend gradually into a hemlock forest and cross small streams with potential camping. Cross another forest road, and the trail passes another register and meanders along more small streams with camping.

Hike along a private property line and begin another gradual climb before crossing two forest roads to the summit of Connecticut Hill, where there is a communication tower but no view. Pass the orange-blazed Bob Cameron Loop to the left as the trail wraps around the top of the mountain. Descend and pass behind a home before reaching Black Oak Road; cross the road and enter the woods. Hike the meandering trail across easy terrain to a power line swath with some views to the east. Descend to Griffin Road, on which the trail turns right. This marks the beginning of the first road walk.

The trail is blazed infrequently along the roads. Follow Griffin Road down to Connecticut Hill Road, on which the trail proceeds straight. Climb to Rumsey Hill Road, on which you will turn right and descend with some views. Turn left onto Trumbull Corners Road, which follows a small stream with cascades. Reach a parking area and turn left into the Stevenson Forest Preserve, which is owned by the Finger Lakes Land Trust. Hike along a small stream and climb into a beautiful hemlock forest. A blue side trail to the left leads to a pastoral view. The white trail continues through this scenic forest and descends back to Trumbull Corners Road, on which the trail turns left. Turn right onto Porter Hill Road and begin the biggest climb of the hike. Near the top are the nicest views of the hike where you can see rolling hills and fields to the east. Turn right off the road and enter the woods behind a house as the trail climbs steadily to a campsite in a pine grove. While this is a nice place to camp, it is dry. The trail makes a sharp turn at the campsite and returns to and crosses Porter Hill Road.

A gradual descent follows through woods and along meadows, which can be wet. Cross Hines Road, pass through a stone wall, and hike along the edge of another meadow with an impressive reconstructed barn. Enter the woods, cross small streams, and descend to the Treman State Park boundary. The trail is hilly and it goes in and out of small stream valleys. Between the valleys is level hiking with pine forests. Pass a register as the trail continues its hilly route to a gravel road. Follow a grassy, old forest road down to a stream; a blue-blazed high-water trail is to the left. This blue trail can be used to access the famous and stunning Gorge Trail in the state park. The white trail crosses a bridge over some cascades, goes down along the stream for a short distance, and then makes a steep climb. Pass the end of a road with a home. The trail then follows a gated forest road in the park, which also becomes the Rim Trail. The white trail leaves the forest road to the right to follow along the park's southern boundary.

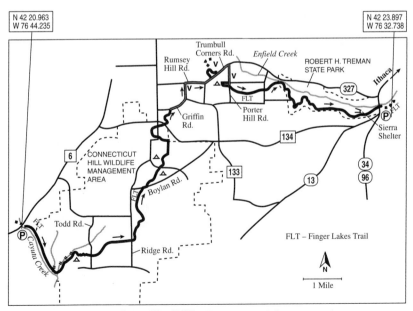

**Hike 17: Connecticut Hill Wildlife Management Area
and Robert H. Treman State Park**

The FLT/NCT basically avoids all the incredible scenic features that make Treman State Park famous. I recommend you at least include the Rim Trail to the overlook of impressive Lucifer Falls. It is well worth your time to follow either the Gorge or Rim Trails through the park instead of the FLT/NCT.

The white trail crosses along the park's southern boundary, going in and out of many small stream valleys, passing behind some homes, and continuing under scenic woodlands. A steeper descent follows as the trail passes an odd, small stone building; soon thereafter, hike behind a group camping or picnic area. The trail is level to the Sierra Shelter, which is along a gated, gravel park road. The shelter is nice, but there is no water nearby and you may hear noises from highways outside the park. The trail stays in the woods, just off the gated park road, and then descends into the woods behind the campground. Follow Enfield Creek and go under the NY 13 and 34 bridge. The gravel parking area is on the right. Keep in mind the only safe way to reach this parking area is by heading north along NY 34.

•   •   •

My career as a backpacker has required me to know rocks intimately. Rocks are a force to be reckoned with and are persistent in their ownership of almost any trail. They have eaten my shoes, clawed at my skin, drawn blood with ease, thrown me off them, and even forced me down on top of them. They can control any hiker like a marionette.

It came as a pleasant surprise to see so few rocks when I hiked this trail. This trail might be the most rock free of any I've hiked. I wish I knew why the rocks surrendered so easily. Maybe glaciers were their mortal enemies.

I sailed along the trail in a deep glen with a placid creek, up a gorge with delicate, sloping cascades, and through forests of pine and spruce. This trail begged me to walk on it, as the forests were beginning to bloom.

At first, my most notable wildlife encounter was the season's initial hatch of black flies that decided to accompany me. Fortunately, they were groggy after a long winter, and I was able to fend them off with a little speed. Later, as I was hiking in a pine forest, I saw a sudden flash of electric red that sparkled in the sunlight. The flash swept from branch to branch before it stopped and I was able to get a good look. It was a lone scarlet tanager, a recent arrival from the Andes. It was here to breed for only a few months before making the long journey back to its exotic home. My journey suddenly felt trivial in comparison.

18. **Finger Lakes National Forest**

Length: 18.5-mile double loop.

Direction of description: Counterclockwise.

Duration: 1¹/₂ to 2 days.

Difficulty: Easy.

Trail conditions: All trails are well signed at junctures and road crossings. The Interloken Trail is also well blazed. The No-Tan-Takto Trail has intermittent blazing and a few confusing areas. The Ravine Trail is well blazed and established. The other trails do not have blazes, but are well established. The trails are notoriously wet and muddy in early to mid-spring, and in the autumn when there is rainy weather. Horse use also makes the No-Tan-Takto Trail muddy in places. Be sure to close the livestock gates where the trails enter and leave the pastures. Cows can be present in the pastures from May to October, but hiking is still allowed.

Blazes: The Interloken Trail is blazed orange; the Ravine Trail is blue; the No-Tan-Takto Trail has intermittent yellow blazes and some older blue blazes.

Water: Generally plentiful, but can be hard to find in a dry summer.

Vegetation: Mostly hardwoods with pine and spruce plantations. Extensive pastures, meadows, and fields. There are some wetlands. There is a hemlock forest along the Ravine Trail.

Highlights: Extensive views, pastures, cows in the warmer months, Teeter Pond, Foster Pond, scenic woodlands, narrow gorge and hemlocks along the Ravine Trail, some large trees and small cascades.

Issues: Backcountry camping is somewhat limited as these trails do not appear to be a well-known backpacking venue. Trails are often wet in the spring and fall. Wind and sun exposure are potential concerns due to the extensive meadows and pastures. Camping is not allowed in the pastures from May to October.

Location: The national forest is north of Watkins Glen.

This figure-eight loop explores New York's only national forest. The scenery of this hike is both unique and surprising, offering a different experience from many trails in this guide. While dayhiking is popular in the national forest, backpacking is less so. This may be because the primary hiking trail is the Interloken Trail (IT). Although scenic, it is only a 12-mile linear trail, which does not lend itself to backpacking. However, by using the other trails in the national forest, an enjoyable overnight backpacking circuit can be created.

From the small parking area for the Burnt Hill Trail on Picnic Area Road, follow the IT across the road in a northerly direction. The trail is level and easy as it explores a scenic forest of hardwoods and some pine. Sections of the trail are very wet and there are many boardwalks (also known as puncheons). Pass the blue-blazed Potomac Trail to the right three different times. Reach Foster Pond and the trail crosses the embankment. There is a potential campsite. Pass a juncture with the Backbone Trail. Follow the IT through a very wet area. The trail continues through the woods; the variety of hardwoods would make this trail ideal in the autumn. The IT turns left and descends gradually before entering a pine and spruce plantation with more boardwalks. Reach another juncture with the Backbone Trail. The IT continues straight and makes a short ascent before a long gradual descent through the woods to County Rt. 1, where there is a trail sign and parking.

The IT cuts diagonally to the left across a field; be sure to keep the livestock gates closed. Reenter the woods and reach beautiful Teeter Pond. The trail follows the earth embankment of the pond, which makes up most of the shore. Sections of this trail will be brushy in summer. There is also a lot of beaver activity, including a beaver lodge right on the trail. Pass a campsite off to the right as the trail continues along an embankment. The pond is home to a lot of birdlife and appears more isolated than it is; a road is just to the north. There is also good camping off the north side of the pond. Reach a larger parking area off Seneca Road and an intersection with the No-Tan-Takto Trail. You will return to this spot via the No-Tan-Takto Trail. Continue on the IT and cross an extensive pasture with many excellent views to the west. This is a good place to see birds of prey such as kestrels and red-tail hawks. The trail follows an old, abandoned country lane covered with grass and bordered by twisted and bent maple trees. Reach the end of the pasture; just off to your left, at the corner of a neighboring pasture, is another superb view of Seneca Lake. The trail follows the old lane into the woods. Turn right, leave the old lane, and reach a small stream with a cascade and potential camping. Look closely, and you will see the remnants of an old earthen dam. Cross the small creek and the trail soon leads to Wilkens Road.

Cross the dirt road and begin a short climb under pine trees. The trail levels off, but becomes very wet for long distances. Circumvent a pasture. The IT bears right and ends at a parking area along Parmenter Road. Now follow the No-Tan-Takto Trail, which is blazed yellow. The yellow blazes are infrequent and the trail is marked across the pastures

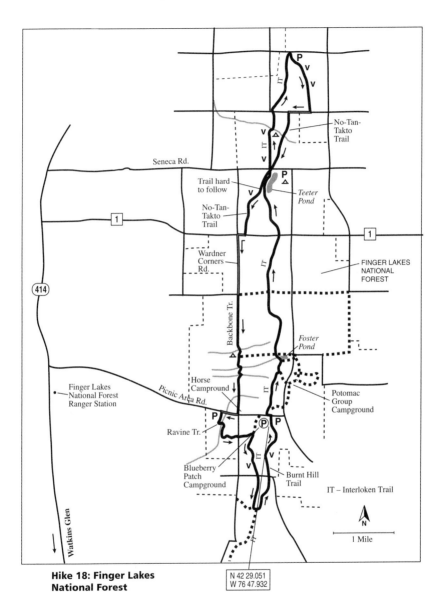

Seneca Rd.

Trail hard
to follow

No-Tan-
Takto
Trail

No-Tan-
Takto
Trail

Teeter
Pond

Wardner
Corners
Rd.

FINGER LAKES
NATIONAL
FOREST

Backbone Tr.

Foster
Pond

Finger Lakes
National Forest
Ranger Station

Picnic Area Rd.

Horse
Campround

Potomac
Group
Campground

Ravine Tr.

Blueberry
Patch
Campground

Burnt Hill
Trail

IT – Interloken Trail

Watkins Glen

N

1 Mile

**Hike 18: Finger Lakes
National Forest**

N 42 29.051
W 76 47.932

by plastic posts; you will also notice some old blue blazes. Much of this trail crosses pastures and fields. The trail leaves the woods and enters a vast pasture with many extensive views. This pasture could be a nice place to camp when not used by cows. As you head south, houses come closer to the trail. Reach Townsend Road, on which you turn right. Follow the road for about a third of a mile; there will be nice pastoral views along it. The trail turns left, leaving the road, at a trail sign. Hike along a grassy path between a series of meadows. Cross a small stream with potential camping. A short climb follows; it is often muddy from horse use. Reach a large pasture with views to the west and intersect the IT at Seneca Road. Continue on the No-Tan-Takto Trail as it crosses meadows with several fine views.

After passing through a hedgerow, there is a "Y" in the trail; bear right as you descend into a woodlot with some old blue blazes. Enter another meadow and the trail becomes a little more evident. Bear left and enter another meadow; the trail overlooks a red barn. The trail can be a little hard to follow with all the herd paths. Reach County Route 1 and turn right to the intersection with Wardner Corners Road, on which you turn left. Follow this road for a mile. At Ball Diamond Road, continue straight on the unblazed, but obvious, Backbone Trail. This trail follows a narrow, abandoned country road lined with maples and brush as it bisects meadows and fields. Some of the trees are very large. There are views just off the trail. Descend to a small stream and pass another juncture with a section of the Backbone Trail; continue straight.

The trail makes a long meander into another small stream valley. Potential camping is possible on the south side of the creek. The trail remains level and straight to the Backbone Horse Campground. Turn right onto Picnic Area Road and follow for a quarter mile to the parking area for the Ravine Trail on the left. The blue Ravine Trail is very scenic and offers a different experience than most of this hike provides. Follow along a spruce plantation and descend toward the creek; reach the beginning of the loop where you can turn left or right. (I turned left.) Cross the small stream over a footbridge where there are some small cascades. Follow the rim of the ravine; it is very steep so it is hard to see the stream. A thick hemlock forest shades the ravine. Descend from the ravine via steps and enter a small side ravine. Reach the bottom of the main ravine and the other end of the loop trail joins from the right. This is a gorgeous spot for a break. Turn left and climb out of the glen with some large trees overhead. Cross Burnt Hill Road and continue the gradual climb to the IT, where you will turn right.

The IT meanders through a scenic forest with occasional boardwalks. Pass a few seasonal streams and reach a large pasture with spectacular views to the west. Cross a road and continue on the trail through the woods. Leave the IT at the Burnt Hill Trail, where you turn left. This trail is not blazed but follows an obvious old woods road. Sections of this trail are wet. Cross a road and enter a woodlot along a pasture. Hike across the pasture with some nice views to the east. Descend and reenter the woods. The woods are scenic as the trail meanders behind some more pastures with partial views. Again, sections of this trail are wet. Reach the parking area where you began.

• • •

A strengthening spring sun slowly rose through the early afternoon sky, burning off the haze to the west. I reached Horton's Pasture following the remains of an old country road, now grown over with grass but still accompanied by ancient maple trees twisted by the wind. Rolling countryside, separated by broad valleys, reached into the distance like swells in the ocean. The wind blew, not with ferocity but as a constant reminder that it was present.

I looked across the fields to see several red-tailed hawks circling each other above the treetops. I saw something rise from the field, levitate in one place, and then drop down into the grass. Several kestrels were looking for prey. They perched in the maple trees, and then flew over the fields, slicing across the surf of the wind. Where they had no place to perch, they flapped their wings to stay in one place until they could locate their next meal. The kestrels were graceful and silent, balancing the wind, gravity, and their elusive prey within a delicate synchronicity. It appeared more like a dance than what had to be done for survival.

I had never been to this place before, and I would likely never return, but in that moment it seemed to be the place where I had to be, if only to witness a few lines in the infinite contours of life.

🚶🚶 19. Letchworth Trail

Length: This route is 21 miles, although the entire trail is 23 miles.

Direction of description: South to north.

Duration: 1¹/₂ to 2 days.

Difficulty: Easy to moderate.

Trail conditions: Trails are well blazed and established. There are many seasonal stream crossings, few have bridges.

Blazes: Yellow. Side trails are usually blue.

Water: Variable. Expect dry conditions in summer or periods of low water. The trail crosses many seasonal streams.

Vegetation: Mostly hardwoods with some areas of pine and spruce. Hemlocks often grow in the ravines. The trail passes some huge oak trees.

Highlights: Genesee River Canyon, views, Upper Falls, Lower Falls, Mt. Morris Dam, numerous seasonal waterfalls and cascades, many deep ravines.

Issues: Call Letchworth State Park about any permits that may be required to use the backcountry shelters. Be very careful enjoying the views along the rim of the canyon—crumbling shale is on the rim, and people have fallen to their deaths.

Location: The trail is in Letchworth State Park, between Portageville and Mt. Morris.

The Letchworth Trail (LT) is a linear trail that explores the east side of beautiful Letchworth State Park and the impressive canyon carved by the Genesee River. The trail is also a spur of the vast Finger Lakes Trail (FLT) system that stretches across New York. The LT begins where it meets the FLT near Whiskey Bridge south of Portageville. It ends in Mount Morris. This description is from the NY 436 bridge that crosses the Genesee River at Portageville to the Mount Morris Dam. Both ends have parking and the shuttle is easy.

The LT is notable for providing backpackers a unique opportunity to explore New York's most impressive canyon—one of the finest canyons in the east. If that's not enough, this trail also offers views of the state's largest waterfalls, aside from Niagara. Sheer shale walls rise hundreds of feet from the Genesee River. When there is a lot of water, seasonal waterfalls plummet from the rim of the canyon.

This is a good trail for beginners. The southern and northern ends of this hike are easy and relatively flat, while the middle two-thirds of the trail is quite hilly. While the trail may be famous for its views of the canyon and two of its three large waterfalls, the time it spends along the rim is fairly limited. In reality, this is a trail of ravines. Numerous side streams and tributaries have carved their own ravines and glens as they descend to the Genesee River. Some of them are of impressive depth and are very precipitous. Seasonal streams flow through these ravines, creating many waterfalls and cascades along the trail when the water is flowing. The LT often follows the rims of the ravines as the trail goes up, down, and around them. This makes

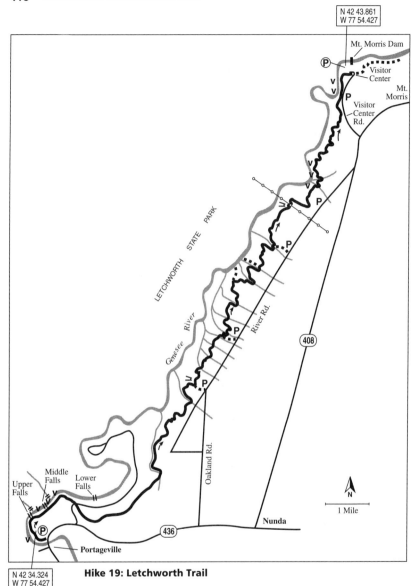

N 42 43.861
W 77 54.427

Mt. Morris Dam

Ⓟ

Visitor Center

Mt. Morris

Ⓟ

Visitor Center Rd.

LETCHWORTH STATE PARK

Genesee River

River Rd.

Ⓟ

Ⓟ

Ⓟ

408

Ⓟ

Oakland Rd.

Middle Falls

Upper Falls

Lower Falls

N

1 Mile

Nunda

436

Ⓟ

Portageville

N 42 34.324
W 77 54.427

Hike 19: Letchworth Trail

the route of the trail circuitous. The trail has some mile markers, others have been chewed up by porcupines.

There are two shelters for backpackers, but they are fairly small and are not very close to water. Be sure to first contact the state park about using them, as a permit may be required.

From NY 436, the trail follows an old, eroded, abandoned road with views of the river and Portageville. Descend and follow another abandoned road. Side trails lead to the rim for views of Upper Falls. The trail stays in close proximity to the rim, but is not right on it. Side trails lead to impressive views of Middle Falls and the sheer canyon walls. Side streams plummet over their own falls across the canyon. Here the canyon is narrow and very scenic, with views of seasonal, 300-foot-high Inspiration Falls.

The trail moves away from the rim and crosses a paved park road at a gate. Continue to follow the level, wide grade through a scenic forest of hardwoods with some large trees. As you head north, the trail passes some huge oak trees. Reach River Road, a narrow dirt road, on which the LT bears left. Follow the road for about a mile as it gradually ascends and then descends. The trail turns left and leaves the road, entering the woods. Descend to beautiful Dishmill Creek amid forests of hemlock and pine. The creek runs all year and has some small cascades. Climb a bank above the creek and get a taste of the first ravine, one of many that dominate this trail. There is also potential camping here, although it is probably not permitted by the state park. A blue side trail goes up to River Road.

Hike along hilly terrain as the trail winds up, down, and around several ravines with seasonal streams and cascades. Descend almost 250 vertical feet along a large ravine, and then climb gradually back up to another blue side trail to the right. Shortly thereafter is the first shelter, in a hardwood forest. Rolling terrain follows for almost 2 miles until the LT reaches another blue side trail to the right. The terrain becomes much hillier as the trail again goes down, up, and around a series of deep and impressive ravines with more seasonal waterfalls. Most of the seasonal stream crossings do not have bridges. Two side trails to the left descend farther down the canyon to some views.

The terrain eases once you reach the next blue side trail to the right. The ravines decrease in size, although the trail still goes around them. Reach the second shelter, set in a nice grove of hemlocks. The trail then passes through a power-line swath and returns to the rim with some impressive views of the canyon. Side trails lead to some beautiful views. The canyon is wider, but still very scenic. Be careful at the views, as the ground is composed of crumbly shale. In typical fashion, the trail goes around ravines and returns to the rim. Reach the Hogback Overlook at a parking area which looks down upon an oxbow loop in the river and a ridge of land. Another nice view soon follows. Continue to hike near the rim until the LT veers to the right in a pine forest; a side trail continues straight along the rim. Hike across some narrow boardwalks and return to the rim where the side trail rejoins. Descend gradually to the parking area at the Mt. Morris Dam, where there are more views, a visitor center, and tours of the dam. (Mt. Morris Dam is a "dry" dam since it does not hold back a permanent reservoir that would otherwise damage the canyon; in fact, there is more water sitting below the dam than above it. The dam is just a big concrete wall whose sole purpose is to hold back floodwaters; when the flooding abates, all the water is drained out.) Here your hike ends, but the LT does continue north for about 1.5 miles before ending in Mt. Morris.

• • •

The direction you take is the destination you seek. This was a hike defined by the Genesee River as it flowed over rolling farmlands to create a stunning canyon. The canyon was eroded hundreds of feet deep for thousands of years as the river flowed in a direction defined by gravity and topography, destined to end in Lake Ontario.

Since I was hiking this linear trail alone I needed a shuttle. After a few emails, I had set up a shuttle with Ellen, who lived nearby. I parked at the Mt. Morris Dam as a massive flock of geese circled above before descending to the river, seeking a place to rest. Ellen soon arrived. Like several before her on my hikes, she did not show any caution or hesitation as she met me, a stranger. She was a friendly, warm woman who talked about her children in Colorado and her memories skiing at the local resort. I asked why her children moved to Colorado, and she mentioned the skiing, the outdoors, and the way of life. Ellen loved visiting them out there, but could not let go of her home in New York. Destinations are most commonly defined by our need for—or avoidance of—change.

I've thought about moving out West to live among fantastic landscapes. But I realized that for me there was no real difference, no real change. I once drove through St. George, Utah, on the interstate after visiting the spectacular Zion and Bryce Canyon National Parks. I passed the same stores, strip malls, and chain restaurants I see at home. And the landscapes didn't change the effect they've had on me. I've been equally amazed by the Adirondacks, West Virginia's Alleghenies, and the sandstone canyons and arches of the Red River and Big South Fork as by any place out West. Beauty is everywhere, and it is always much closer than you realize.

Ellen dropped me off, and I offered some money, but she politely declined. Generosity came easy to her. I insisted, but she was resolute. We said goodbye and I began hiking the trail as she drove away.

I soon noticed small groups of people in tight neoprene outfits and colorful jackets along the trail, walking about randomly and talking in hushed tones. They seemed to be searching for something as they looked at compasses and maps, but I failed to see what could be attracting them. I was at a loss for an explanation. I continued down the trail, half-worried I had stumbled upon a cult lost in the woods. A bunch of them ran by me, sweating, glancing at their watches, and oblivious to my existence. They would turn suddenly and disappear into the woods. They weren't chasing each other, and I concluded they weren't playing hide-and-seek. If they weren't part of a cult, then it was a rather odd race. When I came upon the center of all this activity, it dawned on me that it was an orienteering competition.

I continued my hike as the sun set and twilight filled the canyon. I felt I was on the edge of a pinnacle, on the dividing line between light. The last glow of the sun faded to my left as the cool light of the moon rose to my right. My eyes strained to follow the ribbon of trail through the dark woods. I could see the lights of the Mt. Morris Dam through the trees. In the still night I could hear geese rising into the sky, honking with the whistle of air over their wings. They spiraled higher and higher out of the canyon and continued on their journey south along the moonlit Genesee River.

20. Allegany State Park

Length: 21.5-mile linear trail.

Direction of description: North to south (From ASP 2, a park road, to PA 346 in the Allegheny National Forest).

Duration: $1^1/_2$ to 2 days.

Difficulty: Easy to moderate. Climbs and descents are usually gradual with rolling terrain. Vertical ascents reach up to 700 feet; however, most never exceed 500 vertical feet.

Trail conditions: Trails are well established and usually well blazed. There is a lot of sidehill.

Blazes: The trail is blazed white in New York and blue in Pennsylvania.

Water: There are sufficient water sources along the trail with many streams and springs.

Vegetation: Mostly hardwoods, with hemlock along the drainages.

Highlights: Beautiful forests, scenic streams, three lean-tos. The trail is relatively undeveloped and has an isolated feel to it.

Issues: Camping is limited to the lean-to areas. A few sections of the trail have brush and briars.

Location: The trail crosses Allegany State Park, south of Salamanca and north of Willow Bay, Pennsylvania.

This hike follows the North Country Trail and Finger Lakes Trail (NCT/FLT) across beautiful Allegany State Park into Pennsylvania, ending at PA 346. Allegany State Park has the distinction of being the largest state park in New York, and the largest contiguous block of public land outside the Catskills and Adirondacks. As a result, it is a noteworthy backpacking destination. No other backpack in central or western New York offers so much hiking off roads and away from farms, fields, and development.

While this hike does not offer many vistas, waterfalls, or other stand-out scenic features, it is still an enjoyable hike with varied terrain, scenic forests, hemlock groves, mountain streams, and three very nice lean-to shelters. Simply put, this is a wonderful woodland hike offering solitude. It is an ideal trip in the fall or as a winter snowshoe backpack, where the shelters are an added benefit. The moderate terrain and straightforward shuttle makes this an attractive choice for beginning backpackers.

You can park in a large lot on ASP 2 or on the berm along Bay State Road. Hike down Bay State Road a short distance and turn left onto the white-blazed trail. (In the New York state park, the trail is blazed white; in Pennsylvania it is blazed blue.) The trail crosses a small stream over a footbridge. Footbridges are a common feature on this hike, with bridges even over seasonal streams. Climb past a trail sign and into a large meadow offering views to the north of the rolling mountains and I-86. This is the only significant view of the hike. Begin a meandering 600-foot vertical climb up the mountain. The climb is gradual and the trail follows a lot of sidehill. As you ascend, the forests become more scenic, with hemlocks and a few large boulders. The trail crests and then descends along the ridge, reaching scenic Beck Hollow Lean-to as it overlooks a hemlock-shaded glen with a small stream. A privy is nearby. This is an ideal place to camp if coming in on a Friday night. The lean-to is about 2 miles from Bay State Road.

The rolling terrain continues as the trail explores diverse woodlands of hardwoods and hemlocks. Some trees are fairly large and the forests are beautiful. Pass an orange-blazed trail to the left that descends to Red House Lake. A gradual climb follows into a hemlock forest, followed by an equally scenic descent through more forests. Reach a blue-blazed trail to the left that also descends to Red House Lake. A dilapidated shelter is nearby. Cross a few small streams and begin a larger climb to the crest of a rolling ridge. The forest is mostly hardwoods. Sidehill resumes as the trail crosses the overgrown slopes of an abandoned ski hill. (Watch for briars.) Soon thereafter, cross Bay State Road, and then ASP 1 where there is a trail sign.

Blazes may be a little tricky to follow across ASP 1. The trail climbs gently and reaches a narrow forest road that is also a snowmobile trail in winter. Turn left and follow this forest road for about .6 mile. The trail turns right from the road. This turn is easy to miss, so look out for the double white blazes. Descend gradually along an old grade toward Stony Brook. Cross the brook under some hemlocks as the trail continues down the wooded valley. Cross Stony Brook again, and soon Stony Brook Lean-to is off to the left. The trail crosses some small streams and springs (a dilapidated old shelter is to the right), and then circles around a meadow under hemlocks. Another gradual climb follows to the top of the plateau. For the next 1.5 miles, the trail crosses the rolling terrain of the plateau. Briars are a problem on this section and it is probably the least scenic section of the trail. Descend to beautiful Quaker Run and cross ASP 3.

Make a short climb and turn right onto an old, level grade that wraps around the base of the mountain to beautiful Coon Run where there are hemlocks and a footbridge. Hike across a forest road, and sidehill follows that gradually ascends up the slope of the mountain. Descend into the scenic glen of Willis Creek where there is a lean-to, privy, and piped spring. The trail continues to follow sidehill up the flank of the mountain, crossing small drainages. The climb steepens as the trail reaches the crest of the ridge. The following mile is an enjoyable hike as the trail crosses a narrow ridge where it is possible to look down both sides when the leaves are off the trees. Hemlocks also make a return to the trail. Descend into a col and reach a trail juncture where a side trail goes to the Mt. Tuscarora fire tower. This tower cannot be climbed and does not offer a view.

The NCT/FLT descends into a beautiful stream valley full of hemlocks and large hardwoods. Reach a meadow and Wolf Run where the trail crosses a footbridge. A long, gradual climb follows with sidehill up the flank of the mountain. The trail reaches an old grade which it follows to the top of the plateau. Level hiking under hardwoods follows until the trail reaches the Pennsylvania border and the Allegheny National Forest. Here, the FLT ends and the NCT continues. The trail is now blazed blue. A descent follows into a valley. The trail becomes very scenic as it meanders under beautiful hemlock forests between stream drainages. This hike ends at the trailhead and parking area along PA 346. The NCT continues through the Allegheny National Forest and ultimately ends in North Dakota.

Hike 20: Allegany State Park

• • •

I drove west on a road stained with rock salt, chasing a magenta horizon that was quickly fading. Darkness had already claimed the rolling hills and mountains as their profiles stood in contrast to the last light of the day. I had been on this road dozens of times over the last fifteen years or so. Not much had changed along it, but my perspective felt older and more distant, as if I were a different person looking back on my own memories.

I reached the parking area in the frigid, invisible expanse of night and met the others in my group. The cold was so intense it felt as if it were solid, pressing up against my skin. We hiked down the road to the trail.

A blanket of powder covered the trail, and as we hiked we left a scar across its smooth, flawless complexion. The moonlight was cut by shadows of trees across the snow that sparkled with minuscule diamonds. There were two distinct worlds, one that was illuminated in the silver, metallic glow of the moon, and the second that was engulfed in a deep, absolute darkness. Everything was still and quiet. As we climbed, the trees popped and creaked despite the lack of a breeze. The sap was freezing from within.

We reached the shelter, and I spent the night curled up tightly to conserve warmth in my deep cocoon of clothes, liner, and sleeping bag. I knew I would be fine despite the subzero temperatures and the foot of powder. I was with several others who were facing the same exact conditions. Not only does misery love company; so do safety and security.

The weak morning light unveiled a powdered wonderland. The temperature was –12 degrees. Everything was delicately draped and adorned with snow. The slightest disturbance sent plumes of powder to the ground. I trudged with relentless footsteps on legs that felt like concrete; every mile felt like three.

I reached the next lean-to just before dark and joined the group assembled there, sharing whiskey, warm food, good conversation, and a crackling fire. Together in the frigid cold of a winter's night, we really didn't know each other all that well, but we didn't need to. The trail brings out the best in all of us.

🚶🚶 21. North Country Trail

Length: When complete, the trail in New York will be about 625 miles long; 355 miles are presently complete.

Direction of description: West to east.

Duration: 2 to 3 months.

Difficulty: Moderate.

Trail conditions: The trail follows the Finger Lakes Trail (see page 128) for about half its length in the state, crosses and follows many roads, passes through extensive private land, and passes through urban areas. Between Cazenovia and Rome, the trail follows old canal towpaths and grades. The trail goes through several small towns and villages, and one significant urban area, Rome.

Blazes: Blue. Where the trail follows the Finger Lakes Trail, it is blazed white.

Water: Generally sufficient.

Vegetation: Hardwoods, pine, hemlock, farms, fields, meadows, and wetlands. Spruce and fir become more common in the Adirondacks.

Highlights: Forests, waterfalls, gorges, vistas, ponds, lakes, southern Adirondacks, isolation.

Issues: The trail often follows and crosses roads. There is a lot of private land along the trail, and camping can be limited. The trail is incomplete, and sections of it are closed during hunting season. The trail is often brushy and may have infrequent blazes, particularly on private land.

Location: The trail goes from Allegany State Park to Crown Point on Lake Champlain. It goes through, or passes near, the following towns: Salamanca, Ellicottville, Portageville, Hammondsport, Watkins Glen, Danby, Cortland, Cazenovia, Rome, Boonville, and Forestport.

The North Country Trail (NCT) is the longest of the National Scenic Trails. At about 4,500 miles, it is over twice the length of the Appalachian Trail. The NCT stretches from North Dakota to New York, although the eastern terminus may be extended into Vermont to permit a connection to the Appalachian Trail.

The NCT will also be the longest trail in New York when it is completed. Presently, a little more than half the trail in the state is complete.

I did not hike the entire NCT in New York; few people have. However, I included it in this guide so people are aware of its existence and

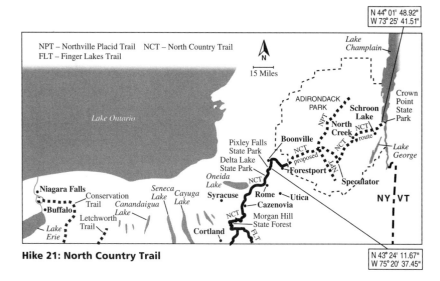

NPT – Northville Placid Trail   NCT – North Country Trail
FLT – Finger Lakes Trail

N

15 Miles

Lake Champlain

ADIRONDACK PARK

Crown Point State Park

Schroon Lake

North Creek

NCT route

Lake George

Pixley Falls State Park

Boonville

NCT

proposed

Forestport

Speculator

Delta Lake State Park

Oneida Lake

NCT

Lake Ontario

Niagara Falls

Buffalo

Conservation Trail

Letchworth Trail

Lake Erie

Seneca Lake

Cayuga Lake

Canandaigua Lake

Syracuse

Rome

Cazenovia

Utica

Morgan Hill State Forest

Cortland

NY VT

FLT

Hike 21: North Country Trail

the incredible, if not unparalleled, hiking opportunities it could provide in the state.

The NCT enters New York in the Allegany State Park and immediately joins the white Finger Lakes Trail, which it follows all the way to near the tiny village of Cuyler. Please refer to the overview description of the Finger Lakes Trail for this portion of the hike.

The NCT leaves the Finger Lakes Trail, and resumes its blue blazing, as it follows the Onondaga Trail, one of the FLT's side trails. The NCT meanders over hills and fields and follows roads to link public lands. The setting is pastoral. A highlight is Morgan Hill State Forest, which features spruce forests, streams, a lean-to, view, waterfall, and ponds. The NCT leaves the state forest and crosses private land on a mixture of footpaths and roads to reach various parcels of public land. Enjoy the view in Highland Forest County Park and DeRuyter Lake. The terrain is hilly, with a mix of fields and forests.

The NCT now heads north—leaving the Onondaga Trail and the Finger Lakes Trail System—to Cazenovia. It passes east of beautiful Chittenango Falls State Park with its 167-foot falls, and then continues to Rome, following a variety of roads, canal towpaths, and rail trails. Hike through Rome on sidewalks, followed by a long road walk to scenic Pixley Falls State Park. The park is named after a 50-foot cascade. The NCT follows the Black River Canal Towpath through Boonville, until the towpath ends at Forestport.

The trail from Forestport through Adirondack Park to Crown Point is currently undefined. A proposal is to route the NCT through the southern area of Adirondack Park. From Forestport, the proposed route goes through Black River Wild Forest, West Canada Lake Wilderness, the town of Speculator, Siamese Ponds Wilderness, the town of North Creek, Vanderwhacker Mountain Wild Forest, Hoffman Notch Wilderness, and north of Schroon Lake before reaching Crown Point.

This proposed route has displeased some hikers who believe the NCT, as a National Scenic Trail, is more deserving of a route through the spectacular High Peaks. While some may believe the NCT will bring even more hikers to the High Peaks, that is unlikely, as the NCT is very different from the Appalachian or Pacific Crest Trails. If anything, the High Peaks would bring desperately needed hikers to the NCT.

There are also efforts underway to extend the NCT into Vermont, through Middlebury, and onto the Long Trail where it can connect with the Appalachian Trail. However, if you were to ask me, a more fitting ending for this vast trail would be at the summit of Vermont's iconic peak, Camel's Hump.

 ## 22. Finger Lakes Trail System

Length: 558-mile linear trail.

Direction of description: West to east.

Duration: 5 to 8 weeks.

Difficulty: Moderate to difficult.

Trail conditions: The trail is generally well blazed and signed, although there are wet and brushy sections. Many stream crossings do not have bridges. The trail may have infrequent blazes and plentiful briars, particularly on private land. There are many road walks and road crossings. The trail often follows old forest roads and grades. Due to all the meadows, farms, and fields, the trail often crosses over stiles.

Blazes: White. In the Catskills, the trail follows local trails that are blazed orange, red, yellow, or blue.

Water: Generally sufficient, although sources dry in the summer, particularly on ridges and higher elevations.

Vegetation: Hardwoods, pine, hemlock, pine plantations, spruce plantations, meadows, wetlands. In the Catskills there are spruce and fir forests.

Highlights: Pastoral views, scenic countryside, gorges, waterfalls, wetlands, and historical features such as rock walls, cemeteries, old foundations.

Issues: There are many road walks and road crossings. The trail crosses a lot of private land, which limits camping opportunities. Sections are closed in hunting season.

Location: The trail traverses the southern tier of New York, from Allegany State Park to the Catskills. Some larger towns the trail passes through or near are Salamanca, Ellicottville, Hornell, Bath, Watkins Glen, Ithaca, and Bainbridge.

The Finger Lakes Trail (FLT) and the Finger Lakes Trail System are unlike any other hiking trails in the nation. No other trail of such length covers so much private land. While most long-distance trails take hikers away from local communities in a search for isolation and wilderness, the FLT does just the opposite. It introduces hikers to the culture, communities, and people of New York. As a result, there has been tremendous local support for the FLT, allowing it to exist in a place with limited public land.

This trail is also unique in its vastness; the entire system incorporates 958 miles of trails, with the main FLT covering 558 miles. This system is the premier hiking and backpacking resource in central and western New York.

From Allegany State Park to the tiny village of Cuyler, east of Cortland, the North Country Trail follows the same route as the FLT. Of the few people who have hiked the entire North Country Trail, several have said the FLT was among their favorite sections.

The FLT is also a very strategic trail. Not only does the North Country Trail follow it, but the Great Eastern Trail connects to it. The FLT also connects to the Long Path, making a hike to the Appalachian Trail possible. The Long Path may also connect to the Northville–Placid Trail in the future. As long-distance hiking grows in popularity, the importance and status of the FLT will rise.

The FLT represents the hard work, determination, and critical importance of volunteers who have created a long-distance trail in the most unlikely of regions. Their commitment has been strong for over fifty years, since the FLT was first conceived in the early 1960s. Thanks to these generations of volunteers, a superb hiking resource has been created for future generations.

I have not hiked the entire FLT, but I felt it was necessary to include the trail as a whole in this book, due to its popularity, scope, and importance. This description is abbreviated; however, five sections of the trail system are described separately in other places in this book.

The FLT is a very hilly and pastoral trail. The trail twists and turns across and along roads to connect public lands such as state forests, parks, and wildlife management areas. Fields, meadows, forests, ravines, streams, and wetlands are often encountered. The trail goes through several towns and villages. Because the FLT cuts across the eroded Allegheny Plateau and valleys, it is more hilly and rugged than you may otherwise expect.

The FLT begins at the Pennsylvania state border and proceeds across New York's largest state park, Allegany State Park. For over 20 miles, it explores the park's forests, streams, and ridges, and you will find three lean-tos along the way. This section is a fine backpacking trip, and is the longest stretch of off-road hiking until the Catskills.

Enter the Seneca Indian Reservation and hike through the town of Salamanca. Follow roads, fields, and footpaths across private land and small state forests. Enter Rock City State Forest to see its large, separated boulders adorned with moss and ferns. Enjoy several more miles of off-road hiking through state forests before arriving at the Holiday Valley and HoliMont ski areas, with views from the slopes. The trail passes just outside of Ellicottville. Hike across hilly terrain with views, meadows, and woodlots. Extensive sections of the trail are closed in hunting season.

Boyce Hill State Forest offers pleasant forest hiking with a lean-to, pond, and pastoral views. Soon thereafter, hike through Bear Creek State Forest. Continue along, hiking a combination of roads, private lands, and small state forests. There is a long road walk between Farmersville and Swift Hill State Forests. After the village of Higgins, the FLT crosses extensive private lands, but with limited road walking. Enjoy easier, rolling terrain with some wet areas. Highlights are the lean-to and campsite at a pond in Boy Scout Camp Sam Wood, another example of the generosity private landowners have shown the trail.

Cross the Genesee River south of Portageville where the Letchworth Trail heads north into its namesake state park. The FLT continues across hilly private land, with short road walks and pastoral views. South of Swain the trail passes through a series of state forests with

N 41° 59' 04.41"
W 78° 54' 08.30"

Hike 22: Finger Lakes Trail System

N 41° 57' 55.55"
W 74° 27' 09.15"

ponds, ravines, small streams, and campsites. Return to private land on roads, cross Interstate 86/17 north of Hornell, and continue on the extensive network of private land that is home to the trail; roads, meadows, small streams, woodlots, and many views await.

The Bristol Hills Trail joins the FLT near Mitchellsville, and here you'll find a series of state forests separated by road walks. The orange Crystal Hills Trail joins from the right at the Moss Hill lean-to, marking the northern terminus of the Great Eastern Trail. The state forests offer more extensive forests, pine plantations, ravines, steep-sided valleys, and small streams. There are several campsites and a few lean-tos before reaching famous Watkins Glen State Park. While the FLT is routed around the glen itself, be sure to hike down the glen to see the beautiful waterfalls, pools, and chasms. Hike through the town of Watkins Glen and begin a long, gradual climb along roads, trails, and old grades up to the Finger Lakes National Forest, where the Interloken Trail joins.

Connecticut Hill Wildlife Management Area provides the next opportunity for a long forest walk, with miles of rock-free trails, plantations, ravines, cascades, and small streams. Follow roads and cross meadows to impressive Robert H. Treman State Park with its gorge and waterfalls. The FLT avoids the best scenery because the gorge is impassable in winter, but leave the FLT to see the falls and gorge. Private land, views, and roads continue to Danby State Forest, another popular area on the FLT, with valleys, small streams, and two lean-tos.

The trail becomes hillier as it connects a series of state forests with road walks. Enjoy views at the Greek Peak Ski Area and pass I-81. The

FLT enters more state forests and off-road hiking. The North Country Trail and Onondaga Trail leave the FLT near Cuyler as they head north into the Morgan Hill State Forest. More state forests and road walks follow as the trail passes a couple of ponds. Reach Bowman Lake State Park, with its campground, lake, beach, and showers.

Private land becomes increasingly common with several short road walks. Enjoy more fields, pastoral scenery, streams, and even some waterfalls. The FLT passes through Bainbridge, where you'll find a grocery store, private campground, and motel. State forests return after Masonville with woodland hiking, lean-tos, and views. The trail stays on a ridge; the terrain is hilly and dry. Reach the Cannonsville Reservoir, part of the New York City water supply. Hike around and past the reservoir on a hilly combination of roads and trails. Enter public land and hike along a ridge, pass the village of Downsville below the Pepacton Reservoir, and enter Delaware Wild Forest.

Here the FLT changes. It is now entering the Catskills, and the trail is blazed with different colors. Follow the trail carefully; there are FLT signs to help guide the way. Now begins the most extensive stretch of off-road hiking since Allegany State Park. The terrain is rugged, with many steep hills, streams, valleys, and occasional plantations of spruce and pine. Ledges and boulders adorn the mountain slopes, and water sources can be limited. There are some views, but they are not very expansive. Big Pond and Alder Lake are both beautiful; the latter has great camping. After Alder Lake, the FLT begins to enter the heart of the Catskills with a long climb up to Balsam Lake Mountain, the highest point of the trail. A deep spruce/fir forest is at the summit, along with a small cabin and a fire tower with superb views.

The trail descends and stays in the valleys, crossing many streams. Return to road walking at Wild Meadow Road. This is a very long road walk of almost 14 miles to the end of Denning Road. Follow the yellow trail a short distance from the end of the road to the Long Path, Peekamoose–Table Trail, and the Phoenicia–East Branch Trail. The FLT suddenly ends at a typical, unremarkable trail juncture. From here, a vast network of trails in the Catskills can be hiked, and the Appalachian Trail can be accessed to the south.

Bryan Mulvihill in Minnewaska State Park on the Shawangunk Ridge Trail.

Island Pond in Harriman State Park.

Wes Atkinson at Blackhead Mountain in the Catskills.

Sunrise on Brace Mountain on the South Taconic Trail.

Letchworth State Park.

View of the Genesee River from the Letchworth Trail.

View of Lake George from Black Mountain in the Lake George Wild Forest.

Leigh Ann Jennings on the Tongue Mountain Range Loop.

View from Cat Mountain on the Cranberry Lake 50.

Latham Pond on the Cold River–Seward Range Loop.

View of Algonquin Peak from the summit of Mt. Marcy in the Adirondacks.

View of Great Range from Mt. Marcy in the Adirondacks.

View from Pyramid Peak in the High Peaks, Adirondacks.

Rainbow Falls in the High Peaks, Adirondacks.

Cedar Lakes on the Northville–Placid Trail.

Cold River on the Northville–Placid Trail.

22a. Conservation Trail

Length: 171-mile linear trail.

Direction of description: South to north.

Duration: 10 to 15 days.

Difficulty: Moderate to difficult. The southern half of the trail is the most rugged, with climbs between 100 and 800 vertical feet. Most climbs are gradual. The section between Erie County Park and Hunters Creek Park features many ravines that the trail traverses.

Trail conditions: The trail follows many roads and fields. Blazing can be hard to follow in sections, and there are many wet areas. The northern section primarily follows bike paths and old railroad grades; it is very urban around Tonawanda and Niagara Falls.

Blazes: Orange.

Water: There are generally sufficient water sources along the trail.

Vegetation: Mostly hardwoods with some pine and hemlock often along streams. There are many fields along the trail.

Highlights: Views, scenic streams, ponds, waterfalls, pastoral scenery, Niagara Falls.

Issues: Camping opportunities are limited on this trail, and it follows many roads. The northern section follows long stretches of a multi-use bike trail. Some sections are closed in hunting season.

Location: The trail passes through or near the following towns and villages: West Valley, Holland, Wales Center, Akron, Tonawanda, and Niagara Falls.

The Conservation Trail (CT) is maintained by the Foothills Hiking Club and is a component of the vast Finger Lakes Trail System. The Foothills Hiking Club was formed in 1962, with the goal of building a hiking trail from Allegany State Park to Niagara Falls. The CT was the result of that effort. The CT connects with Canada's Bruce Trail. To build and maintain trail that crosses so much private land is truly a herculean effort on behalf of the volunteers.

The southern 55 miles of the CT from the Pennsylvania border co-exists with the Finger Lakes (FLT) and North Country Trails (NCT). Once the CT leaves those trails heading north, it is blazed orange. Due to the extensive road walking, developed areas, and private land along the trail, it does not receive a lot of backpacking use. I have not hiked the entire trail and the description that follows is abbreviated. The CT

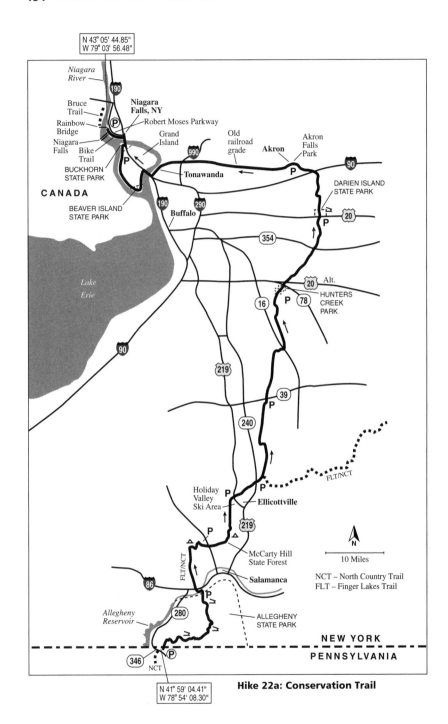

N 43° 05' 44.85"
W 79° 03' 56.48"

Niagara
River

190

Bruce
Trail

Rainbow
Bridge

Niagara
Falls

Bike
Trail

**Niagara
Falls, NY**

Robert Moses Parkway

Grand
Island

Old
railroad
grade

Akron
Falls
Park

Akron

990

90

P

BUCKHORN
STATE PARK

Tonawanda

DARIEN ISLAND
STATE PARK

CANADA

BEAVER ISLAND
STATE PARK

190

Buffalo

290

20

354

Lake
Erie

Alt.

20

16

78

**HUNTERS
CREEK
PARK**

P

90

219

39

P

240

Holiday
Valley
Ski Area

P

Ellicottville

FLT/NCT

N

10 Miles

NCT – North Country Trail
FLT – Finger Lakes Trail

219

McCarty Hill
State Forest

FLT/NCT

86

Salamanca

280

Allegheny
Reservoir

P

ALLEGHENY
STATE PARK

NEW YORK

346

NCT

P

PENNSYLVANIA

N 41° 59' 04.41"
W 78° 54' 08.30"

Hike 22a: Conservation Trail

is included in this guide so that hikers will be aware of it. Keep in mind several sections of the trail are closed in either the fall or spring hunting seasons, so refer to the Finger Lakes Trail Conference map and guides. Many sections of the trail are wet, particularly between Hunters Creek Park and Akron, and some of these areas are addressed with boardwalks. As a general rule, the trail is hillier in its southern section, but levels out as it heads north.

At the Pennsylvania border, the CT heads north for 21 miles through Allegany State Park. This is an enjoyable trail featuring beautiful forests, nice streams, three shelters, and moderate climbs of 300–500 vertical feet in and out of drainages. The CT enters the Seneca Indian Reservation and passes through Salamanca. Enter private land where the trail is closed during hunting season. The trail traverses hilly terrain and fields and follows roads. Most of the off-road hiking is found in the Bucktooth, Rock City, and McCarty Hill State Forests where primitive tent camping is allowed. In Rock City State Forest, be sure to explore Little Rock City, just off the trail, with its huge boulders, crevices, and caves. Leave McCarty Hill State Forest and traverse the top of Holiday Valley Ski Area with some views from the slopes. Pass through Ellicottville. The next 11 miles are primarily private land with road walking, fields, and wooded hills. Again, sections of the trail here are closed in hunting season, in both the fall and spring. The CT leaves the FLT and NCT near Fancy Tract Road.

The CT continues its journey north alone. The terrain is gradual, yet hilly. The trail is pastoral and rural, with fields, streams, and woodlots. The CT divides its time among roads, woods, and fields. North of NY 55 is a long road walk; however, there is a camping area off Bolton Road, reached by a blue-blazed side trail. Enter Erie County Forest where the trail enters a nice pine forest with some small streams. North of Erie County Forest, the CT stays mostly off the roads before descending along ravines into the Cazenovia Creek Valley. Cross NY 16 and a railroad, and begin an ascent up the other side of the valley. While the CT stays near the crest of the valley, it does wind in and out of many ravines. This section is closed in the spring hunting season. Road walking follows to Hunters Creek Park where the trail follows boardwalks over wet areas. The CT primarily follows roads to NY 354.

From NY 354 to Darien Lake State Park, the CT is mostly off the roads as it traverses the countryside, with meadows, streams, ravines, and several wet areas. The Norfolk Southern Railroad is fairly busy, so be careful. Darien Lake State Park offers a shelter for backpackers, and is essentially the last place for primitive camping along the trail. After leaving the state park, the next section of trail was flooded by beavers, so a road walk is required. Cross another railroad and NY 33; the trail hopscotches among roads, fields, and hedgerows. Cross I-90, pass a pond, and follow a power line, which is also an old railroad grade, to Akron. Just off the CT is Akron Falls Park, which is worth seeing. Follow a bike path, and then return to the old railroad grade. The CT follows this old grade west into the Buffalo metropolitan area; as a result, the surroundings become increasingly urbanized, and heavy traffic is a concern.

Cross I-990 and follow a bicycle trail to Tonawanda Creek. Follow the creek down to the scenic River Walk, a popular, paved multi-use trail along the huge Niagara River in Isle View County Park. Cross the Niagara River on the I-190/South Grand Island Bridge. The CT follows a paved bike path along the South Parkway to Beaver Island State Park. Follow the West River Parkway, where the trail follows the grassy strip along the parkway. There are views across the Niagara River as the trail traverses the western shore of Grand Island. Reach Buckhorn State Park and cross the I-190/North Grand Island Bridge. Take the first exit, turn right onto Buffalo Avenue, and then turn right on the Niagara River Bike Trail.

The bike trail is between the Niagara River and Robert Moses Parkway; it passes the hydroelectric power plant intakes. As the CT nears Goat Island, there are impressive rapids in the river. Reach spectacular Niagara Falls. The CT ends at the Rainbow Bridge. Across the bridge, in Canada, a bike path leads to the Bruce Trail, which continues for about 550 miles to the tip of the Bruce Peninsula along Lake Huron, near Bruce Peninsula National Park.

22b. Bristol Hills Trail

Length: 54.2-mile linear trail.

Direction of description: North to south.

Duration: 2¹/₂ to 4 days.

Difficulty: Moderate with a few steep sections.

Trail conditions: The trail is generally well blazed and signed. Some sections can be brushy and wet. The northern half of the trail is more rugged and difficult than the southern half. Old forest roads and grades are often followed.

Blazes: Orange.

Water: Generally sufficient, but sections of the trail can be dry in summer.

Vegetation: Hardwoods, pine, hemlock, meadows, wetlands, pine plantations.

Highlights: Views, pastoral scenery, small ponds, small waterfalls, nice shelters, old cemetery, and foundations.

Issues: About 8 miles of road walking. Sections of the trail are closed to dogs and closed completely during hunting season. The trail crosses a lot of private land. Camping is basically limited to existing shelters and designated campsites.

Location: The trail passes near, or through, the following towns and villages: Bristol Springs, Naples, Italy, Prattsburgh, and Mitchellsville.

The Bristol Hills Trail (BHT) is a spur trail of the Finger Lakes Trail System and has been attracting the attention of backpackers. The BHT offers some of the most scenic and enjoyable backpacking in Western New York, with relatively limited road walking. To create a trail across so much private land with limited road walking is a reflection of the hard work and commitment of the volunteers who maintain this trail and the support the trail has from the community. The BHT is known for its views, pastoral scenery, small ponds, and nice lean-tos.

The northern end of the trail begins at Ontario County Park, and it starts with a bang. The park has a campground and picnic facilities, but the premier highlight is along the trail with a superb view to the west from the Jump Off. Look over deep valleys and broad, forested ridges. Hike over a ridge, the highest point of the trail, and descend to Beaver Pond and its lean-to. Cross Route 33 and climb steeply into a Boy Scout camp until the trail levels off along the edge. Enjoy views to the south and east. Descend to a road, which you will walk along for 2 miles. Turn right off Seman Road into the West Hill Nature Preserve as the trail makes a gradual ascent, and then a meandering descent. A blue side trail on the left leads to a view. Descend to the town of Naples, where there are restaurants and a grocery store.

Walk on roads through Naples and begin a steep 1,000-foot vertical ascent with some switchbacks. The BHT enters the High Tor Wildlife Management Area, and other trails intersect the BHT. After reaching the top, descend along a ridge to Conklin Gully, a deep ravine. Hike

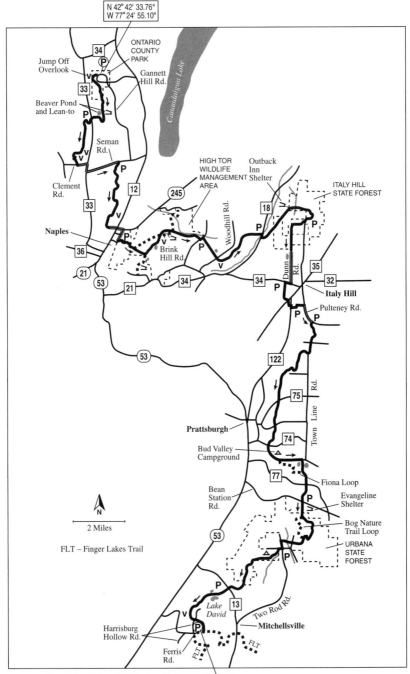

N 42° 42' 33.76"
W 77° 24' 55.10"

ONTARIO
COUNTY
PARK

34

P

Jump Off
Overlook

Gannett
Hill Rd.

V

33

Beaver Pond
and Lean-to

P

Canandaigua Lake

Seman
Rd.

V

P

Clement
Rd.

12

33

V

HIGH TOR
WILDLIFE
MANAGEMENT
AREA

Outback
Inn
Shelter

ITALY HILL
STATE FOREST

245

18

Woodhill Rd.

P

P

Naples

P

36

V

Brink
Hill Rd.

P

P

21

V

Dunn Rd.

35

53

21

34

34

P

32

Italy Hill

53

P

Pulteney Rd.

P

P

122

75

Town Line Rd.

Prattsburgh

74

Bud Valley
Campground

N

77

Fiona Loop

Bean
Station
Rd.

Evangeline
Shelter

2 Miles

Bog Nature
Trail Loop

FLT – Finger Lakes Trail

53

P

URBANA
STATE
FOREST

P

P

Lake
David

13

Two Rod Rd.

Harrisburg
Hollow Rd.

V

P

Mitchellsville

Ferris
Rd.

FLT

FLT

Hike 22b: Bristol Hills Trail

N 42° 24' 09.16"
W 77° 19' 24.11"

up, and above, the small stream to a road. Follow the road for 1 mile. Reach the edge of the ridge with another nice view, and then descend steeply over 800 vertical feet to the bottom of the valley. Cross the valley, enter Italy Hill State Forest, and begin a long, gradual climb to the Outback Inn Shelter. The BHT crosses and follows a variety of abandoned forest roads across level terrain in the state forest. Leave the state forest and follow roads for 2 miles. Continue to head south, crossing several country roads as the trail explores fields, hedgerows, and woodlands.

Hike past the Bud Valley Campground to the left before a .75-mile road walk. Leave the road and cross several streams to Bean Hollow Road. Cross the road and climb to the impressive Evangeline Shelter in scenic woodlands. The climb continues into the Urbana State Forest where the BHT reaches a side trail, the Bog Nature Trail Loop, which encircles a bog with the BHT. Continue the level and rolling hike through the state forest with scenic forests and several forest road crossings. Granma's Campsite is one place to stay the night. Descend to Route 13 and then gradually climb to beautiful Lake David and hike along the shore. The BHT climbs gradually, passing some views, crosses Harrisburg Hollow Road, and then descends to a couple of steep gullies. Hike through the gullies and reach the BHT's southern end at the Finger Lakes Trail. The closest road access is to the right, at Ferris Road.

22c. Crystal Hills Trail

Length: 49-mile linear trail.

Direction of description: North to south.

Duration: 2^1/$_2$ to 4 days.

Difficulty: Moderate. Climbs tend to be gradual, averaging between 100 and 600 vertical feet. Much of the trail is on roads.

Trail conditions: The trail follows many roads and fields. Blazing can be hard to follow in sections, and there are some wet areas.

Blazes: Orange.

Water: There are generally sufficient water sources along the trail.

Vegetation: Mostly hardwoods, with some pine and hemlock often along streams. There are many fields along the trail.

Highlights: Views, scenic streams, ponds, pastoral scenery.

Issues: Camping opportunities are limited on this trail, and there is extensive road walking.

Location: The trail is near or goes through Painted Post, Addison, and Pinnacle State Park.

The Crystal Hills Trail (CHT) is a component of the vast Finger Lakes Trail (FLT) system. The CHT is a spur trail to the FLT, connecting the FLT and North Country Trail (NCT) to Pennsylvania's Mid State Trail. The CHT is also the northern end of the Great Eastern Trail, which goes from Alabama to New York. I have not hiked the entire CHT. Because it is such a strategic trail in a national system of interconnecting trails, it is included in this guide so hikers will be aware of it. The description that follows is abbreviated.

The description is from north to south. The CHT begins at the Moss Hill Lean-To along the FLT and NCT. The first 4 miles of the trail feature rolling terrain with forests and fields; descend to Wixon Road and cross CR 26. Leave the road and ascend through woods and fields. Enter the Watson Homestead property, where hiking is allowed. The homestead is named after Thomas Watson, the founder of IBM. A meandering ascent continues with side trails on the homestead property. Reach Woodstock Road, which the CHT follows to West Hill State Forest, where the trail leaves the road and explores the forests, small streams, and a beaver pond in the state forest. After the state forest, there is a long unblazed road walk down to Painted Post.

The unblazed rural road walk continues for over 9 miles to Mose Road, where the trail enters the woods. The next highlight is Goodhue Creek and its gorge, where a blue spur trail goes down to a waterfall known as "Little Niagara." Pass through a cemetery and reach the small town of Addison. Begin a meandering 600-foot vertical climb into Pinnacle State Park, which features views, many side trails, a golf course, and other typical state park amenities. The CHT becomes circuitous and loops into McCarty Hill State Forest where there is a shelter, one of only two along the entire trail. Reenter Pinnacle State Park and pass scenic Levi Pond. A 9-mile road walk follows along rural, backcountry roads to the Pennsylvania border and the Mid State Trail (MST). Although road walking is not ideal, the countryside is scenic.

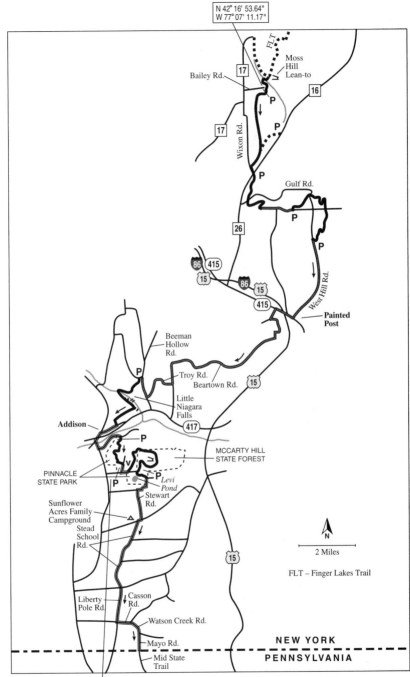

N 42° 16' 53.64"
W 77° 07' 11.17"

FLT

Moss
Hill
Lean-to

Bailey Rd.

17

16

17

Wixon Rd.

P

P

P

Gulf Rd.

P

26

P

86 415

15

86 15

West Hill Rd.

415

**Painted
Post**

15

Beeman
Hollow
Rd.

P

Troy Rd.

Beartown Rd.

15

Little
Niagara
Falls

Addison

417

P

MCCARTY HILL
STATE FOREST

PINNACLE
STATE PARK

V

P

P *Levi
Pond*

Stewart
Rd.

Sunflower
Acres Family
Campground

Stead
School
Rd.

15

N

2 Miles

FLT – Finger Lakes Trail

Liberty
Pole Rd.

Casson
Rd.

Watson Creek Rd.

Mayo Rd.

Mid State
Trail

NEW YORK

PENNSYLVANIA

N 42° 05' 30.92"
W 77° 12' 57.42"

Hike 22c: Crystal Hills Trail

The MST is also blazed orange and it stretches across Pennsylvania to Maryland; much of this trail is off the roads and it is a scenic, rugged trail with isolation, waterfalls, views, gorges, and scenic streams. If you have a couple of months free, continue south to Alabama.

Adirondacks

The Adirondacks are beyond description. They are simply the premier backpacking destination in New York, the outdoor recreation epicenter of the state. The beauty, trails, and limitless outdoor recreational opportunities of these mountains easily rival, if not exceed, most national parks. Not surprisingly, the Adirondacks have attracted hikers from around the world.

The 'Dacks are also home to the Adirondack Park, a unique private and public partnership to protect and properly manage this special place. The so-called blue line defines the boundary of this vast park, which covers 6.1 million acres; 2.4 million acres of that is public land. The park is also home to the largest state-owned wilderness system in the entire nation, encompassing almost 1.1 million acres.

The 'Dacks are not simply mountains, a park, or a wilderness. They are something more. They are a cathedral, a sanctuary that invites a journey that is as spiritual as it is physical. This is a place that can change, and empower, lives. Go there, and you will see. The trails are waiting.

Trails maintained by: Adirondack Mountain Club and its various chapters, www.adk.org. Volunteers build and maintain these trails.

23. Lake George Wild Forest

Length: 21-mile loop.

Direction of description: Counterclockwise.

Duration: 1^1/$_2$ to 2 days.

Difficulty: Moderate to difficult.

Trail conditions: Generally good, although the trails in the southern part of the loop are not as well established, with few blazes.

Blazes: Various. Trails are marked red, yellow, and blue. Most trail junctures have signs.

Water: Generally sufficient.

Vegetation: Mostly northern hardwoods, with hemlock and spruce.

Highlights: Views from Sleeping Beauty and Black Mountain, several beautiful ponds, cascading streams, Lake George.

Issues: Some trails are not well established or blazed, particularly in the southern part of this loop. Trails may have multiple colored blazes. Trail junctures along Lake George are not well established and are easy to miss.

Location: This trail system is located on the east side of Lake George, about 10 miles north of Route 149.

This loop makes for a very enjoyable weekend backpacking trip. It offers a wide variety of scenic features, great camping, nice trails, and some solitude. These trails do not appear to get a lot of backpacking use, but areas are very popular with dayhikers. The trail to Sleeping Beauty is very popular. You can also expect to see people at Fishbrook Pond and Black Mountain. For the remainder of the trails, you may see few other people.

These trails offer a diverse range of ponds, views, streams, and forests. Aside from Black Mountain, the terrain tends to be moderate. Many of these trails are also multi-use, where horses and snowmobiles are allowed, but I did not find the trails to be significantly degraded due to such use. The hike along Lake George is beautiful, with many places to relax and swim.

The first issue is deciding where to park. This description begins and ends at Dacy Clearing. Keep in mind this parking area is at the end of a one-lane 2-mile dirt road from the Hogtown parking area along Shelving Rock Road. The road to Dacy Clearing is passable to cars, but you'll have to pull over if a vehicle approaches the opposite way. This road may also be gated in winter. The other option is to park at the Shelving Rock No. 3 lot, which is much smaller than Dacy Clearing, but located right along the road. Shelving Rock Road is steep and twisty in places.

From Dacy Clearing, follow the yellow trail and sign the register. The trail follows a wide grade that gradually ascends under a scenic forest. Reach a trail juncture; left goes to Bumps Pond, which you will see later. Turn right on the blue trail to Sleeping Beauty. At first the trail is level, but it becomes increasingly rocky as it follows the base of a cliff. Begin a steeper climb over rocks and slabs of bedrock. Reach a spur trail to the left that goes to Sleeping Beauty, where there are spectacular views to the south and west over Lake George. You can also hear the voices of hikers far below, echoing off the cliff.

Return to the blue trail and bear left, heading north. The trail is narrow and brushy as it winds through areas where there was storm or fire damage to the forest. The trail ascends and enters a scenic forest of hemlock and spruce. Descend gradually through this scenic forest and reach the odd-looking outlet of Bumps Pond. (It looks odd because it almost appears to be a canal chiseled into the rock.) Cross the footbridge. Bear left to see the pond, otherwise bear right on the yellow trail to Fishbrook Pond. The trail is wet in areas as it passes marshes and meadows. Descend gradually, and beautiful Fishbrook Pond comes into view with a nice campsite on a peninsula; a faint red trail is to the left and goes around the lake. The yellow trail turns right and passes behind a lean-to. The pond is a beautiful spot and a great place to camp. Another lean-to is on the opposite shore. The trail becomes a little brushier and moves away from the lake until it crosses the outlet.

It can be a little confusing to know where to go from the outlet. A snowmobile trail, with infrequent white blazes, goes straight, while the yellow trail turns left. Both rejoin in about a quarter mile. Follow the yellow trail along the shore of the pond. Avoid the trail to the left that goes to the other lean-to. Proceed straight and climb gradually to a point where you'll rejoin the snowmobile trail. The yellow trail is not well established through here, and blazes are infrequent. You'll know you're in the right place if you see a faded red trail to the right; it descends for a mile to Greenland Pond, an isolated place to camp.

Continue on the yellow trail as it ascends gradually over loose rock. Descend gradually and cross a small stream. The gradual descent continues to serene and isolated Millman Pond. There is a lean-to, and a unique boardwalk goes out into the pond to reach a small bedrock islet where you can enjoy the water. This is another gorgeous place to relax or camp. The trail climbs away from the pond, and then descends to its outlet stream. Continue down along the stream, crossing it twice; you'll see several small cascades. Your hike levels off through a beautiful forest; to the right are meadows and wetlands. Reach a blue trail to the left that leads to a lean-to at the Black Mountain Ponds. This blue trail is also a bypass if you do not want to hike

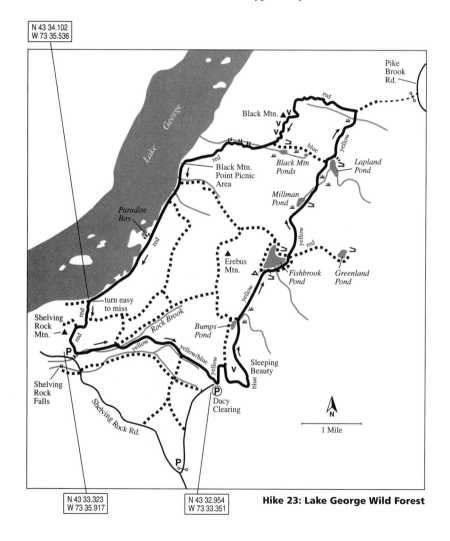

N 43 34.102
W 73 35.536

N 43 33.323
W 73 35.917

N 43 32.954
W 73 33.351

Hike 23: Lake George Wild Forest

Black Mountain. Continue on the yellow trail as it keeps its distance from Lapland Pond, which you can see through the trees. A side trail to the right leads to the pond and a lean-to. The yellow trail is level, and often wet, but soon begins a gradual descent along a wide grade. Cross a bridge over a bog with a beaver dam. Black Mountain rises in the distance, marked by an antenna tower. Reach the juncture with a red trail. Turn left to begin the climb up to Black Mountain. The 1.5 mile climb is never very steep, but it is rocky as it winds its way up the mountain. Spruce becomes more common as you near the summit. Reach a great view to the north as it looks up the length of Lake George. The High Peaks and Green Mountains rise in the distance. Climb a short distance farther to the antenna tower and a small windmill. Follow the trail to the right behind the fenced-in tower to an even more impressive northern panorama overlooking Lake George, over 2,000 feet below. It is an amazing view.

The descent from Black Mountain follows a trail that is narrower and steeper, with many switchbacks; blazes are infrequent. Surprisingly, there are two more views looking south and west over Lake George. There is also a third view looking south and east over the narrow valley harboring the Black Mountain Ponds. Another steep descent brings you to a trail juncture where you turn right on the red trail down to Lake George. The descent is long, but somewhat gradual as it follows an old grade. The trail also meets a small stream at a few spots with mossy grottoes of angled bedrock with flumes and cascades. The descent ends at Black Mountain Point, a picnic area for boaters along Lake George. Here the red trail turns left and follows the shoreline of this gorgeous lake, heading south.

The red trail follows the shore for 3 miles. The trail is level or rolling and follows an old carriage road with a stone retaining wall. The red blazes are infrequent, but the trail is obvious. You will pass numerous campsites for boaters; I believe these sites must be reserved. Regardless, they would also be perfect for backpackers. The trail offers extensive views of the lake and many opportunities to swim and enjoy its clear, cool water. The National Geographic maps show four trail junctures to the left; these are easy to miss and most do not have signs. The level terrain, fine views, and stunning lake make for a sublime hiking experience.

About 1.5 miles from Black Mountain Point, you will reach a confusing spot that lacks a sign or blazes. The trail goes straight, but you will see an obvious grade turn right. Take it. It leads to Paradise Bay, a secluded cove with rocks and views of the Tongue Mountain Range. It is popular with boaters and another nice place to relax. Retrace your steps to the red trail.

The trail generally stays close to the lake, with more views of bays, coves, islands, and the Tongue Mountain Range. Pass another picnic area on a narrow peninsula. About .7 mile farther, look for a narrow trail to the left that climbs up a slope. There may be some surveying tape and a small cairn. This is the turn you must make. The trail climbs steeply up the slope and blowdowns are a problem. There are infrequent red blazes; you will notice some other blazes for horses. Cliffs and ledges rise over the trail. The terrain levels off and the trail reaches a juncture; left goes to Erebus Mountain, right to Shelving Rock Mountain. Turn right. The trail meanders through a scenic forest, dips into a small valley, and soon reaches a wide, old carriage road that winds up to Shelving Rock Mountain. The hike up to the mountain is not really worth it as the view is largely grown over, so it is best to turn left here.

The old carriage road is at first level, but soon begins a series of switchbacks down the rocky slope. Reach another trail juncture; to complete the loop back to Dacy Clearing, turn left. To reach the parking area along Shelving Rock Road, turn right. If you want to see Shelving Rock Falls, turn left on the road, walk for .3 mile, and then turn right onto a trail and follow for .4 mile down to the falls.

Otherwise, continue the hike to Dacy Clearing. The trail follows a wide grade in a beautiful forest. Cross a small stream, and when you reach a trail juncture, bear right. Cross another small stream via a footbridge. This route follows a faded yellow trail to the left; the easier route continues straight to the Dacy Clearing road.

The yellow trail, which follows a stream, has infrequent blazes, blowdowns, and is not well established, although a treadway can generally be followed. The stream has some nice flumes and cascades; it is a scenic, rarely hiked place in the wild forest. Reach a trail juncture with signs and turn right on the yellow trail with the same conditions. The trail is wet, with moss-covered rocks and little treadway. The treadway becomes more evident as you climb, but blowdowns remain a problem. The trail levels off, but you will need to keep any eye out for blazes since the trail can be a little hard to follow. Reach a trail juncture and turn left on a yellow- and blue-blazed trail. Cross a small stream and hike around a wet meadow. The trail continues up the valley, staying close to the base of a mountain slope and passing rocks. Reach a pine grove, a trail sign, and soon thereafter, the parking area at Dacy Clearing.

• • •

The day was hotter than I expected as I hiked along Fishbrook Pond. I walked by a young family swimming in the water as a little boy squealed with delight. Across the pond, a couple of hikers ate and camped at a lean-to. I wished I could have camped right there at the pond, but it was too early in my hike. I had more miles to go, and to be honest, I didn't know where I would end up that night. Sometimes it is impossible to predict where the trail will take you.

The trail returned to the woods as it followed an old forest road now covered in weeds, eroded by water into loose rock and gravel. I kept walking when I noticed something hanging from a narrow branch just a couple of feet from me. It was a chipmunk, trying to find a meal among some blossoms and unripened berries. The chipmunk just hung there, like a heavy Christmas tree ornament, oblivious to my looming presence. It stuck its head in the blossoms, until its instinct sensed something was amiss. The chipmunk looked up and its eyes didn't quite believe I was standing there. Finally, reality set in and the chipmunk flew from the branch with a squeak. For good measure, it chattered at me with annoyance as I walked away.

I walked down to Millman Pond and followed the trail above its shore. Looking down to the water I saw a narrow boardwalk reaching out into the pond, inviting me to visit a small bedrock isle. I walked on the narrow, creaking walk as it skimmed the surface of the water. When I reached the tiny isle it seemed like a perfect spot to take a break. I dropped my pack and took off my shirt, shoes, and socks.

Dozens of dragonflies darted to and fro in search of bugs. Their maneuvers defied what was possible as they suspended themselves in the air, only to move left or right, up or down, in an instant. They chased each other when one intruded into the other's territory, marked by invisible boundary lines. The air was filled with the quick flapping of their wax paper wings.

The sky was blue and the sun was warm; the water danced with sparkling light. I tried to think about things, but I couldn't. I gave up the effort and allowed myself to enjoy this moment of absolute peace and contentment; soon it was time to return to the trail.

24. Tongue Mountain Range Loop

Length: 13.2-mile loop.

Duration: 1¹/₂ days.

Difficulty: Moderate to difficult.

Trail conditions: Trails are well marked and established. All trail junctures have signs. Sections of the trail along Northwest Bay are often wet.

Blazes: Red, blue, or yellow.

Water: Generally sufficient. In the summer, do not expect any water sources along the ridge.

Vegetation: Scenic and diverse forests of pine, hemlock, and hardwoods. Several summits along the ridge have hardwood forests with carpets of grass.

Highlights: Several excellent views, Lake George, waterfalls in wet weather, nice campsites.

Issues: The traverse of the ridge of the Tongue Mountain Range is surprisingly difficult due to the numerous ascents and descents over the mini-summits. This terrain exists from Fifth Peak to almost the end of the peninsula. The trailhead parking area along NY 9N is small and easy to miss. It is located along a bend, so watch out for traffic.

Location: Along NY 9N, north of Lake George.

This beautiful and challenging loop is one of the most popular hiking venues in the scenic Lake George region. While fit hikers can easily dayhike this route, it also serves as an excellent overnight backpacking option. Do not let the relatively modest length and elevation fool you; this is a challenging hike along the serrated crest of the Tongue Mountain Range. There are numerous ascents and descents over mini-summits and the cols and narrow valleys that divide them. This can be frustrating to some hikers. The payoffs are breathtaking vistas that are nearly nonstop. This loop also offers beautiful forests, small streams with waterfalls, and enjoyable lakeshore hiking. What more could you want?

The parking area is at a small pond hemmed in by cliffs; it appears to be an old quarry. The blue trail begins just to the south along NY 9N. Pass a register and hike through a pine plantation. Descend to a long footbridge over Northwest Bay Brook and climb gradually to the beginning of the loop. The blue trail goes right and marks your return; follow the red trail to your left as it makes a steady climb up the mountain along the glen of a small and beautiful mountain stream. A nice falls is just off the trail. This stream has many small falls and cascades, but the trail keeps a little distance from the stream. The climb is along an old forest grade and never particularly steep, but the climb does not relent. The forests are beautiful, with pine, hemlock, and hardwoods. Cross a side stream over a wooden bridge. The trail switchbacks up along some ledges and then soon levels off in a small and beautiful forest valley. The creek babbles along moss-covered rocks. This is a good spot to take a break.

Climb the switchbacks out of this valley and hike along the small stream. Pass large moss-covered ledges to the right and a bog to the left. A gradual climb continues to the four-way intersection with the blue Tongue Mountain Range trail, where you turn right. The climb up to this point was about 1,000 vertical feet over 1.6 miles. The blue trail begins easy enough as it ascends gradually along sidehill. Reach a yellow side trail to the left that climbs .3 mile to the Fifth Peak lean-to. This trail is worth taking as there is a narrow view to the east over the lake, and an expansive view to the southwest over Northwest Bay. A privy is behind the lean-to, but there are no water sources. Few leantos offer such superb views. Retrace your steps on the yellow trail and return to the blue trail.

You will now begin to hike the challenging crest of the Tongue Mountain Range. Expect several ascents and descents ranging from 50 to about 400 vertical feet.

The blue trail descends, crossing rocky terrain, and climbs to a summit with nice views to the southwest; you can see Lake George to both the east and west, separated by the ridge on which you are hiking. A steep, rocky descent follows, but it is manageable. Hike up and over two more summits separated by deep, narrow valleys, and then begin a climb up to French Point Mountain. The summit has camping potential and features a hardwood forest with grass covering the ground. The view is to the east and is remarkable. From here, you can look up and down the lake, which is surrounded by mountains and dotted with islands. The trail descends from French Point Mountain along a ridge with more views. The trail drops steeply into a small stream valley, and then another climb is required up the serrated ridge to First Peak, where there are more superb views. In typical fashion, descend from First Peak along a ridge with many views of the lake. These views are almost nonstop and continue for about a mile. Do not expect a continuous descent. The trail seems to climb over many mini-peaks as much as it descends, so it takes a while to get close to the lake. Evergreen shrubs often border the trail.

Reach a sloping crevice that will require a little scrambling to descend. The terrain levels off soon thereafter. Reach the south end of the loop and a spur trail that leads to Montcalm Point. The trail to the point is easy and rolling. You will see a "No Camping" sign near the point, although there are a couple of established sites. The point appears to be a popular spot for kayakers to camp; it offers nice views across the lake and Northwest Bay.

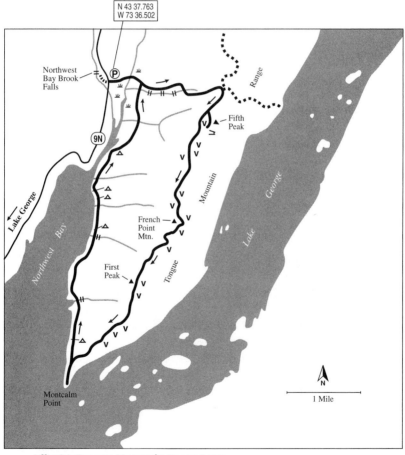

Hike 24: Tongue Mountain Range Loop

Back on the loop, the blue trail now follows the shore of the Northwest Bay. The trail is much easier than it was on the ridge, although you can expect several wet sections and small stream crossings. There are also four to five small campsites along the lake.

The trail stays in fairly close proximity to the shore and passes a campsite. Begin to climb away from the shore, but a descent soon follows back to the water. Continue to hike along the shore; the shore tends to be steep and the trail generally stays about 5 to 10 feet above the water. Cross a small stream with a cascading waterfall. The trail reaches a bay and a very wet meadow; expect to get wet feet as there is no boardwalk or logs to cross. Return to the woods, cross another small stream, and continue to hike along the scenic shore. Cross a boggy inlet of the lake and continue up along the shore. Up ahead is a small cascading waterfall. The trail continues to follow the shore, wrapping around small bays and coves, as it passes small campsites. Reach the Northwest Bay Brook inlet in a scenic forest of pine and hemlock. The inlet resembles a marsh with its winding channels and shallow water. The trail climbs up the mountain about 200 vertical feet, crosses some small streams, and then descends more steeply. Cross another stream and reach the end of the loop. Turn left and return to your car.

•   •   •

My hiking partner and I underestimated the difficulty of this trail. The spectacular, serrated ridge of Tongue Mountain with its relentless ups and downs sapped our energy despite its breathtaking views. By the time we reached the shore of Lake George, the level trail to come was little consolation. The sun shimmered across the pristine water as boats effortlessly skimmed the surface. The water lapped the shore, bouncing between the rocks and splashing us.

The trail followed close to the shore and the sunlight reflected off the water, illuminating the forest with golden light and dancing ripples. The trail was beautiful, but it was difficult to appreciate it through our exhaustion. The steps became monotonous as we wondered how much farther it would be to the trailhead. Every mile felt like three. To the west a massive thundercloud rose, looking otherworldly.

As we hiked up yet another slope and descended in the twilight, a heavy wind filtered through the forest, pushing branches and treetops out of the way. We heard the low grumble of thunder. When the storm hit, we were too tired to panic or hike any faster. Resigned to our fates, we pulled out our headlamps. Sheets of rain began to fall, cascading off leaves and branches. The soaking rain brought us some energy, or at least a sense of urgency. We reached Route 9N, glad to be off the trail, as the rain eased and the storm moved across the lake.

25. Pharaoh Lake Wilderness

Length: 24-mile loop.

Direction of description: Clockwise.

Duration: 1¹/₂ to 2 days.

Difficulty: Moderate to difficult.

Trail conditions: Trails are well established and most trail junctures have signs. Some sections are wet.

Blazes: Various. Trails are blazed yellow, red, or blue.

Water: Plentiful.

Vegetation: Northern hardwoods, with pine and hemlock. Spruce on Pharaoh Mountain.

Highlights: Beautiful lakes and ponds, waterfall and cascades, views from Pharaoh Mountain, superb camping, old mine, historical features.

Issues: Beginners may find navigating the network of trails a little difficult. Some trails are popular, and there can be competition for lean-tos depending on the time of the year. The terrain is hillier and more rugged than you might expect.

Location: This hike begins and ends at Crane Pond Road, north of Schroon Lake.

Pharaoh Lake Wilderness is one of New York's finest backpacking destinations. It is accessible, very scenic, and allows backpackers to hike a loop. The trails feature beautiful lakes, tremendous views, historical ruins, and even a waterfall. The wilderness area is famous for its stunning locations for campsites and lean-tos. This hike is notable for offering a lot of scenery for the effort. As a result, you can expect to share the trails with others.

This description begins at the parking area at the end of Crane Pond Road. The road does continue into the wilderness area and is open to public use. At first the road is in fairly good condition, but does degrade with some ruts and mud puddles. Regardless, it is passable by a vehicle with some clearance. There are a few places to pull off and park, particularly at the Goose Pond Trail. The road is no longer drivable where it crosses a marsh and becomes muddy. The road also makes for a decent walk, particularly at the beginning where it is above a scenic stream with cascades and pools. A side trail circumvents the marshy road crossing, but it is easy to simply hike the road if the water isn't too high. Pass a blue trail to the right and continue on the road. The road ends at a grove of pines and the trail begins to the right, where it crosses a bridge at the outlet of Crane Pond. It is marked blue.

Pass a register and follow the wide trail along an old forest grade. At the first intersection, go left (the trail to the right marks your return route). Reach Glidden Marsh, a scenic pond, and turn left again on the blue trail to Oxshoe Pond. Climb a hill and descend to the beautiful pond; ledges and outcrops rising over the water provide interest. A lean-to looks over the pond. Continue on to Crab Pond across rolling terrain and cross the outlet of the pond. Turn left at the next intersection. There are two nice campsites along the shore of this pond. Leave Crab Pond and hike steeply up a ridge to see Horseshoe Pond; a side trail to the left leads to a campsite. Descend gradually to another trail intersection, and then turn right on the red trail to Lilypad Pond. The trail passes the lean-to of this pond; it is a nice location, but not as beautiful as the others.

The trail becomes hillier as it climbs a ridge with exposed bedrock. Reach Rock Pond Brook where a side trail to the left leads to a 30-foot falls. The main trail climbs up the hill steeply, keeping its distance from the falls. Reach Rock Pond, one of the most scenic ponds along this hike. This pond has many bays, islets, and sloping ledges along the water. I recommend hiking the red trail to the left that explores the pond's northern shore. Although the trail is rocky, it offers great views of the water and surrounding hills. It also passes two fine campsites, and the sloping ledges are great for sunbathing or swimming. Another highlight of this trail is a large mine shaft and ruins. Bear right on the yellow trail and continue hiking around the shore of the pond toward the Rock Pond lean-to.

The lean-to is in a beautiful location, surrounded by pine and hemlock, and faces away from the water. Islands are just offshore. There is also space to camp. The beautiful trail soon reaches the outlet of Little Rock Pond; a trail to the left goes to the Little Rock Pond lean-to. Continue straight across the bridge, and soon you'll reach another intersection. The trail to the right continues around Rock Pond; turn left onto the yellow trail as it gradually climbs through a forest. Descend to beautiful Clear Pond where you can take either trail that goes around it. I took the yellow trail to the left which offered nice views and passed Clear Pond lean-to at a blue trail. This lean-to is stunning and offers great views of the pond and the mountains. As the name indicates, the water does seem clearer than most ponds on this hike. The blue trail soon meets the red trail that was on the opposite, or western, shore of Clear Pond. Bear left onto the blue trail.

Descend gradually and reach a four-way intersection. Continue straight. The spur trail to the right goes to the top of Treadway Mountain, which is a popular dayhike and has great views of the wilderness, but it would add over 4 miles to your hike. Reach another juncture with a trail that goes left around Putnam Pond and the Putnam Pond campground. Go straight on the yellow trail as it climbs gradually along a stream with some cascades. A side trail to the left goes around Grizzle Ocean and accesses its lean-to; go straight and cross a long boardwalk at the outlet. The same side trail rejoins from the left. Continue straight to Pharaoh Lake. The trail ascends, and then descends to a wetlands area, which is circumvented with a long half-loop. The trail

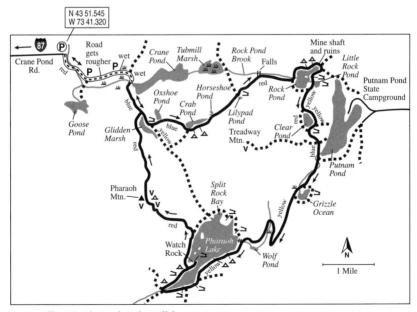

Hike 25: Pharaoh Lake Wilderness

follows some mini-ridges through the forest before descending to a trail that loops around Pharaoh Lake. A cascade and pool are nearby.

The trail to the right is shorter, but the trail to the left is more scenic and offers more camping opportunities. Keep in mind that Pharaoh Lake is a popular destination. The yellow trail is rocky—and surprisingly rugged as it climbs up and down—but offers occasional views of the stunning lake with Pharaoh Mountain rising across the water. As you proceed, the terrain moderates, and there are more views of the lake from ledges and cliffs—the scenery is superb. After passing a couple of campsites, turn right at the next trail juncture and continue your way around the lake. The trail passes two beautiful shelters and soon reaches a register and the outlet of the lake. Cross the outlet and turn right on the red trail to continue around the lake, passing more campsites and a shelter. On this side, the trail keeps its distance from the water. Reach a yellow spur trail to the right that you cannot miss. It goes out to a peninsula, known as Watch Rock, which juts out into the water and is home to a shelter. There are big rocks at the end of the peninsula with awesome views of almost the entire lake, its islands, and surrounding mountains. It is spectacular.

Return to the red trail as it makes its way around the lake, still keeping its distance from the water. Turn left at the red trail that climbs up Pharaoh Mountain. This is the most difficult part of this hike; the trail is steep in places and the climb is long. You will climb about 1,400 vertical feet over 1.5 miles. The climb is never technical or exposed, but the trail does traverse slabs of bedrock. Watch for a place where the trail turns right and is level as it traverses the slabs, but take care because springs can make the rock slick. There are partial views here before the steep climb begins, the forest changes to more spruce, and there are some rock scrambles that must be negotiated. Reach the top in a mini-col between two peaks or ridges. Side trails to the left and right all lead to awesome views of the wilderness area, the High Peaks, the Green Mountains, and much of the Adirondacks. It is truly breathtaking. The side trail to the right from the mini-col leads to more awesome views and a small campsite. To continue on the hike, proceed straight on the trail through the mini-col, which is blazed red.

The descent is more gradual than the ascent, but, again, watch your footing on the spring-soaked slabs. The forest soon transitions back to hardwoods. Reach the bottom near Glidden Marsh and reach the trail intersection that began this loop. Turn left and retrace your steps back to the car.

· · ·

I began this hike on a Sunday afternoon. As I walked along the old forest road into the wilderness, I saw several people hiking out, including some who were obviously on their first backpacking trip.

It brought back memories of my own first trip. A friend and I decided to go hiking and camping in an effort to find Schmitthenner Lake in the state game lands near where we lived. I drove my old Ford Escort up a dirt mountain road; we found a place to park, gathered our gear, and began to walk. We didn't have any idea where to go or how to get to the lake. My gear consisted of an old-school book bag with a big flannel sleeping bag strapped to it with bungee cords. We didn't even bother with a tent.

I did have the wisdom to bring a topographical map, and when I thought we had reached the proper side road, we took it. The area was very isolated and wooded, miles from any village. We found ourselves in a maze of massive blueberry bushes, the largest I had ever seen. With no luck finding the lake, we stumbled upon an old white farmhouse and asked the residents for directions. In a place with no landmarks, though, it was no use, and we were soon lost again.

As darkness approached, we gave up on finding the lake and found a place to camp. We didn't have a tent or a fire. We simply lay down our bags as the night was overrun with stars. I remember deer snorting at us with annoyance as I tried to sleep. Somehow we survived the bugs. The next morning we managed to retrace our steps back to the car. We had survived, despite our oblivion.

That first backpacking excursion was doomed from the start. Camping wasn't allowed on state game lands, and Schmitthenner Lake was privately owned. Even if we had found the lake, we surely would not have been allowed to be there. I can't imagine now sleeping outside in the summer without a tent. We bumbled without a clue across the woods and meadows, trespassing most of the way. Despite the utter futility of our hike, I look back on it with a smile. Ignorance can surely be bliss.

I entered the Pharaoh Lake Wilderness almost twenty years later a much more enlightened hiker. Finding the gorgeous lakes on this hike was easier. When I reached the sublime Pharaoh Lake, I took the trail to Watch Rock, a narrow peninsula that juts into the water. The stunning panorama across the lake included islands, cliffs, and mountains. The clear, deep water lapped against the smooth ledges and cliffs lining the shore. A wind blew across the lake with a biting chill, and the veil of rain showers coming from the north no longer carried the warmth of summer. Red maples burned in a forest of green. Autumn would soon be here.

I sat at Watch Rock and thought about all the places I've been in the last twenty years. It is more than I thought was possible when I was a young man. Even being at Watch Rock was once beyond the scope of my life. We may be blind, but we can always choose to see.

26. West Canada Lakes Wilderness Loop

Length: 23 miles.

Direction of description: Clockwise.

Duration: 1½ to 2 days.

Difficulty: Easy to moderate.

Trail conditions: Expect several wet and muddy sections. The trails are usually well established and most junctures have signs. Trails often follow old forest roads and grades.

Blazes: Red, blue, yellow.

Water: Generally plentiful.

Vegetation: Northern hardwoods with pine, spruce, and fir.

Highlights: Several beautiful and isolated lakes, superb camping, isolation, West Canada Lakes Wilderness, side hike to the summit of Pillsbury Mountain.

Issues: Muddy and wet conditions. There is no bridge across the outlet of West Lake, which can be difficult and dangerous in high water. The road to the trailhead, called Old Military Road, has some very rough and eroded sections. A vehicle with clearance is recommended. There are some places to pull off along this road. The trailhead is very isolated.

Location: This trail is located southwest of Indian Lake.

The West Canada Lakes Wilderness is one of the most scenic and isolated areas in the Adirondacks. Comprised of numerous lakes, ponds, wetlands, streams, and hills on an elevated plateau, the wilderness experiences a cooler climate than surrounding areas. Covering over 156,000 acres, it is the second largest wilderness area in the Adirondacks. This loop is an ideal way to explore some of the most scenic areas in the wilderness without having to hike long miles on a linear trail. The loop also follows a section of the famed Northville Placid Trail (NPT), the longest trail in the Adirondacks.

The hike begins on an old grade, with a steady, gradual climb of 400 vertical feet over 1.6 miles up a stream valley carved by the diminutive Miami River. This is the French Louie Trail, marked red. Reach the loop and turn left onto the French Louie Trail, named for a trapper, guide, and hermit who lived in the area and died in 1915. After a short ascent and rolling terrain, the trail drops gently to Pillsbury Lake, where there are wet areas and some boardwalks. A side trail to the right goes down to this scenic lake, featuring islands and a lean-to for camping. Noisey Ridge rises across the lake.

Hilly terrain follows as the trail proceeds west toward Whitney Lake. Follow a ridge above the lake and descend gradually toward Sampson Lake, another beautiful and isolated gem. A side trail to the left goes down to the water and a lean-to. Otherwise, the trail keeps its distance from the lake. Hilly and rolling terrain follows until the trail drops down to the blue NPT, which this route joins on the right. Reach the outlet of Mud Lake, the source of West Canada Creek, where there is a bridge. Enjoy some partial views of Mud Lake. Pass a nice lean-to and

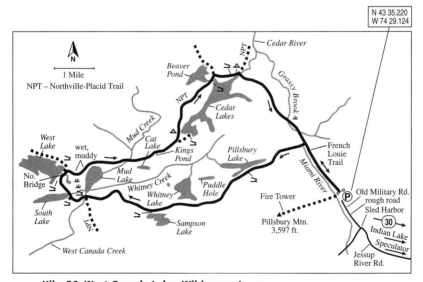

Hike 26: West Canada Lakes Wilderness Loop

hike across more hilly terrain under a pine forest. A side trail to the left goes to the South Lake Lean-to, a beautiful place to camp at a sandy and shallow lake.

The blue NPT reaches a grassy—but wet—meadow before crossing a long, wooden bridge at the outlet of South Lake. This bridge offers great views across the vast wetlands, meadows, and rolling hills. Reenter the woods and the hills soon return. Drop down to beautiful West Lake, although the trail never gets close to it. An inconspicuous side trail to the left leads to the two lean-tos on this gorgeous lake, which features islands and rolling mountains in an isolated and serene setting. The lean-tos are great for sunsets. Reach a meadow with a register and trail sign.

Cross the outlet of West Lake by rock hopping, as there is no bridge. Be careful in high water. The NPT now circumvents Mud Lake and, as the name implies, this section is famous for its muddy, rocky, and wet conditions along a tight and narrow trail. Cross a bridge over Mud Creek and hike in a pine and spruce forest up a larger climb of about 150 vertical feet. Descend and cross the outlet of well-hidden Kings Pond. Continue a gradual climb followed by hilly terrain. Descend gradually to Cedar Lakes. A trail to the right goes to a lean-to on a peninsula with views across the lake. Continue on the NPT and pass some nice campsites to the right along the lake. Hike across level terrain before beginning a long ascent up Cobble Hill, and then a steeper descent to Cedar Lakes and Beaver Pond. A trail to the right goes to a lean-to on Cedar Lakes. Cross a tilted and somewhat unstable wooden bridge above the channel between Beaver Pond and Cedar Lakes, with views of both. Begin to hike along an old, level grade, and then turn right on the blue NPT; the trail to the left goes to Lost Pond. Continue to follow an old forest road across rolling terrain. The trail passes a lean-to in a tall grassy meadow, and soon thereafter, a nice campsite. Brush inundates the trail before it reaches the dam of Cedar Lakes. Reach a trail juncture and trail sign. Turn right and leave the blue NPT, cross the bridge on a yellow trail over the Cedar River, and pass a campsite.

Follow an old forest road as it gradually ascends. Enter a spruce forest and cross a meadow, where you will have to negotiate some muddy sections. Soon thereafter, cross a twisted wooden bridge across Grassy Brook. Begin a steeper climb and cross Stony Brook before reaching the end of the loop. Retrace your steps back to the car. While at the trailhead, you may also want to take the red trail to the summit of Pillsbury Mountain, where there is a fire tower and spruce forest. From the fire tower, enjoy impressive views of Indian Lake, Lewey Mountain, and Snowy Mountain.

• • •

It was another hot day on the trail. The heat pressed against my skin, spreading sweat across my clothes. Some mosquitoes did their best to be an annoyance and a couple of deerflies tried to show them up. But the bugs weren't bad—the dreaded black flies were gone. However, their resurrection will surely come in May. I'm sure black flies have their ecological purpose and probably feed some kind of critter. Whatever that critter is, it doesn't eat enough of them.

Later, after a day of slogging through mud, I found a great campsite near the lake. I took off my shirt, socks, and boots, tempted to jump in, but something told me not to. I stepped into the water and my feet sank into the muck, but I didn't much care. I walked in up to my waist, and the water felt great as I scrubbed the caked mud from my legs.

I strained to extract myself from the lake bottom as the muck held onto my feet with suction. As I finally freed my legs, I looked down to see a worm on my ankle, wiggling. I looked closer. It was a leech attached to a bloody blister, sucking away. I pulled, and it stretched with slippery ease but remained attached. Undaunted, I pulled harder and managed to dislodge it. A rivulet of blood leaked from the wound. I had an electric shock of panic. Were there more? I dropped my shorts and stood along the lake naked, searching as much of my body as I could see and feel. No more leeches. Thank God I hadn't gone swimming. I crawled into my sleeping bag with the nightmarish vision of a leech attached to my back, sucking my blood as I slept. I'd wake up withered and pale, next to a huge, moist, wiggling leech as it rolled itself out of the tent and down to the lake.

Maybe black flies weren't so bad after all.

27. Woodhull–Bear Lake Loop

Length: 24-mile loop.

Direction of description: Clockwise.

Duration: 1^1/$_2$ to 2^1/$_2$ days.

Difficulty: Easy to moderate.

Trail conditions: Trails are sufficiently blazed and signed at junctures. The treadway may be a little faint along the trails in the southern part of this loop. There are some wet areas without bridges or boardwalks. Trails often follow old forest roads and grades.

Blazes: Blue, yellow, red, and orange.

Water: Plentiful.

Vegetation: Mostly hardwoods with some pine and spruce.

Highlights: Bear Lake, Woodhull Lake, Woodhull Mountain, Remsen Falls.

Issues: This circuit requires some road walking and a long out-and-back to Woodhull Mountain. Sections of trail are very wet, and one is flooded.

Location: The trail begins near the tiny village of McKeever, south of Old Forge.

This loop offers the typical scenery of the western Adirondacks—ponds, lakes, streams, wetlands, and rolling mountains. The added benefit of this hike is the fire tower on Woodhull Mountain where there are some views.

At the main parking area, you will notice two roads, one to the left and one to the right. The road to the left is an older, grassy forest road. It is gated and has a small parking area a short distance from the main parking area. The road to the right is a single-lane gravel road that is usually in good condition. Although gated, the gate is usually open in the warmer months and you can drive it almost all the way to Wolf Lake Landing. To avoid additional walking on either road, you can drive down the gravel road and park where the blue Bear Lake Trail crosses. There is some space to pull off on the right. However, parking here is very limited, so this description begins at the main parking area.

Begin by taking the older, grassy forest road to the left. It is level and soon passes a small parking area, gate, and register. The level road tunnels through the forest and features a few meadows, vernal ponds, and some spruce trees on the right. After about a mile, reach a blue trail to the right that gradually ascends to a gravel road and continues on to Bear Lake; this is a potential return route. The old forest road continues for about 2 more miles to a four-way intersection. The trail to the left descends for a half mile to Remsen Falls and the South Branch Moose River. The falls are really a set of rapids, and the river is quite large. It is a beautiful spot to take a break.

The trail to the right goes to the gravel road. The trail straight ahead goes to Woodhull Mountain; this intersection marks the beginning of the 4.5-mile (for a total of 9 miles) out-and-back hike to Woodhull Mountain. The trail continues on the old, grassy forest road for about 3 miles, and then follows a trail that gradually ascends about 500 vertical feet up to the summit of Woodhull Mountain. This trail may be marked with a variety of colored blazes. The top of the mountain is forested with spruce, but the highlight is a fire tower you can climb for some nice views of the surrounding hills, mountains, and lakes. The cab on top of the fire tower is locked. Retrace your steps back to the four-way intersection. Some maps show a southern route from Woodhull Mountain to the gravel road, but it no longer exists.

Turn left at the four-way intersection and reach the gravel road; turn left onto the gravel road and hike it for about 1.5 miles as it gradually

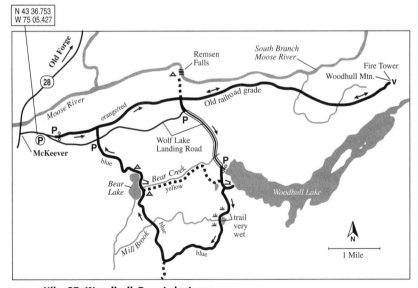

Hike 27: Woodhull–Bear Lake Loop

ascends and crosses some small streams. Leave the gravel road and turn right onto a blue trail, which descends to Wolf Lake Landing on Woodhull Lake. The blue trail follows an old forest grade and descends to a yellow trail to the right, which is also a shortcut to Bear Lake. Continue straight on the blue trail. Cross a stream and then reach a red side trail to the left that goes to Woodhull Lake Lean-to. This side trip is worth taking as it provides the only real views of this massive, untouched lake. The lean-to is very close to the water and is in a beautiful location. Some small campsites are nearby. This would be a wonderful place to camp and see the sunrise.

Continue on the blue trail, which also doubles as an orange snow-mobile trail. The trail continues to follow an old forest grade along hilly terrain. The blue blazes can be infrequent. Be prepared for some very wet and muddy sections, including one where the trail is essentially flooded. The water is a couple of feet deep, but some spruce trees and stumps can help with the crossing. The trail reaches a scenic beaver pond and passes through some grassy glades that are also muddy. Descend and hike along a wet meadow. The trail turns right and becomes drier as it gradually ascends under a hardwood forest on the old, wide grade. Enjoy a period of level hiking followed by a gradual descent where you will reach an intersection with a blue trail; turn right.

The hike now takes you back onto a footpath in the woods. The trail may be blazed a little infrequently and the treadway is a little over-grown, but it can be followed. The terrain is hilly and passes some large hardwoods interspersed with spruce saplings. Cross a moderately sized stream without a bridge. The National Geographic maps indicate that Coleman Dam is somewhere near here, but there is no sign of it from the trail. The trail is easy and level to Bear Lake.

Bear Lake is gorgeous and is a perfect place to camp. The yellow trail mentioned previously joins from the right and crosses a small stream with some small campsites nearby. A side trail to the right leads to the newer shelter, which faces a large boulder. The blue trail wraps around the lake, with views of it through the trees. Rounded hills rise over the water to the northwest. Reach the north shore, where you'll find a small, sandy beach and another campsite. In late May, expect to see many pink lady's slippers along this section of the trail.

Climb gradually away from the lake and enter a small stream valley. The terrain is hilly once again, but overall the trail descends as it crosses some small streams. Reach the gravel road. Here, you have a choice. You can turn left and follow the gravel road about a mile back to the main parking area, or you can continue straight on the blue trail, descend along a small stream, and reach the old, grassy forest road, where you can turn left back to the main parking area.

• • •

Not every hike can be a life-affirming experience, filled with daisies and butterflies. Sometimes it is an effort in blood, pain, and determination. On this day, despite the promise of gorgeous weather, blue skies, and warm temperatures, an ominous threat lurked in the shadows: mosquitoes and black flies. I came prepared with an arsenal of DEET and a head net.

I reached the trailhead and opened the hatch of my car to see a squadron of mosquitoes already swarming all over my gear, as if I had brought them from home. I had to retreat into my car to put on my shoes, but I wasn't going to give up. I threw on my head net, got my pack on, and hurried down the trail with the mosquitoes in hot pursuit.

I reached beautiful Bear Lake in bright sunshine and followed trails north toward Woodhull Lake. And then I felt it: a sharp, piercing pain around my lower back, then my shoulder. At first I pretended it wasn't happening, since I was already in misery from the mosquito attacks. But soon I had to face reality: The black flies had found me. They burrowed under the straps of my backpack and bit me repeatedly through my shirt. In a moment my attention was diverted again to battling the mosquitoes. Could I survive fighting a two-front war?

The situation became so desperate that I had to assault myself to kill the bugs. I took too much pleasure in seeing their mangled, twisted corpses littering my shirt. Then I noticed blood—my defenses were failing. They were getting to me, testing my sanity and using my blood to hatch their next generation. My defenses felt futile. If I couldn't fight them, I could always flee. Speed was my only hope as I hiked fast, covering 3 miles per hour along an old, grassy forest road. The level road passed meadows, streams, and forests, but I saw no other hikers. I was alone in these beautiful, infested woods. As the daylight faded, I was alone in my pain.

Retreat was my only option, so I raced back to my car, vainly hoping that the cool night would bring relief from my attackers. As I loaded my gear into my car, they saw an opening and invaded, swarming my final defense. I turned my air conditioning on high and lit the interior light to distract them. They buzzed around, crazy and confused, wanting both the light and the blood. I drove quickly away with all the windows open to flush them out, and the wind rushing through my car slowly calmed me down. My defensive tactics helped, but I was still reminded of their presence on the interstate as they whispered sweet nothings in my ear so I would know they were there, watching and waiting. When I got home and took off my shirt, I saw that my back was covered in welts.

The next morning I went to get my gear out of my car. A few determined mosquitoes were still buzzing, nosing the glass. I just let them out, my defeat now complete.

28. Remsen Falls–Nelson Lake Loop

Length: 21-mile loop.

Direction of description: Counterclockwise.

Duration: 1½ to 2 days.

Difficulty: Easy to moderate.

Trail conditions: Sections of trail are often wet, blazes may be infrequent, some sections are in poor condition with blowdowns. Trails often follow old forest roads and grades.

Blazes: Orange, blue, yellow.

Water: Plentiful.

Vegetation: Forests of hardwoods, spruce, and pine.

Highlights: Nelson Lake, Nicks Lake, rapids on the Middle Branch and South Branch Moose River.

Issues: The northern part of this loop follows faint trails along old grades with infrequent blazes. One stream crossing beneath a beaver dam is a wet crossing.

Location: The hike begins off Bisby Road, Thendara, New York.

This is a relatively easy weekend backpacking loop that offers the unique feature of hiking along large rivers with whitewater rapids in an area where the water features tend to be ponds, lakes, or swamps. This loop also has two lean-tos, one at Nelson Lake and the other along the South Branch Moose River overlooking Remsen Falls. Because so much of this hike is along rivers, this is a perfect summertime backpack when you can wade and swim in the rivers when the water is low. Do not attempt to swim or wade when the water is high, as both rivers have powerful rapids.

From Bisby Road, sign in the register and follow the blue trail along a forest road as it descends under hardwoods. Pass a trail to the right, and soon thereafter, a yellow trail to the left, which is part of the Nicks Lake loop trail. Stay on the blue trail as it levels off and passes a second intersection with the yellow trail to the left. The blue trail gradually descends and reaches another intersection; follow the trail to the right along another old forest road. This is an older snowmobile trail, blazed orange. The trail is not in the best of shape, with

Hike 28: Remsen Falls–Nelson Lake Loop

some blowdowns and branches, but the trail route is evident. Cross a stream and a wet meadow below an impressive beaver dam. The boardwalk is in poor shape, so expect wet feet. Continue the meandering descent, passing many vernal pools in spring when you can expect conditions to be wet. The trail follows the grade as it begins to stay higher on the slope and enters a verdant spruce forest with carpets of moss and several vernal pools. Reenter the hardwoods and descend to a nice view of the Middle Branch Moose River and a large pool. The trail leaves the river but soon returns with another large pool and some potential camping.

The grade bends left, away from the river, and passes several wet areas with a diverse forest of hardwoods, spruce, and pine. The terrain is easy and rolling. Pass an unblazed side trail to the right that I presume goes to the railroad viaduct, which gives hikers access to NY 28. An impressive series of rapids, off trail, are downstream of the viaduct. On the orange trail you will soon reach more views of the river, with its rapids, and some camping. Cross a small stream, and the trail follows a grassy grade right along the river. The trail bears left, away from the river, with blue and orange blazes.

Be sure to follow a side trail to a new lean-to at Nelson Lake. The lean-to is away from the water, but a trail leads down to a privy and the lake, where there is a campsite. This is a gorgeous lake surrounded by rolling mountains. Keep in mind that this is the only good view of this lake along the hike.

Back on the blue trail, hike up along a gradual grade to another intersection where you will turn right onto a blue trail. This trail also follows an old forest road that is level, and then descends to a small stream, with rapids and boulders. This stream enters Nelson Lake. Follow the contour around a hill and descend to another small stream where the old forest road ends. The trail now follows the Middle Branch Moose River downstream with many views of this beautiful river. The trail at first keeps its distance from the river, but you can see through the trees its impressive and powerful series of rapids. Hike closer to the river where you can see more rapids; in some places, the trail is so close it will be flooded in high water.

The trail continues to stay close to the river where you can both see and hear the rapids. Hike away from the river and enter a scenic spruce forest. Cross a small side stream and enjoy more views of the river. The trail bears left and turns away from the Middle Branch Moose River to continue up along the much larger South Branch

Moose River. The trail also degrades, with more blowdowns and infrequent blazes. The trail comes close to the river, with many views. After passing an island in the river, you will see that the rapids begin. The South Branch is a huge river and is an impressive sight. A cascading side stream tumbles down from the left.

Be careful to watch the blazes before reaching the second side stream. The trail turns left and ascends up a slope where blowdowns are a big problem. The trail is in rough shape and is poorly established. Descend back to the river where you will soon reach a second island. Here the river's side channel separating the island from the shore is a narrow mini-gorge framed by cliffs. Cross another side stream and the trail soon reaches Remsen Falls Lean-to at the edge of a meadow. This lean-to offers views looking up the river to its namesake, which is really a rapid. It is a beautiful location, although this lean-to has a reputation of being a little bit of a party spot.

Hike across the meadow and begin the hike up Nicks Creek valley. The blue trail is better established and blazed. The terrain is easy and gradual as it explores a diverse forest of birch, maple, spruce, and pine. Cross three side streams and begin a steadier climb to a juncture with the yellow Nicks Lake Loop. The quicker hike is to continue left on the blue and yellow trail that will soon complete the main loop, but avoids Nicks Lake. I followed the yellow trail to the right as it descended steeply to a footbridge over Nicks Creek and followed the meandering shore of the lake. The only drawback of the route I took would be the crowds in the campground and at the beach on summer weekends.

Along Nicks Lake, both the forest and the lake are very beautiful, and you are treated to views of the water and large pine, hemlock, and birch trees. Cross a boardwalk with more views of the water and reach a beach. Follow the road and turn left at the intersection. Continue on the road into a campground and reach two roads that form a loop. Follow either road to the end of the campground loop where the yellow trail resumes along the hilly shoreline for more views of the lake. The trail passes behind campsites and follows unique narrow ridges over the water under scenic forests of white pine. Descend and cross a stream via a footbridge. The trail begins to move away from the lake and crosses small streams. The terrain is easy and rolling. Complete the loop where the yellow trail joins the blue. Turn right and retrace your steps back to the car.

• • •

The trail entered a deep pine forest as sunlight littered the ground. Despite the soft pine needles, my feet felt sore, raw, and tired. I descended to a small stream that I was able to cross on a decomposing spruce log, resisting the enticements of gravity and the water below. I made it to the other side and climbed a bank, where I had a nice view of the Middle Branch Moose River.

Despite the mild terrain, I needed a break; I felt I was rushing the trail without appreciating anything. I sat down on the soft bank, carpeted with a bed of amber pine needles. I stripped off my shoes and socks, relishing the fresh air on my feet as I munched on some trail mix. I watched the river as it rolled by. Its deep, powerful current seemed to be the work of muscles and tendons, pushing and surging within a body of water. The river seemed alive, the shore the boundary of its skin. If I entered, I would be at its mercy. It may release me back to land, or it may absorb me deep within its muscular current.

 # 29. Ha-De-Ron-Dah Wilderness

Length: 24-mile loop.

Direction of description: Counterclockwise.

Duration: 1½ to 2½ days.

Difficulty: Easy to moderate.

Trail conditions: The northern trail along Lost Creek, Big Otter Lake, East Pond, Little Simon Pond, and the headwaters of the South Inlet is not well maintained; blazes are infrequent, and the trail is not always evident. The trail can be followed with some effort. Blowdowns are also a problem. The northern trail is easier to follow in the spruce forests, but more difficult in the hardwood forests; it may be overgrown in the summer. This is not a bushwhack, but you will have to stop several times to find your way. The remainder of the trails are better established, blazed, and have signs. The trail is wet in many locations as it passes many streams, bogs, lakes, ponds, wetlands, and beaver ponds. The terrain is level and rolling, with no major climbs.

Blazes: Various trails are blazed yellow, blue, and red.

Water: Plentiful.

Vegetation: Hardwoods mixed with forests of spruce, pine, and hemlock.

Highlights: Isolation and many beautiful lakes, ponds, and streams. Do not miss East Pond, Pine Lake, Lost Lake, Middle Settlement Lake, and Middle Branch Lake.

Issues: Northern trail is not well maintained, the trail is often wet, and some streams do not have footbridges. There is one significant wet crossing at a stream and marsh. The trail is impacted by flooding from beaver dams in a few places.

Location: Thendara and Old Forge, New York.

This beautiful loop is an ideal weekend backpack as it explores a diverse wilderness. The terrain is easy, with rolling hills. This hike could be good for beginners; just keep in mind the northern trails in the wilderness are not well maintained, but they do exist.

Most backpackers seem to park along NY 28 and hike in to Middle Settlement and Middle Branch Lakes. This route shows more of everything this wilderness has to offer by following a longer loop that begins at Herreshoff Road in Thendara, just off NY 28.

There is a parking area at the gate. Follow a dirt road through private property and turn left on a woods road. This woods road enters the wilderness, where there is also a register. This trail is blazed blue. The terrain is hilly as the trail follows the old woods road through small valleys, over streams, and above wet meadows. The forest is primarily hardwoods. There is a small campsite on the left where the trail crosses Indian Brook via a culvert. When I hiked here, a trail to the right was marked with red tape, so there may be a relocation in the future. The trail becomes wet as it skirts a large wet meadow and reenters the woods. The blue trail goes through deep spruce forests and reaches the beginning of the loop at a trail juncture and sign.

Follow the yellow trail to the right; you will return via the blue trail to the left. The yellow trail marks the beginning of the northern trail, which is not well maintained but can be followed with some effort. The yellow trail descends to a branch of the South Inlet and a large bog. Here the trail is wet and usually flooded; the boardwalk that is here is dilapidated. Expect wet and muddy feet when you cross this stream and bog. Hilly terrain follows to the other branch of the South Inlet, where there is a sturdy new log bridge. The trail from here to Little Simon Pond is gorgeous, with deep spruce forests and hilly terrain. Cross a small stream and reach the outlet of Little Simon Pond, where there are cascades. The pond is scenic and isolated but does not appear to offer much in the way of camping. Hilly terrain follows and the hardwoods return as you reach another trail juncture near East Pond.

I recommend you follow the yellow spur trail to the right to go to East Pond, where there are fine views of this beautiful, island-studded pond. This is also a great place to camp. I do not recommend you follow the red spur trail out to Blackfoot Pond. There is only a narrow view of the pond, no camping, and blowdowns are a problem out to the mica mine. The trail to Blackfoot Pond follows a narrow valley with spring-slicked ledges.

Back at the loop after the detour to East Pond, the trail is now blue and begins to degrade. Blazes are infrequent, and it is hard to follow at times. The trail climbs away from East Pond, and then descends to the pond's outlet, where there is a series of small ponds formed by beaver dams. The trail here is often wet. Continue down a stream valley as the trail stays above the stream. The trail continues to be hard to follow in sections; keep an eye out for blazes.

The blue trail comes close to the creek, which I'll refer to as East Pond Creek, and suddenly the trail is blazed red. This appears to be

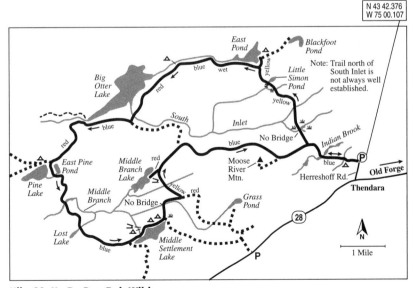

Hike 29: Ha-De-Ron-Dah Wilderness

the place of the spur trail out to Lost Creek, except that there is little sign of this trail. I could not locate any blazes across East Pond Creek. However, the good news is that there is potential camping along this creek. The red trail is hard to follow, so try to discern the remnants of an old forest grade. Enter a scenic spruce forest as you near Big Otter Lake. The trail never gets close to the lake, and blowdowns are a problem, as well as infrequent blazing. Reach the beautiful South Inlet, where there is a footbridge. The red trail ends, and you can celebrate your survival of the northern trail. Despite the maintenance problems, the isolation and scenery of the northern trail make it worthwhile. It also provides the opportunity for a larger backpacking loop.

Turn right on the blue trail as it follows an old forest road. From here on out, the trails are easier to follow. Hike to the outlet of Big Otter Lake and turn left onto the red trail. A long wooden bridge is to your right. The red trail is also a snowmobile trail, and it continues along an old forest road. The forest becomes stunning as you near East Pine Pond, with deep green spruce and pine. Reach another trail juncture at Pine Lake; the loop/blue trail continues left, but it is worth your while to explore to the right a little bit to see this gorgeous lake with a superb campsite on the north shore. I did not find a lean-to as indicated on the National Geographic map.

Otherwise, continue on the blue trail as it follows a ridge under a pine forest with views through the trees of both Pine Lake and East Pine Pond. It is a wonderful section of trail. Descend from the ridge and cross a very long footbridge across the outlet of East Pine Pond. Hardwoods return as you gain elevation. Descend to Middle Branch, where there is another footbridge across a bog. Hilly terrain follows as the trail meanders under hardwoods to a small stream valley where you pass along a large, broken beaver dam. Ascend to Lost Lake; a cascade marks the outlet of this beautiful lake, which is actually a small, narrow pond bordered with large boulders and ledges. The hilly terrain continues as you hike across several small streams and pass another beaver dam that creates a spooky bog with many dead, bleached trees. A gradual climb follows up along a small stream valley. As you reach the top of the ridge, large boulders begin to appear. Reach a trail juncture. The blue trail goes right, but you will turn left onto the yellow trail as it descends to the outlet of Middle Settlement Lake where there are tiers of beaver dams. Cross the outlet on a bridge and ascend to a ridge above the lake. Descend to campsites and a very nice lean-to with views of this attractive lake area. There are also canoes that hikers are free to use. As you might expect, this beautiful area is also very popular.

The trail follows the north shore of the lake, passing three or four other campsites. Reach the inlet of the lake where there is a cliff to the left; here the trail winds through massive, jumbled boulders. Reach a juncture with a blue trail, but continue left on the yellow trail as it skirts along wet meadows. Hike through hardwoods along hilly terrain and descend to Middle Branch. This is a larger stream crossing, and there is no bridge, so be very careful in high water. The trail turns right and follows the creek upstream. Reach a juncture with a red trail; follow the yellow trail to the left. For the next mile, the hike is hilly and there is one small stream crossing. Descend to a red side trail to the left that goes down to Middle Branch Lake and lean-to. This is also a gorgeous spot, but this shelter is a little tilted and more exposed to the weather; it sits on a peninsula, so it is surrounded by water. A small campsite is nearby.

Return to the yellow trail as it crosses level terrain to the blue trail, where you turn right. The blue trail follows an obvious old forest road, which is the same one you initially hiked in on from Thendara. The trail is blazed infrequently, but the route is obvious. Cross several small streams in a spruce forest, and begin a gradual but long climb as the forest changes to hardwoods. Reach a juncture with the Moose River Mountain Trail. This red spur trail goes to the top of its namesake, but there are no views.

The blue trail gradually descends and completes the loop at the yellow trail. Retrace your steps back to your car.

• • •

The cold sky became a battleground between clouds and sun, and the sun was losing. I pressed on to beautiful Pine Lake as shafts of fading sunlight illuminated the low clouds. I could camp here, I thought, but I felt the need to go farther. Lost Lake's scenery was appealing, but it was otherwise inhospitable, lacking a campsite to shield me from a cold, passing shower. I continued on to Middle Settlement Lake, crossing logs over its outlet in the twilight. I reached the shelter overlooking this gorgeous lake. Across the lake I saw a tent and a dim fire. The shelter was filled with older men who looked cautiously at me, indicating that there was no place for me. I asked if there was any place to pitch a tent, and one of the men pointed me back up the trail.

I rushed to pitch my tent in the blackness of the night, hoping to finish before it rained again. I fell asleep as the rain gently began to tap the nylon.

From the warm depths of sleep, I heard a piercing, ghostly call that echoed across the water. I was awakened suddenly, as if from the grip of unconsciousness. The midnight siren was so clear, so vivid, that it felt as if it were both miles away and right next to me. The call was repeated—it was haunting, but not malicious—and I realized it was a loon on the far shore. The call carried an absolute sense of wildness. While this place was a weekend escape for some of us, it was home for another, and the call was its proclamation.

30. Cranberry Lake 50

Length: 50-mile loop.

Direction of description: Clockwise.

Duration: 2^1/$_2$ to 4 days.

Difficulty: Easy to moderate.

Trail conditions: The trails are generally well blazed and established. Some areas are wet, and beavers have impacted several sections of the trail, particularly north of Olmstead Pond and the High Falls area. Expect sun exposure and brushy conditions from High Falls to north of High Rock. Trails often follow old forest roads and grades.

Blazes: The overall loop is blazed blue, but those blazes are infrequent. The trails along the loop have red, blue, and yellow blazes.

Water: Generally plentiful.

Vegetation: Northern hardwoods, wetlands, some areas of spruce, hemlock, and pine. There is some old-growth hemlock and pine.

Highlights: Cranberry Lake, Olmstead Pond, Cat Mountain, High Falls, great campsites, meadows, beaver dams, isolation, and scenic ponds, lakes, and streams. The scenic village of Wanakena offers services for backpackers.

Issues: The various colors of the blazes on the different sections of the trail may confuse beginner backpackers; sections of the loop are flooded or wet due to beaver dams; muddy areas; trail crosses the tops of several beaver dams. Almost 8 miles of road walking are required to complete the loop.

Location: Cranberry Lake and Wanakena.

The relatively new Cranberry Lake 50 (CL 50) has quickly established itself as one of New York's premier backpacking destinations. The trail is unique for the state, offering a long loop along a
single trail system. Most backpacking trails in the state are linear, or
part of a larger web. The CL 50 also offers mild terrain, scenic forests,
isolation, streams, and great camping. As an added benefit, it can also
be divided into smaller loops for weekend trips.

Begin the hike at the Burntbridge Pond/Brandy Brook trailhead. The
trail is marked red and doubles as a snowmobile trail. The terrain is
rolling and easy as the trail crosses several small streams in a hardwood forest. The trail is also wide and follows an old forest grade. Pass
a trail to the right that leads to the Cranberry Lake Campground and
Bear Mountain. Continue straight, cross more small streams, and
descend slightly to Brandy Brook. Cross the brook and the first view of
Cranberry Lake peeks through the trees. Reach a trail juncture; the
trail to the left goes to Burntbridge Pond. Continue straight, passing a
side trail to the right that leads to a campsite.

The hike now follows a traditional footpath, leaving the old grade.
The terrain is hilly, and the trail keeps its distance from the lake as it
winds in and out of drainages. Eventually the trail moves closer to the
lake, passing some more campsites and offering nice views of the
beautiful, and seemingly vast, Cranberry Lake. After a short stretch of
shoreline hiking, the trail leaves the lake and begins a gradual, hilly
climb. Pass an intersection with a yellow trail; to the left the yellow
trail goes to Hedgehog Pond. Descend and reach the East Inlet of Cranberry Lake. Here you will find several beautiful campsites and more
nice views of the lake. The trail, now marked blue, gradually climbs
away from the lake along East Creek. Cross the creek over boulders at
the outlet of a spooky swamp. A steady climb begins in earnest as the
trail reaches its highest elevation, passing a series of large boulders.
The trail reaches a side trail to the right that goes down to the lake.
The terrain then levels off and reaches beautiful Curtis Pond; there is a
campsite near its outlet. Hilly terrain follows as the trail crosses the
outlets of two more ponds with beaver dams. The CL 50 bears right at
the next trail intersection and passes Dog Pond, which also has a
campsite. The pond is largely out of view, and the trail negotiates
beaver flooding on the pond's inlet stream.

Begin a gradual descent and negotiate more beaver dams. Reach a
register and an intersection with a horse trail. Turn right onto the
grade as it climbs, and then levels off. Descend and cross two streams

before a steeper climb. The trail levels off along rolling terrain on the side of a mountain. Pass through what appear to be the remnants of a hunting camp, complete with rusting appliances. Descend to Chair Rock Flow and cross small streams. Chair Rock Creek has a campsite and is a beautiful stream with large boulders. Enjoy views of the lake through the trees. Climb along a small stream, and then descend to South Flow as the trail switchbacks along ledges. Cross Six Mile Creek, with its waterslides and pools. A quick climb and descent bring you to a well-established trail that goes right to West Flow on Cranberry Lake. (I believe the trail to the left might lead to Sliding Rock Falls.) The CL 50 turns right onto the well-established trail before turning left at a register. The trail is now blazed yellow.

The trail to Olmstead Pond is hilly and negotiates a few beaver dams. The trail passes Spectacle Pond, but is high above it. Olmstead

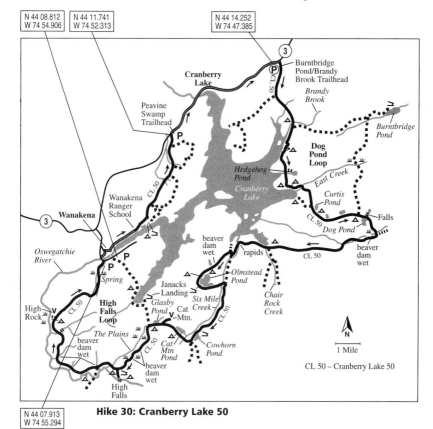

Hike 30: Cranberry Lake 50

Pond is beautiful and well worth the hike. The trail meanders close to the shore, offering great views, and passes a few small campsites. It will take a little time to hike around the pond. There is one lean-to, but not a lot of space to camp near it. Descend along the outlet stream and cross Six Mile Creek on a log. Climb up a short ridge and turn right to Cowhorn Pond. The trail is now marked blue.

The hike to Cowhorn Pond follows a dry, wooded ridge line with rolling terrain. The ridge is fairly narrow and you can see both sides fall away into the lowlands. This section is a nice respite from the beaver dams and wet conditions. Cowhorn Pond is another beautiful spot, and a side trail to the left leads to the lean-to. The trail stays above the pond, continuing along the ridge. Reach a trail intersection and turn right onto a yellow trail as it descends off the ridge. Enter a valley, cross a stream, and pass another campsite. The trail is easy to Cat Mountain Pond, where there is a brief view of the water, but it begins to climb and becomes rockier as it enters a pass between the mountains. Descend slightly and reach the .7-mile side trail to the top of Cat Mountain. The hike to the top is well worth the effort, although the trail does get steep near the summit. The views are outstanding and overlook a vast wilderness that appears untouched. Rolling mountains are separated by ponds and wetlands. To the east, Blue Mountain looms on the horizon. There is also a dry campsite at the top of Cat Mountain. The mountain is a popular destination for dayhikers.

Back on the CL 50, begin another descent, passing a small clearwater spring. Reach Glasby Pond, with a campsite near the outlet. The pond offers a view of Cat Mountain, which looks more like a hill. The trail follows a stream with some cascades. Reach a juncture with a trail that goes to Janacks Landing and Wanakena. However, turn left onto the red trail to High Falls. Hike along a meadow with some wet areas and forests of spruce. The trail is level and rolling. As you continue, conditions become wetter as the trail is increasingly impacted by beaver dams. At one point, the trail crosses the top of a dam, and then crosses a long, narrow log over a putrid swamp created by a beaver dam. Climb up a hill and descend to a .4-mile side trail to High Falls. On the side trail is an interesting piece of logging machinery, now abandoned and rusting in the woods. The falls are worth the visit, but are not very high. The river spills over a large ledge and slides into a pool below. A maze of trails leads to campsites and a lean-to, and another lean-to is across the river. High Falls is a popular place to camp for both hikers and paddlers.

Back on the CL 50 loop, the trail follows an old railroad grade almost all the way to Wanakena. There are some things to keep in mind. First, the trail is often brushy and overgrown, although a treadway is present. Second, expect a lot of sun exposure. Third, the trail crosses three beaver dams, one of which had been a wet crossing.

The red trail follows an obvious and level grade and enters a vast meadow through which Glasby Creek flows. Reenter the woods, where there will be some views of the Oswegatchie River. Cross the first beaver dam and reach the blue Five Ponds Trail to the left; continue straight on the grade. A half mile farther the trail returns to the river on a high bank. Here the trail passes a nice campsite on the left—this was the best campsite I saw between High Falls and High Rock. Soon thereafter, cross the second beaver dam. About a mile farther is the third and last beaver dam, and there are nice views of a large wetland. Continue on the grade as it circumvents a swamp; reach another stream, this one with a bridge and a cascading waterslide. The grade makes a slight ascent and reaches a side trail to the left that goes to High Rock, where there are campsites and a privy. The rock ledge offers nice views over the wetlands and meandering Oswegatchie River. It is also a great place to see the sunset or catch a breeze. The CL 50 continues along the grade as it traverses the side of a series of wet meadows. Climb slightly to the top of a ridge and descend along the old grade, crossing small springs, including one that is piped. The grade crosses more meadows along Skate Creek. The level trail soon reaches an inlet or bay of Cranberry Lake, and then ends at a road in Wanakena; a town park and a parking area are to your right.

The CL 50 follows roads and streets through Wanakena for the next 2 miles. Wanakena is a beautiful little town and the people are friendly. Turn left on the street and cross the Oswegatchie River. Turn right and enter the "downtown" where there is a general store and post office. The CL 50 turns left and then right on the road to the Ranger School. Pass a bar and restaurant with views of the lake. Follow the road as it climbs and reach the Wanakena Ranger School. The CL 50 turns right onto a yellow cross-country ski trail system. The trails are fairly wide and hilly as they explore a scenic forest with some large hemlocks. A total of three cross-country ski trail loops intersect the CL 50. Camping is basically limited to a lean-to a half mile off the trail at the first loop intersection. It is a nice lean-to and a great place to see the sunrise. There are places to camp around the lean-to.

The CL 50 becomes wet and muddy as you proceed north; it also crosses some small streams. The forest is mostly hardwoods, with some large hemlocks. The trail ends at the Peavine Swamp trailhead at Route 3.

To complete the loop, a 5.7-mile road walk is required along Route 3 back to the Burntbridge Pond/Brandy Brook trailhead. As far as road walks go, it isn't too bad, and the route goes right through the town of Cranberry Lake where there are a few restaurants and stores. Route 3 provides some nice views of the lake and even passes a small beach. Once through Cranberry Lake, Route 3 makes a long and gradual climb before leveling off and arriving at the Burntbridge Pond/Brandy Brook trailhead.

• • •

After enduring hikes with heat, black flies, thunderstorms, mosquitoes, sleet, rain, cold, and leeches, I finally had a hike with perfect conditions. I drove to the trailhead under deep blue skies and warm sunshine. The fall colors were at their peak, covering the hills and surrounding the lakes with red, orange, and yellow. The colors were so absolute, it almost seemed the forests always looked this way. And the bugs could no longer muster the energy to chase me.

Fallen leaves dotted the forest floor as the rolling trail meandered over hills and across stream valleys. Across the vast Cranberry Lake, the sunshine danced across the water and electrified the fall foliage. On the summit of Cat Mountain, bare cliffs and ledges overlooked amazing views to the west as rolling mountains blended with countless ponds and swamps. The rich tapestry of the flaming foliage spread across the entire landscape, uninterrupted.

After surviving the gauntlet of beaver dams and bogs, I reached the side trail to High Falls. I passed a massive piece of corroded logging machinery. After so many years abandoned and entrenched in the woods, the machinery still looked solid and formidable, waiting to be put back into service. What is now a vast wilderness was once logged and mined. The mark of industry cannot be completely erased, even by wilderness. The grades, logging roads, and bridge abutments remain; they once carried the rumble and smoke of trains, now they are home to a footpath. These remnants will be slowly eroded and erased, as the mountains will.

I hiked into Wanakena as the sun began to set. After a long day on the trail, I was looking forward to getting something to eat. I reached the bridge over the river and saw a lone, thin woman looking intently into the water, her stringy blonde hair hiding her face. People passed her by with their bicycles and golf carts. I said hello, and she revealed her mottled face, aged and worn from too many tough years lived. She responded with a surprisingly strong and appreciative, "Howya doin'?" and promptly returned to staring at the water, looking for something in the reflection below.

I walked through town. The general store was closed and the other restaurant was busy, packed with locals enjoying the fall foliage across the water. I didn't feel like going in with my backpack and dirty, sweat-streaked skin. I kept walking along the road until it ended, and then disappeared into a twilight forest.

31. Dog Pond Loop

Length: 19-mile loop.

Direction of description: Counterclockwise.

Duration: 1¹/₂ to 2 days.

Difficulty: Easy to moderate.

Trail conditions: The western and southern part of the loop follows the Cranberry Lake 50. The northern and eastern sections of the loop are less hiked, have more brush, and may be less established. Blowdowns may be an issue. There are wet sections of the trails. Trails often follow old grades. Most trail junctures have signs.

Blazes: Blue and red.

Water: Generally plentiful.

Vegetation: Northern hardwoods, with some spruce and fir.

Highlights: Cranberry Lake, Dog Pond, Burntbridge Pond, Curtis Pond, scenic streams, isolation, nice campsites.

Issues: The northern and eastern sections of the loop are less hiked and may be less established. Blazes can be infrequent.

Location: Cranberry Lake, New York.

The Dog Pond Loop is an easy and enjoyable weekend backpacking trip. Like so many trails in the Adirondacks, this loop features several beautiful ponds, scenic streams, and isolation. This hike also makes a fine introduction to the Cranberry Lake area and its extensive trail system.

Begin the hike at the Burntbridge Pond/Brandy Brook trailhead. The trail is marked red and doubles as a snowmobile trail. The terrain is rolling and easy as the trail crosses several small streams in a hardwood forest. The trail is wide and follows an old forest grade. Pass a trail to the right that leads to the Cranberry Lake Campground and Bear Mountain. Continue straight, cross more small streams, and descend slightly to Brandy Brook. Cross the brook and see the first view of Cranberry Lake through the trees. Reach a trail juncture; the trail to the left goes to Burntbridge Pond and marks your return route. Continue straight, passing a side trail to the right that leads to a campsite.

The hike now follows a traditional footpath, leaving the old grade. The terrain is hilly, and the trail keeps its distance from the lake as it winds in and out of drainages. Eventually the trail moves closer to the lake, passing some more campsites and offering nice views of immense Cranberry Lake. After a short stretch of shoreline hiking, the trail leaves the lake and begins a gradual, hilly climb. Pass an intersection with a yellow trail; to the left the yellow trail goes to picturesque Hedgehog Pond, where you'll also find a campsite. Descend and reach the East Inlet of Cranberry Lake. Here you will find several beautiful campsites and more nice views of the lake. The trail, now marked blue, gradually climbs away from the lake along East Creek. Cross the creek over boulders at the outlet of a dismal swamp. A steady climb begins in earnest as the trail reaches its highest elevation, passing a series of large boulders. The trail reaches a side trail to the right that goes down to the lake. The terrain then levels off and reaches beautiful Curtis Pond; there is a campsite near its outlet. Hilly terrain follows as the trail crosses the outlets of two more ponds that are home to beaver dams. At the next trail intersection in a meadow, this hike continues to the left on a blue trail. However, if you want to see this loop's namesake, follow the CL 50 to the right and hike to Dog Pond, where you will find a cascading stream and another campsite. The beautiful pond is largely out of view from the trail, which negotiates beaver flooding on the pond's inlet stream. Retrace your steps back to the loop.

Proceed north on the Dog Pond Loop toward Burntbridge Pond. The terrain is rolling until you reach the col between Bear and Dog Pond Mountains, where there is a longer, gradual climb. The trail then makes a longer, gradual descent to East Creek. Cross the creek near some bogs and wetlands. Hike across rolling terrain, crossing some small streams along

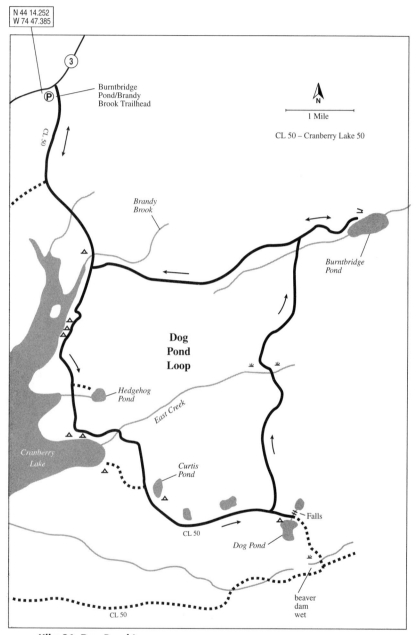

Hike 31: Dog Pond Loop

the way. Descend slightly to another stream and cross it. A short climb brings you to the side trail to Burntbridge Pond, to the right. The side trail is less than a mile and descends to scenic, isolated, albeit marshy, Burntbridge Pond, where there is a nice, lonely lean-to on the northwest shore.

Back on the loop, follow the trail back to Brandy Brook Flow at Cranberry Lake along an old grade. The trail is level with a slight incline before descending and crossing some streams. Reach Cranberry Lake and complete the loop. Turn right and retrace your steps back to the trailhead.

•   •   •

My legs grew too accustomed to the easy, rolling terrain along wide, forgiving trails. The path left the lake and tightened as it threaded its way between the trees. And soon it climbed. The hill was by no means significant, but my legs expressed their displeasure after being spoiled for so many miles.

The forest was divided by color. The higher canopy was painted with red, orange, and yellow. The colors were at peak. The leaves beneath were still green, biding their time until the canopy was stripped bare. The sun was lower in the sky, a retreating journey across the changing seasons. The sunlight glowed through a kaleidoscope forest.

We mark and measure time, organizing it carefully on our calendars. How can we wonder where it all goes when we plan it so meticulously? The trees and leaves know no time; the forest is oblivious to it. Everything grows and lives while it can, adapting to the endless cycles of seasons.

Massive rocks along the trail captured my attention. They were out of place in the rolling, gentle forest, blatant trespassers in a world of trees. Topped with crowns of ferns and garments of moss and lichens, they leaned against each other as if sharing a secret. They were rounded and had been deposited randomly across the landscape.

Thousands of years ago, glaciers covered the land. They grew and shrank, acquiring rocks along the way that were crushed and worn by the relentless ice. The rocks moved with the ice, changing as their edges were ground along the surface. Despite their capture, the boulders had a secret—they would outlive the ice. After a timeless journey, measured in years rather than miles, the ice began to melt. The rocks were left wherever they were, to inhabit random forests.

And there the boulders will remain, long after the final generations of hikers pass and the trail fades back into the forest.

🥾 32. High Falls Loop

Length: 16-mile loop.

Direction of description: Clockwise.

Duration: 1¹/₂ to 2 days.

Difficulty: Easy to moderate.

Trail conditions: Trails are generally well established and most junctures have signs. Blazes can be infrequent. Trail is overgrown and brushy in sections from High Falls to High Rock, although the treadway is established. The trail also crosses and circumvents several beaver dams. There are wet areas.

Blazes: Red and blue.

Water: Generally plentiful.

Vegetation: Northern hardwoods, with areas of spruce and fir.

Highlights: Cat Mountain, Oswegatchie River, High Falls, High Rock, Cranberry Lake, Glasby Pond.

Issues: Overgrown conditions between High Falls and High Rock with sun exposure. Wet areas and impacts from beaver dams.

Location: Wanakena, New York.

The High Falls Loop is a popular and scenic weekend backpacking loop. It is an excellent introduction to the Cranberry Lake trails and includes some of the finest natural features in the region. The trails are easy, although sometimes wet, and are good for beginners. The trickiest part of this hike may be traversing the large assortment of beaver dams. Much of this loop also follows the Cranberry Lake 50 (CL 50).

From the parking area on South Shore Road follow the red trail across level terrain. Hike across several meadows and along beaver ponds and marshes. Reach Dead Creek Flow of Cranberry Lake. Enjoy views of the lake and pass a nice campsite. Cross Dead Creek and follow the trail as it moves away from the lake. Reach a yellow side trail to the left that leads to the lean-to at Janacks Landing, a popular spot for paddlers, anglers, and hikers.

Return to the red trail and continue toward Cat Mountain along a gradual ascent. Reach a juncture with the CL 50. While the High Falls Loop continues to the right, on to its namesake, you should go left to hike to Glasby Pond and Cat Mountain. The pond is a typical, scenic

Adirondacks pond with a campsite at its outlet. The trail climbs away from the pond and reaches the .7-mile side trail to Cat Mountain. The hike to the top is well worth the effort, although the trail does get steep near the summit. The views are outstanding and overlook a vast wilderness that appears untouched from this height. Rolling mountains are separated by ponds and wetlands. To the east, Blue Mountain looms on the horizon. There is also a dry campsite at the top of Cat Mountain. The mountain is a popular destination for dayhikers. Retrace your steps back to the loop.

Continue on the red trail to High Falls. Hike along a meadow with some wet areas and forests of spruce. The trail is level and rolling. As you continue, the trail becomes soggy as it is increasingly impacted by beaver dams. At one point, the trail crosses the top of a dam, and then crosses a long, narrow log over a decaying swamp. The trail meanders around the ponds created by these dams. Climb up a hill and descend to a .4-mile side trail to High Falls. On the side trail is an interesting piece of logging machinery, now abandoned and rusting in the woods. The falls are worth the visit, but are not very high. The river spills over a large ledge and slides into a pool below. A maze of trails leads to campsites and a lean-to; another lean-to is across the river. High Falls is a popular place to camp for both hikers and paddlers.

Back on the loop, the trail follows an old railroad grade almost all the way to Wanakena. There are some things to keep in mind. First, the trail is often brushy and overgrown, although a treadway is present. Second, you can expect a lot of sun exposure. Third, the trail crosses three beaver dams, one of which is a wet crossing.

The red trail follows an obvious and level grade and enters a vast meadow through which Glasby Creek flows. As you head back into the woods, there will be some nice views of the meandering Oswegatchie River. Cross the first beaver dam and reach the blue Five Ponds Trail to the left; continue straight on the grade. A half mile farther the trail returns to the river on a high bank. On the left the trail passes the best campsite between High Falls and High Rock. Soon thereafter, cross the second beaver dam, and about a mile farther, the third and last dam, with nice views of a large wetland. Continue on the grade as it circumvents a swamp, and you'll reach another stream, but this one has a bridge and a cascading waterslide. The grade makes a slight ascent and reaches a side trail to the left that goes to High Rock, where there are campsites and a privy. The rock is a cliff or ledge that offers nice views over the wetlands and the winding river. It

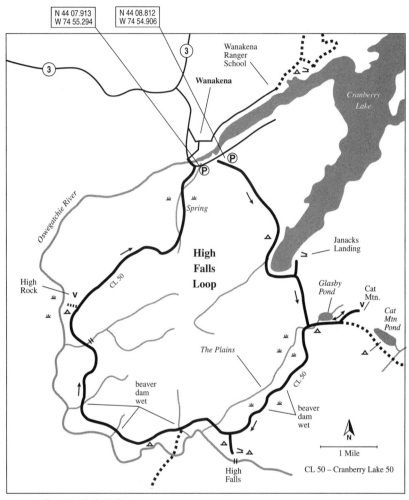

N 44 07.913
W 74 55.294

N 44 08.812
W 74 54.906

3

3

Wanakena
Ranger
School

Wanakena

*Cranberry
Lake*

P

P

Spring

Janacks
Landing

**High
Falls
Loop**

High
Rock

CL 50

Oswegatchie River

V

*Glasby
Pond*

Cat
Mtn.

V

*Cat
Mtn
Pond*

The Plains

beaver
dam
wet

CL 50

beaver
dam
wet

N

1 Mile

High
Falls

CL 50 – Cranberry Lake 50

Hike 32: High Falls Loop

is a great place to see the sunset or catch a breeze. The trail continues along the grade as it traverses the side of a series of wet meadows. Climb slightly to the top of a ridge and descend along the old grade, crossing small springs, including a small, piped spring. The grade crosses more meadows along Skate Creek. The level trail soon reaches an inlet or bay of Cranberry Lake. The trail ends at South Shore Road in Wanakena; a town park and parking area are to your right. Follow the road to the right a short distance back to your car.

• • •

I walked through the tall grass of a baking savannah. The languid Oswegatchie River, dark with water from countless swamps, bogs, and beaver dams, barely had a current. It meandered crazily across the marshy lowlands. Within just a mile were many loops that nearly turned back on themselves.

Just before the trail returned to the forest, I saw a couple wading through the grass, hiking in my direction. As they approached, I saw that the man and woman, probably in their seventies, were unaffected by the heat or the miles they had walked from Wanakena. They looked refreshed, and their movement was effortless. Being alone in a wilderness caused them no concern. They seemed to have a synergy with each other: being in each other's presence was enough, without the need to talk. I stepped aside to let them pass, and they said a quick, friendly hello without any suspicion or hesitation. They were soon gone, fading away across the savannah.

This couple exhibited a vitality, an energy, in a way that was sublime and understated. It was as if their age made them stronger, more potent. Their age was not a limitation, but a reflection of all that was possible.

The couple still had so many miles to go, and now I realized I did as well. More than I ever imagined.

33. Cold River–Seward Range Loop

Length: 30-mile loop.

Direction of description: Clockwise.

Duration: 1$\frac{1}{2}$ to 2$\frac{1}{2}$ days.

Difficulty: Easy to moderate.

Trail conditions: The trails are well established and signed. Some sections may have infrequent blazes and are brushy. There are wet areas. The trails often follow old forest roads or grades.

Blazes: Red, yellow, and blue.

Water: Generally plentiful.

Vegetation: Northern hardwoods, cedar, spruce, fir, and pine.

Highlights: Cold River, Latham Pond, beautiful campsites, scenic streams, isolation.

Issues: The road to the parking area is gated and closed from December to May. The trail is very isolated.

Location: Coreys, New York.

This loop is a backpacking delight, so I'm surprised it isn't more popular. The terrain is fairly easy, and the route gives access to the beautiful Cold River, one of the most isolated areas in the Adirondacks. The trails also feature diverse forest types, the site of a hermit's camp, and easy access to popular Duck Hole and sublime Latham Pond. This hike's greatest attribute may be its beautiful lean-tos, particularly along the Cold River. If you want an easy weekend backpack to enjoy nature and get away from it all, this is it.

From the parking area, follow the wide trail for about .5 mile to a red hiking trail on the left, and a yellow horse trail on the right. Take the red trail. The terrain is rolling and hilly under a hardwood forest with several large moss-covered boulders crowned with ferns. The trail follows along a private property line with "No Trespassing" signs. Reach a trail juncture next to a road (on private property) to the left. This hike continues straight on the red trail to the Blueberry and Ward Brook lean-tos. The return route is to the right.

The trail continues to follow rolling terrain, crossing several small streams and some wet areas with boardwalks. Reach the Blueberry lean-to to the right; this is a popular place for base campers looking to hike the peaks in the Seward Range. There are tent sites around the lean-to. The trail crosses a stream where a side trail to the right, marked by a cairn, goes up to Seward Mountain, one of the High Peaks. Continue straight on the red trail. Reach a small meadow and turn right; you will soon reach Ward Brook lean-to, another popular place for peak baggers to camp. Cross a small stream where another side trail to the right, marked by a cairn, goes to the summit of Seymour Mountain.

The trail is easy to the Number 4 lean-tos (there are two of them). Although these are intended more for horse riders, hikers often use them. They are in a scenic spot with a small stream flowing behind them. From this point on, you can expect to see few, if any, other hikers. The trail continues to follow an old grade or forest road. Begin a long, gradual climb above a stream. The forest turns to fir and spruce, which nearly crowds the trail in places, creating a mysterious feel. Rolling terrain follows until the trail descends and crosses a wet meadow. After another short climb, you'll descend to the blue Northville–Placid Trail (NPT). This route follows the NPT to the right; however, the two Cold River and Duck Hole lean-tos are 1 to 2 miles to the left. Duck Hole is a popular destination, although the dam that formed its beautiful pond is now breached.

The blue NPT is the longest single trail in the Adirondacks, stretching for over 130 miles from Northville to near Lake Placid. The trail stays well above Mountain Pond and traverses hilly terrain as it climbs in and out of small valleys and streams; there are several more streams than shown on most maps. Reach the Rondeau hermitage,

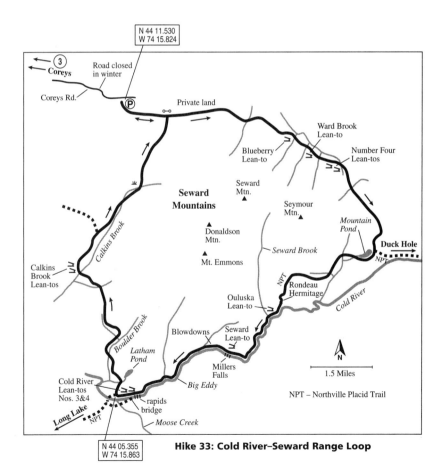

Hike 33: Cold River–Seward Range Loop

home to a well-known hermit who lived here from the 1920s into the 1950s. Now the camp is marked by a sign and some rusted utensils and kitchen items.

The trail now stays in close proximity to its scenic highlight, the Cold River. This gorgeous, pristine river features waterslides, boulders, rapids, and huge pools. The first lean-to, Ouluska, is also the least popular. While in a scenic spot next to the river, it simply does not compare to the stunning scenery of the remaining three lean-tos along the river. Ouluska lean-to is also somewhat run-down, but still usable. (Its best feature may be its journals, covering several decades and transcribed into type. What an impressive labor of love to preserve this history of trail culture.) Cross Seward Brook, where the bridge has been washed to the side and you may find a wet crossing in high water.

The sublime scenery along the river continues, although the trail can be brushy. The forest is quite diverse, with pine, spruce, fir, and cedar. Reach beautiful Seward lean-to near Millers Falls, a huge ledge rapid and slide that tumbles into a deep pool. Several tent sites are near the lean-to. The setting is simply gorgeous. After Seward lean-to the trail becomes tighter as it weaves up and down across the terrain. Reach an old grade and hike around several large blowdowns. The trail becomes easy once again as it follows the grade and passes huge Big Eddy, a pool the size of a pond. Over a mile later, the trail reaches Cold River No. 4 lean-to and the impressive suspension bridge over a series of rapids and pools. Leave the blue NPT, which crosses the bridge. Follow the trail to Cold River No. 3 lean-to, located in another stunning spot, perched on a ledge looking up the river. These lean-tos are some of the finest in the High Peaks.

Follow an unblazed trail from the No. 3 lean-to, heading southwest along the river. The trail is level, established, but brushy in places. Enter a large white pine forest and reach the yellow Calkins Brook Trail, a horse trail. Turn right onto the yellow trail as it goes through the beautiful pine forest. Hike across a cleared, windblown area and begin to hike up some hills. When you reach a short side trail to Latham Pond, take it. The pond, a serene and enchanting place, offers views of the Seward Range. This hike is unique in that it has few ponds or lakes compared to other Adirondack hikes.

The hilly terrain continues and the trail crosses a bridge over Boulder Brook. The forest changes to hardwoods. Cross another stream, and then a long, gradual ascent follows. Descend to Calkins Brook and its two lean-tos, a nice place to camp but intended for horse riders.

The trail makes a short, steeper climb and then traverses the side of the ridge with rolling terrain. Reach a trail to the left that goes to the Raquette River and Stony Creek trailhead, but continue straight. The trail slowly brings you back to Calkins Brook with its boulders, pools, and small rapids. Cross the brook twice before reaching a side trail to the right that goes up to Donaldson Mountain; it is marked by a cairn.

The yellow trail turns left and makes another long, gradual climb before an equally gradual descent. Continue straight at a juncture with a yellow horse trail to the left. A short distance farther is where you began the loop. Turn left and retrace your steps back to the car.

• • •

We didn't get on the trail until 3:30 P.M., the latest I've ever started a backpacking trip. The air was chilled and moist. Autumn was quickly fading into winter, and the trees were stripped bare, with their crooked, naked branches clawing the milky sky. The understory still had drops of yellow and orange.

Darkness moved in quickly, spreading from the shadows in the forest, across the trail, and up into the sky. A rain shower accompanied the dusk and my headlamp reflected off the droplets.

We soon reached the Northville–Placid Trail (NPT) and I took a moment to reflect. I had thru-hiked that trail a month or so prior and it was odd to be on it again. On that trip, by the time I had reached this point of my journey on the NPT, I was eager to be done. I felt differently this time: determined, resolute, and tougher than before. I was back in the place where I tested my limits and fears and became an ever so slightly different person in the process. This place was the same, but I felt new.

We reached the Ouluska lean-to and stopped for the night as the invisible Cold River called through the trees. I read through three volumes of the trail journals kept at the lean-to. It was fascinating and inspiring to read of the thousands of people who had passed through, their experiences so different and yet so similar to my own. I read the entries after the 9/11 attacks and recalled my own thoughts as I sat at a view on the Standing Stone Trail that same day, hundreds of miles away. I was alone, looking over a vast panorama. I remember seeing the sun set, without a single plane in the sky. The silence was haunting. My mind felt empty and drained after such a tragic day; my heart didn't know where to go. So I just sat there as the sun was absorbed by the horizon, offering the hope of a new day.

34. Algonquin Peak–Indian Pass Loop

Length: 22-mile loop.

Direction of description: Counterclockwise.

Duration: 1^1/$_2$ to 3 days.

Difficulty: Moderate to very difficult.

Trail conditions: Trails are generally well blazed and established, with signs at most junctures. North of Indian Pass, the trail is on the edge of the creek and in the water if the creek is high. Indian Pass is very rugged, and some scrambling is required.

Blazes: Red, blue, or yellow.

Water: Generally plentiful.

Vegetation: Northern hardwoods and pine at lower elevations, fir and spruce at higher elevations. Algonquin Peak is above tree line and has alpine vegetation.

Highlights: Beautiful streams, Flowed Lands, Lake Colden, waterfalls, Algonquin Peak, Heart Lake, Rocky Falls, Indian Pass Brook, Indian Pass.

Issues: The climb up Algonquin Peak is very steep, often in the creek, and rugged. Indian Pass is also very rugged, and the trail to the pass is in the creek.

Location: This hike begins and ends at the Upper Works trailhead. You can also begin and end at Adirondack Loj.

This challenging loop gives backpackers a taste of the scenic features that make the High Peaks famous. Here, you will find lakes, waterfalls, alpine summits, beautiful streams, great camping, one of the tallest cliffs in the east, and an incredibly rugged pass with jumbled, house-size boulders. If you want to avoid the taxing climb up and over Algonquin Peak, you can opt to complete the loop via Avalanche Pass and Marcy Dam instead. This route is easier, but still challenging.

From the parking area, sign the register and follow the trail along an old forest road. The Hudson River is to the right and is the size of a large stream; it has many rapids. Cross a bridge and pass a side trail to the left that goes to Henderson Lake. Soon reach a second trail juncture, which is the beginning of the loop. Turn right onto the red

Calamity Brook trail to Flowed Land. You will return via the yellow trail to your left. The red trail begins a rolling climb, with several wet and muddy spots. Hike along some meadows with nice views of the mountains; the creek is to your right. Reach a blue trail and bear right (or straight) onto it, crossing a small stream. The steady climb steepens along an old forest grade. The trail crosses Calamity Brook over rocks, but a bridge crossing is available just upstream. The climb continues and becomes rockier, but it does ease up. The trail levels off and reaches some wet and muddy areas as it goes around a marshy meadow. Pass the Henderson monument to your left. Reach a trail intersection at Flowed Lands, where you will find a register and a lean-to. Enjoy the mountain views from Flowed Lands, particularly the slides on Mount Colden. The loop continues left, but if you have time, consider the 1-mile hike to impressive Hanging Spear Falls, one of the finest in the High Peaks. Keep in mind there is no bridge to cross the outlet of Flowed Lands, and it is usually a wet crossing.

To continue the loop, turn left onto the red trail to Lake Colden. The trail is hilly and meanders, passing lean-tos and campsites, but keeps its distance from the pond in Flowed Lands. Pass a side trail to the left that goes up to Mount Marshall, and soon thereafter, a small stream. The trail levels and reaches beautiful Lake Colden and its low wooden dam. Enjoy more fine views of the mountains and continue straight along the shore as the trail comes close to the water. Pass more lean-tos and campsites. Cross Cold Brook over a bridge and reach the Interior Outpost to your right. The Cold Brook Pass trail is to your left; it can serve as a cross-connector for this loop. Reach the yellow trail to the left that goes to Algonquin Peak. Now your fun begins.

This is about a 2,000-foot vertical climb to the col between Algonquin and Boundary Peaks. The climb is never really technical, but it is steep and follows an eroded, rocky, and rooted trail. The trail crosses a small stream several times, without bridges, and is even in the streambed at times. As a result, this is a trail you must avoid in high water. The stream is beautiful, with many waterfalls and cascades. The trail at one point even ascends the bedrock slabs right next to a long series of slides and falls where you can enjoy views of Mt. Colden. As you ascend, the trail steepens and the creek diminishes in size. Scramble up some bedrock slabs as the forests turn to fir and spruce, and then climb to the col, which is surrounded by stunted trees. A side trail to the left goes to Boundary and Iroquois Peaks. The yellow trail turns right to ascend Algonquin. The climb isn't very steep here as the trail leaves the trees and enters an alpine environment of grasses, lichens, and exposed rock ledges. Follow the cairns and stay on the ledges. Reach the exposed summit, where you will find spectacular views in all directions, including Mt. Colden, Lake Placid, Mt. Marcy, and the Great Range. Down in the valley to the west is Wallface Cliff and the steep notch of Indian Pass, where you will be tomorrow. Algonquin is popular with dayhikers, so expect company.

The descent is not as steep as the climb, although you will have to go down some steep slabs. Reenter the forest and pass a side trail to Wright Peak. The descent eases up and crosses a small stream with a

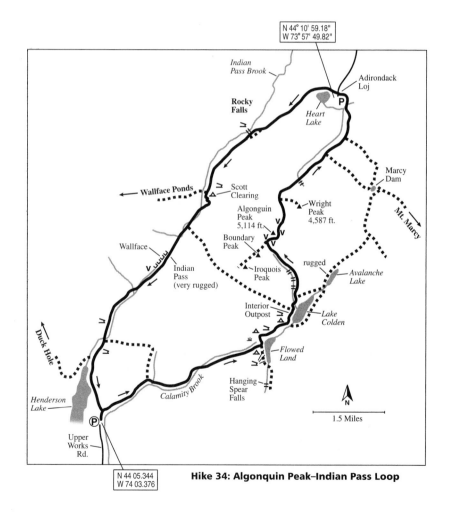

Hike 34: Algonquin Peak–Indian Pass Loop

falls. The hike down feels endless, dropping 3,000 feet over 3 miles, and is rocky and wet in places. The farther down you go, the more the terrain eases. Pass a side trail to Whales Tail Mountain, and a little farther, the popular blue trail right to Marcy Dam. Continue straight for a mile to Adirondack Loj. Cross a marshy stream on a boardwalk, traverse hilly terrain, cross another small stream, and climb gradually to the Adirondack Loj parking lot, where there is a register. The Loj is a good place to take a break and check the weather.

Walk to the exit of the parking area and follow the trail across the road to your right to Mt. Jo and Indian Pass. The trail is level and stays above the shore of scenic Heart Lake. Trails leave to the right to climb Mt. Jo; continue straight to Indian Pass. Reach a four-way trail intersection and continue straight on the red trail to Indian Pass. Begin a mild ascent along an old forest grade under a hardwood forest. The trail levels and reaches a side trail to the right that descends to Rocky Falls and a shelter and camping site across Indian Pass Brook. The falls are beautiful and feature a deep pool. There is no bridge to the shelter and campsite, so be very careful crossing this sizeable stream. Indian Pass Brook is very scenic, with rapids, pools, and rocks. The side trail is a half-loop that ascends and rejoins the red trail.

The trail stays away from the brook and is easy, although it crosses some small streams and is muddy in sections. Reach Scott Clearing lean-to next to a small stream. Continue .3 mile to a trail juncture; the blue trail to the right goes to Wallface Pond. Just ahead is a nice camping area with three or four tent sites. Here there is an old stone dam that is breached, leaving a high grass meadow with some views of the mountains. It is a nice place to camp. The red trail climbs away from the brook along a side stream with several falls and some pools. Turn right along sidehill and climb in and out of the drainages of small seasonal streams; the terrain is a little difficult. Return to Indian Brook for some beautiful views of the water. Crossing Cold Brook can be challenging, but then you'll reach the Cold Brook Pass trail to the left that goes to Lake Colden. This is a cross-connector for this loop.

The red trail continues up Indian Pass Brook and becomes challenging, particularly in high water. The trail follows the stream closely, and then goes up the streambed itself. If the stream is high, you will have to walk in the water. Hike on land for only short distances before returning to the streambed. The trail crosses the creek at a spot that is easy to miss. Hike on land for a short distance and cross the creek again over boulders. Indian Pass Brook is beautiful, with rapids and cascades over boulders. Leave the brook and follow a side stream into a hidden glen that will surely test you.

The trail enters this mystical, moss-carpeted glen, full of jumbled boulders and oozing water. It is picturesque, but also very difficult. You will have to scramble over rocks, moss, roots, and water, and the trail itself is often wet. Cascading rivulets and springs adorn this gorgeous, forbidding place. As you reach the height of the pass, the Wallface Cliffs come into view, but your scrambling is not done. Look for alternative routes; there may be one. Traverse the side of the pass along ledges, as the bottom of the pass is filled with boulders and moss. Begin a descent and enter a realm with jumbled, towering house-size boulders as the Wallface Cliff looms overhead. There is no other place in the Adirondacks like this. Reach a short side trail to the right that goes to Summit Rock and its nice views of the pass and cliffs.

The terrain steepens below Summit Rock; however, instead of boulders, you must descend over ledges. There are ladders in several places. Large boulders continue to be part of the landscape. Drop steeply to Indian Pass Brook, which marks the end of this gauntlet. For backpackers, it can take $1^1/2$ to 2 hours to traverse Indian Pass. The trail from here on out is much easier as it follows scenic Indian Pass Brook along an old forest grade. Cross Pass Brook without a bridge; you will also cross several smaller streams without bridges. As you descend, the valley opens up and hardwoods return. The trail is often muddy. Pass Wallface lean-to and a campsite, and then cross a new, high footbridge over the rapids of Indian Pass Brook.

Reach a trail juncture with a blue trail to the left that goes to Calamity Brook. Turn right and pass Henderson lean-to. Reach a red trail to the right that goes to Duck Hole, but continue straight on the yellow trail along an old forest road. The trail ascends gradually and goes up sidehill to avoid muddy sections. Enjoy views of Henderson Lake through the trees. Hike through some small meadows and reach the end of the loop. Turn right to return to your car at Upper Works.

• • •

It was a cool, moist morning as a layer of clouds stretched across the sky, levitating above even the highest peaks. Despite the mid-August date, autumn was in the air. The maples were already dotting the mountainsides with crimson. I began at the isolated Upper Works trailhead. This was my first backpacking trip in the High Peaks, and I felt like a stranger. Everyone else looked like they knew exactly where they were and where they were going. They had a goal, a purpose, and I felt like I wasn't even sure what I was getting myself into. I had a route in mind, but I didn't know if it was feasible. I couldn't afford to underestimate the trail, but I wouldn't know until I hiked it. I carried my backpack, while others zipped by with their daypacks, out to bag a peak.

As I made my way up along Calamity Brook, I heard a man huffing behind me, walking with powerful steps. I turned around and saw that it was a white-haired fellow, maybe in his late sixties. He had a determined look in his eye, with a gleam of joy. I said hello, and he announced that he was going to climb Mount Marshall today, his forty-sixth and final peak. Climbing all forty-six of the Adirondack peaks above 4,000 feet in elevation is a popular goal for many. Even though I had no idea who this man was, and would never see him again, it suddenly felt like this occasion was historic, if not a little ironic. This was my first backpacking trip in the High Peaks, and this was his final peak. I congratulated him and he was off, up the trail toward his prize.

What comes after the goal? Mount Marshall gave that man a vitality and a purpose many half his age do not have. Once accomplished, what comes next? Maybe, in the end, the forty-sixth peak isn't really the goal. Maybe the objective is to live our lives by allowing new experiences to challenge our fears and bend our routines. For some, this means climbing the forty-sixth peak. For others, it is stepping into the woods for the first time.

I camped at Scott Clearing next to an old, breached logging dam made up of round boulders stacked incongruously on top of each other, somehow holding in place. I went to sleep as rain dripped through the trees and tapped my tent.

The next morning I awoke early and hiked up to Indian Pass. The creek was high and had long ago washed away the trail. The creek was the trail. I splashed through the cold water, preferring it to the mud and dirt. I clawed my way up moss-covered boulders and spring-slicked ledges. I wrapped my body along some of the ledges and inched my way up. Knotted, ancient roots provided the only assistance.

I followed a narrow ledge through the pass as mist rifled across Wallface Cliff. Moisture dripped from the cliff, each drop landing with an echo. The trail finally began to descend, and numerous streams seemed to flow from everywhere. This place had as much water as rock. Massive, house-sized boulders were jumbled and stacked, clothed with moss, ferns, lichens, and trees. Each was a world unto itself. I reached a series of ladders, and my knees shook on the slick wood as I descended. Indian Pass requires a price, and I was paying it.

I finally reached the bottom and crossed a stream. Light returned to the woods. The trail was inviting. I knew where I was and where I needed to go. I belonged. In the shadow of Mount Marshall, one man's journey was coming to an end, and mine was beginning.

35. Mt. Marcy–Avalanche Pass Loop

Length: 21-mile loop.

Direction of description: Counterclockwise.

Duration: 1¹/₂ to 2 days.

Difficulty: Moderate to difficult.

Trail conditions: Trails are well established, fairly well blazed, and most trail junctures have signs.

Blazes: Blue, yellow, and red.

Water: Generally plentiful.

Vegetation: Northern hardwoods at lower elevations, fir and spruce forests at higher elevations. Alpine vegetation at the summits.

Highlights: Avalanche Lake and Lake Colden, Opalescent River, Mt. Skylight and Mt. Marcy, Indian Falls.

Issues: Some spots of the trail are wet. Trails often crowded on weekends and there can be competition for lean-tos and campsites. The terrain is very challenging along Avalanche Lake.

Location: This hike begins and ends at the Adirondack Loj parking area.

This is a classic route in the High Peaks, and an ideal introduction for backpackers to this remarkable place. This route has challenging sections, but is moderate in difficulty, by Adirondack High Peak standards. I feel it is easier than the Algonquin Peak–Indian Pass Loop. This hike has it all—easy access, lakes, waterfalls, alpine peaks, and spectacular views.

This description follows the loop counterclockwise. You will want to determine your route depending on the weather on the peaks. Keep in mind the western side of this loop has far more camping options than the eastern side. If you hike the loop clockwise, there are no camping opportunities between Phelps and Feldspar Brooks.

From the Adirondack Loj parking area, sign the register and follow the trail through a spruce forest toward Mt. Marcy. Several of Heart Lake's cross-country ski trails intersect. Descend and cross McIntyre Brook over a bridge and boardwalk. The trail begins a hilly gradual ascent to a Y intersection. Turn left on the blue trail to Marcy Dam. The trail remains hilly, but easy, as it crosses several small streams and uses an extensive network of boardwalks in wet areas. The climb steepens over some steps. Reach Marcy Dam, a popular place to camp. Several campsites and lean-tos surround the former pond. The log dam is scheduled to be removed as it was damaged by a flood. The pond is gone; it is now a mud flat and will eventually become a meadow. The open area is a good place to see the surrounding peaks.

Reach another Y intersection, and here the loop begins. Turn right onto the yellow trail to Avalanche Lake and Lake Colden. The trail makes a gradual incline along Marcy Brook with its pools and rapids. Pass more lean-tos and tent sites. At the next Y intersection, continue to follow the yellow trail to the right and cross Marcy Brook. Pass another lean-to and tent site. The climb steepens over rocks and roots, but it is not that difficult. Sections of the trail are eroded, and it becomes steeper as you near the pass. Enter the pass and descend as cliffs tower along the trail. Sections of this trail are often wet and there are several boardwalks. Hike along the base of Mt. Colden, including the bottom of a landslide where there is now a twisted mess of white birch trees. The landslide exposed a scar of bedrock. The wet conditions continue as the trail descends to the north end of Avalanche Lake.

Surrounded by towering cliffs, this narrow lake is impressive. It resembles an inland fjord. It is also a fun place to make echoes, and listen to your voice bouncing off the cliffs. The trail traverses the muddy northern end of the lake and follows the western shore. Hiking along Avalanche Lake is one of the most challenging parts of this hike; it is almost a Chutes and Ladders game for adults. The trail weaves over and around large boulders, with the help of many ladders, and some scrambling is required. It will take time to negotiate this section of the trail. In two places, the trail follows a boardwalk bolted into the side of cliffs above the lake. Leave Avalanche Lake and descend to Lake Colden where there is a register at a trail intersection. Turn left to hike around Lake Colden's east shore. This trail only has a little scrambling and is much easier than the hike along Avalanche Lake. There

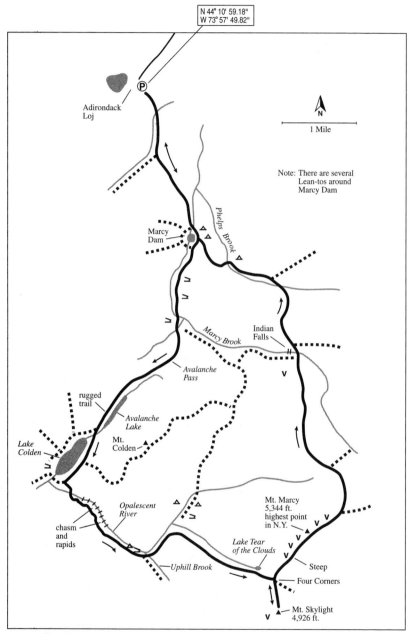

N 44° 10' 59.18"
W 73° 57' 49.82"

Adirondack
Loj

N

1 Mile

Note: There are several
Lean-tos around
Marcy Dam

Marcy
Dam

Phelps Brook

Marcy Brook

Indian
Falls

*Avalanche
Pass*

rugged
trail

*Avalanche
Lake*

Mt.
Colden

*Lake
Colden*

*Opalescent
River*

chasm
and
rapids

Mt. Marcy
5,344 ft.
highest point
in N.Y.

*Lake Tear
of the Clouds*

Uphill Brook

Steep

Four Corners

Mt. Skylight
4,926 ft.

Hike 35: Mt. Marcy–Avalanche Pass Loop

are several fine views of the lake and the MacIntyre Range. Pass a trail that goes up to Mt. Colden. Reach the south end of the lake and turn left onto the red trail.

Hike up the red trail and cross the gorgeous Opalescent River, really only a moderately sized stream, over a bridge. The hike up along the river offers stunning scenery, with rapids, cascades, and pools over white bedrock. The climb is steep in places, but never technical. The trail begins to climb higher above the river. The two soon meet where there are a couple of incredible, narrow chasms into which the river disappears. It is impressive to see how narrow these chasms are as the water plummets into darkness. High water can impact this trail. The trail moves away from the river and the terrain levels off. Reach Uphill lean-to and tent site, a good place to stay the night. The unblazed trail to the right climbs up to Mt. Redfield.

The yellow trail continues its gradual climb over wet areas and boardwalks. Reach a blue trail to the left that goes down to Feldspar lean-to and tent sites. Continue straight on the yellow trail. As you climb, the trail becomes narrower, steeper, and rockier. The forest also changes to fir and spruce. The terrain levels off and the trail soon reaches the well-known Lake Tear of the Clouds, the source of the Hudson River. The tiny lake isn't that impressive—it is mostly an open-water bog or swamp. The imposing summit of Mt. Marcy looms in the distance. Negotiate some muddy spots and reach a four-way trail intersection. The trail that leads straight goes down into Panther Gorge. The yellow trail to the left ascends Mt. Marcy and is the route for this loop. The red trail to the right is a spur trail that climbs to the top of Mt. Skylight. The climb is steady and continuous, but not particularly difficult. Mt. Skylight is worth the side trip, as its broad summit is above the tree line and offers views in all directions. It is considered one of the finest views in the Adirondacks. The mountain is particularly noteworthy for its views to the south, where the distinctive peak of Snowy Mountain rises in the distance, but you can also see the Seward Range, Algonquin Peak, Whiteface, the Great Range, and Panther Gorge. Mt. Marcy dominates the view to the north. If you decide to skip Mt. Skylight, continue on the yellow trail to the summit of Mt. Marcy.

The climb up Mt. Marcy is more challenging than the one up Mt. Skylight. There is some moderate scrambling over sloping bedrock. The trail soon breaks free of the tree line and ascends the exposed southern flank of the mountain where there are some remarkable views. The trail is very exposed, and fairly steep, as it climbs the sloping bedrock. Follow the cairns and yellow blazes. The trail is not near any cliffs or ledges; however, descending this trail in wet or bad weather can be dangerous. Reach the top where there is a plaque and spectacular views, especially over the Great Range, with its jagged ridges and peaks.

The descent from Mt. Marcy is not nearly as steep as the climb. Hike down ledges and bedrock and across several wet areas. Impressive views abound before the trail returns to the woods. Follow the blue trail left at the first intersection and continue a gradual descent. Stay left on the blue trail as it passes a yellow trail to the right. The descent steepens as the trail becomes rocky and eroded. The terrain moderates as the trail crosses some small streams before making a gradual descent to a yellow trail to the left; stay on the blue trail. Reach another stream, but before crossing it, follow the side trail to the left to see Indian Falls. You can only really see the falls from the top; it is a broad sloping ledge that is impressive in high water. The falls provide superb views of Algonquin Peak and the McIntyre Range. Return to the blue trail and cross the stream. A steeper descent soon follows down to Phelps Brook. Cross the brook and hike along this scenic stream with its cascades, pools, and boulders. The trail crosses the brook again, and a footbridge is available further downstream. Follow the trail above an eroded grade as it passes through the woods. The trail soon returns to Marcy Dam and completes the loop. Retrace your steps back to the Adirondack Loj.

•   •   •

This was my second backpack into the High Peaks. I was alone, but felt the excitement of climbing Mt. Marcy. I felt the electricity of the mountains; their presence filled me.

I made my way toward popular Marcy Dam. As I hiked, I passed many others hiking out. I was surprised by the number of children hiking, maybe as young as seven or eight. They were muddy and wet, but they had a look of excitement, joy, energy, and innocence. They seemed to be truly alive. They knew of the world beyond video games, malls, and social media. They had already tasted the peace of nature and they'll be back, decades from now, to fill their cups. The mountains will be in very good hands.

The next morning brought vivid, blue skies. I was anxious to get on the trail. I climbed through a chilled spruce forest as the bright morning light seared my eyes. I needed to get to the top of the mountains.

When I reached the top of Skylight, I had the rounded, alpine peak to myself, with infinite views in all directions. The Great Range cut a jagged spine as Mt. Marcy, with its slopes of bare rock, rose to the north. Whiteface peaked above a ridge in the distance, as Algonquin and the Sewards rose to the west. Lakes and ponds glistened like distant gems. The great, mysterious gulf of Panther Gorge hid in the shade of the morning sun. The Green Mountains were soaked in a morning mist. I couldn't contain my joy, my excitement. The air was so light and crisp, it not only filled my lungs, but my entire body.

Every kid needs to see something like this.

Every kid needs to feel something like this.

36. High Peaks Loop

Length: 32-mile loop.

Direction of description: Counterclockwise.

Duration: $2^1/_2$ to $3^1/_2$ days.

Difficulty: Very difficult.

Trail conditions: Trails are generally well marked and signed. There are many wet areas, and some streams do not have bridges. The profusion of trails around Johns Brook Lodge can be confusing. Scrambling over ledges is required on Upper Wolf Jaw and Armstrong Mountains. The descent from Pyramid Peak into the col with Sawteeth is very steep and demanding. The trail through Elk Pass is very wet and muddy.

Blazes: Blue, red, and yellow.

Water: Generally sufficient, although the mountain ridges and peaks are often dry in summer.

Vegetation: Northern hardwoods, with pine, hemlock, spruce, and fir. Gothics has an alpine environment.

Highlights: Spectacular views, Johns Brook Lodge, Great Range, Gothics, Pyramid Peak, Rainbow Falls, Indian Head, Lower Ausable Lake, Nippletop, and Dial Mountains.

Issues: The terrain is very challenging, particularly for a backpacker. This loop passes through the Adirondack Mountain Reserve where camping and dogs are prohibited. Sections of this trail can be crowded depending on the weather and time of year.

Location: Keene Valley, New York.

This is the most challenging, and arguably the most beautiful, back-pack in this guide. This route explores the rugged heart of the High Peaks, offering a taste of its diverse scenery while including some of its iconic views. This route also has strategically located campsites, the first around Johns Brook Lodge, and the second at Gill Brook or Elk Pass.

This is a very difficult hike and you should be in very good physical condition. It is essential that you pack light and compact.

After including the Algonquin Peak–Indian Pass and Mt. Marcy–Avalanche Pass Loops, I wanted to add a third in the High Peaks. Naturally, the High Peaks has a vast web of trails and countless loops are possible. I considered including the iconic Great Range Traverse, but decided against it. While incredibly beautiful, the traverse is a tough route for backpackers because of the formidable terrain, dry conditions, and limited campsites, which often require backpackers to descend into the valley, only to climb back out again the following day. Backpackers would also face stiff competition for the campsites and lean-tos that do exist, since peak baggers and base campers often reach camp earlier in the day. As a result, the traverse is more commonly dayhiked or hiked from basecamps.

However, I wanted a route that included at least a portion of the Great Range while minimizing technical scrambles and exposure that can place backpackers at risk. After poring over the maps, this is what I came up with. An added bonus is that you can easily shorten this loop, use the northern Great Range Traverse as a cross-connector, or utilize a number of side trails as bailout options if the need arises.

It is best to park at the Rooster Comb trailhead along Route 73 to avoid having to pay at the Garden trailhead. Unless you have access to two cars, you have to walk the road anyway, so you might as well get it out of the way first. Hike up Route 73 to the village of Keene Valley and turn left onto Johns Brook Lane at the sign for the Garden parking area. Hike up the road for over a mile, crossing over Johns Brook with its rapids and boulders. Reach the Garden and sign the register at the end of the parking area. Promptly turn right onto the blue trail to the Brothers (a group of three mountains you hike to reach Big Slide) and Big Slide Mountain. Begin a gradual climb and cross a few small streams. As you ascend, the climb steepens and you soon reach ledges and boulders. Some scrambling is required at the Brothers—an exposed ridgeline with extensive views from ledges and cliffs—although it is not that technical. Enjoy the views of the Great Range and Johns Brook valley.

Continue the steady climb up the ridge as the trail returns to the woods. Descend into a stream valley with wet conditions in a spruce forest. Cross a stream and climb gradually to an intersection with a red trail that descends to Johns Brook. Turn right onto the blue trail as it climbs steeply up ladders over ledges to the summit of Big Slide Mountain. Reach some exposed ledges at the summit, where you will find great views to the south. Descend gradually along a ridgeline through a beautiful spruce and fir forest. Expect mud in the cols. Climb gradually to the forested summit of Yard Mountain. The descent

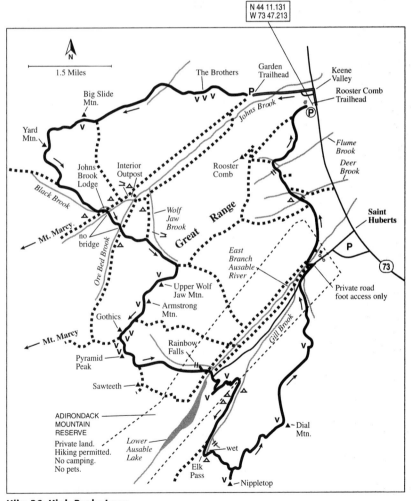

Hike 36: High Peaks Loop

is much steeper and passes ledges and large boulders. The trail also features a seasonal waterfall. The descent eases and you soon reach an intersection with a red trail. Turn left on the red trail and descend to Johns Brook Lodge. It is a steady descent that crosses scenic Black Brook on a bridge not long before you reach the lodge.

Johns Brook Lodge is a center of activity when it is open in season. There are many camping options and lean-tos within a half mile of the lodge, particularly along the yellow trail to the left or right. This route proceeds straight on the blue trail across Johns Brook. This is a wet crossing and should not be attempted in high water. There are footbridges downstream to the left that can be reached via the yellow trail. The blue trail rises over a ridge and descends to Ore Bed Brook, another wet crossing. Reach a trail intersection and proceed straight on the yellow trail. A steeper ascent follows under a hardwood forest into a col, but then the trail levels and offers pleasant hiking. Descend slightly and hike across a massive landslide with tossed and fallen trees, inhabited by a small stream that tumbles over bedrock. It is hard to imagine a stream so small can cause so much destruction. Enjoy the views of Big Slide Mountain. Reach the red trail up to the Wolf Jaws; there is camping and a lean-to to the left. Otherwise, turn right.

The climb is steady, but not very steep. Cross some small side streams and enter a spruce forest. Reach the yellow Great Range Traverse trail in the col between Lower and Upper Wolf Jaw Mountains. Turn right on the yellow trail and begin an ascent, negotiating ledges and some short scrambles. Descend into a col and begin an ascent to Upper Wolf Jaw Mountain with more ledges and scrambles. There are some views on the mountain. Descend gradually into a col and begin the climb up Armstrong Mountain. This ascent has larger ledges and is more technical, so take your time. The top features some nice views to the west from a ledge. Descend into another col where a blue trail joins from the left; this trail is popular with dayhikers climbing Gothics. Continue on the yellow trail across a muddy and wet col. The climb up to Gothics is relatively mild with no significant ledges. Reach the alpine zone and the exposed ridge with expansive views in all directions. Stunted spruce surrounds the summit, and landslide scars mark the surrounding mountains as Saddleback, Basin, and Haystack mountains rise ominously to the south.

Turn left onto the blue trail, passing a spectacular view over Shanty Brook gorge and the surrounding mountains with scars of white bedrock. Pyramid Peak rises like its namesake. The descent is steep over some slabs and ledges. Reach the bottom of the col and begin a more gradual climb up to Pyramid Peak. The ledge at the summit is considered by some to have the finest view in the High Peaks. There is an awesome panorama of the Great Range, the deep valleys and gorges, and the distant lakes to the south. Bedrock exposed by landslides is visible throughout the mountains. It is simply breathtaking.

The blue trail descends from Pyramid, and it is steep and unrelenting. While not technical, there is one slab that will take some negotiation. The trail bends right and the descent moderates to the col with Sawteeth. If you want to summit Sawteeth, stash your pack and hike the half mile to the summit. There are some ledges, but no technical scrambles. The summit has an exposed ledge with a great view to the west. Retrace your steps.

The blue trail descends gradually, with a few steeper slopes. Enter a hardwood forest and cross some side streams with small waterfalls and cascades. To your left, you can see larger waterfalls through the trees on Cascade Brook. Reach an impressive overlook of Rainbow Falls as it plummets into a gorge below; the falls is well over 100 feet high. The trail drops down into the valley, passing under hemlocks. Take the side trail to the left to see Rainbow Falls from the bottom. Enter a beautiful gorge surrounded by towering cliffs, but be careful— the trail gets rocky and slippery. The falls soon come into view, and they are a stunning sight. Retrace your steps. You are now in the Adirondack Mountain Reserve, which is private property. Camping and pets are prohibited. Pass the Scenic Trail to the right and cross the East Branch Ausable River on a long footbridge below the Lower Ausable Lake dam. Turn right and climb on a gravel road, continuing up the road a short distance as it curves uphill. Take the trail to the right to Indian Head, marked by a sign.

Begin a series of switchbacks up the steep slope, hiking along and over ledges. Reach the top and turn right on the side trail to Indian Head (the loop will continue on the blue trail to the left). Indian Head is an iconic view of the Adirondacks as it looks down narrow Lower Ausable Lake, surrounded by cliffs and towering mountains. It almost looks like a fjord. The lake acts like a wind tunnel, so expect strong gales in unsettled weather.

Return to the blue trail and follow it along a bedrock ridge with spruce. Descend, with some steep spots over ledges. A side trail to the left goes to a view to the north. Descend more steeply and enter a hardwood forest. The terrain eases before reaching the red trail at Gill

Brook. Turn right and hike up the red trail. There are three campsites along Gill Brook, a scenic place to camp. The first is to the left, across the brook. The other two are a short distance uphill and are on the right. The red trail makes a gradual climb uphill and enters a spruce forest. Expect several wet areas. Catch a glimpse of Fairy Ladder Falls across the thick, wooded valley. Continue the climb and reach a juncture where the red trail goes to Mt. Colvin; bear left and continue to Elk Pass and Nippletop. The terrain levels in a beautiful forest as the trail meanders between two scenic ponds surrounded by mountains. The trail is very wet and muddy. Negotiate a tricky small stream crossing and pass a campsite to the left.

The climb now begins up to Nippletop; you will climb over 1,000 vertical feet in less than a mile. It is steep and unrelenting, but not technical. There are some small ledges to climb. As you ascend, the trees are smaller and the trail becomes comprised of sloping bedrock. Enjoy views to the west from the trail. Reach the top of the ridge and take the .2-mile side trail to the summit of Nippletop. The trail follows a narrow ridge. Hike over one knob, descend into a col, and climb briefly to the summit where there is a great view to the west; the steep slopes just fall away.

Back on the loop, you will hike on a yellow trail that is an anomaly in the High Peaks—a high elevation trail along a ridge with forgiving terrain. The trail begins a rolling descent with short ascents in a spruce forest. There are a few steep sections; otherwise it is a fairly easy trail. Climb and descend over a knob, and then make a steeper climb of 200 vertical feet up to Dial Mountain where there is a glorious southwestern view from a boulder and ledge. The trail drops more steeply to a col, followed by a brief climb up forested Bear Den Mountain. Descend steeply again into a notch between the mountains, where there is a small stream. Turn left and climb into a forest of saplings, new growth after a forest fire. Enjoy views of the impressive ridge you just descended, as the peak of Nippletop looms in the distance. Continue to climb, with more fine views to the south from exposed ledges. A 1,600-foot vertical descent follows.

The trail is wet as you begin your descent, passing between ledges and down seasonal stream drainages. The trail bears left and follows a pine ridge, where there are some small dry campsites. Reenter the Adirondack Mountain Reserve. The trail continues the long descent over a series of switchbacks. Enter hardwoods as a small cascading stream in a deep glen comes into view from the right. Hike under an impressive hemlock forest with some old-growth trees above the stream. The terrain is steep in places, but not badly eroded; the large hemlocks continue to dominate the forest. Reach the private dirt road for the Ausable Club and follow it to the right. Hike the road for a quarter mile or so until you reach a sign for the East River Trail to the left; follow it. The trail takes you to the East Branch Ausable River. Turn right and cross the footbridge over the scenic river. Turn right onto the yellow trail and continue to follow the river downstream with views of the rapids and mountains. A numbered nature trail joins the same route as large hemlocks tower overhead. Another footbridge comes into view to the right; it spans impressive rapids in a chasm. However, turn left onto the red trail toward Snow Mountain and Rooster Comb.

This is an enjoyable, forgiving trail to hike as it follows a rolling ascent over small streams along an old grade. Large hemlocks and boulders adorn the trail. The trail has some short, steep slopes. Reach a trail juncture where the red trail ascends to the left; proceed right on the blue trail. The trail soon reaches state land and the old grade ends as the trail follows a footpath where more hemlocks and boulders enhance the scenery. Far below is the glen of Deer Brook and its several waterfalls. Cross beautiful Deer Brook. There are cascades here and a larger falls just downstream. A mild ascent follows as the trail crosses a seasonal stream over a bedrock waterslide. Enter a col with Snow Mountain to the right. A yellow trail joins from the right; it descends to Route 73. Continue on the enjoyable blue trail and pass another yellow side trail that goes to the summit of Snow Mountain. The blue trail stays at mid-elevation and crosses another stream, possibly Flume Brook, between a series of cascades. Descend to a small stream and turn right on the red trail down to Keene Valley and the parking area.

The descent is long and gradual, with some steep slopes under a scenic hemlock forest. Cross a small stream near the bottom and bear left as the trail follows the contour of the rolling terrain. Reach the yellow trail (to the left, this trail leads to the Great Range Traverse) and turn right, descending along switchbacks in a pine forest with ledges and boulders. The trail levels and crosses some boardwalks before reaching a pond; continue straight and avoid the boardwalk to the left. Hike along the pond and descend slightly to a series of boardwalks that end at the Rooster Comb parking area.

Your incredible journey through the High Peaks is done. Now, grab a meal and beer at one of Keene Valley's fine restaurants to celebrate.

• • •

Cold, gray clouds concealed the Great Range as my friend Wes and I began this loop with a vigorous climb up to the Brothers. This would be my final hike in the Adirondacks for this book. I couldn't count all the miles I had driven on Interstates 87, 88, and 81 at all hours of the day and night. My journey in this spectacular region was about to come to an end.

The forests were bare, congealed into shades of brown, gray, and purple as their foliage littered the ground. Only some birch trees clung to their bright yellow leaves in the valley below. Mist rose straight up from the valley floor like a geyser of vapor.

As we climbed the ridge, I suddenly heard the smashing of glass. Ice that covered the tops of the spruce trees had begun to melt and had crashed to the ground. Little cubes of ice covered the forest floor, making it appear as if an ice-making machine had run amok through the woods.

We descended from Yard Mountain through thick forests of spruce, passing cascading springs that flowed from every crack and crevice in the rock. The water pooled on the trail or claimed it with a running stream. The Adirondacks are made of water as much as rock.

On the hike up to Gothics, the trail was again littered with fallen ice. Massive slabs of clear ice had formed on the trees and had started to melt. One chunk had hit a man in the head. There are so many ways a tree can kill you.

On the second day, Wes and I reached the summit of Pyramid Peak and took a break. The atmosphere was transforming as sheets of mist swept over the ridge, shot up the face of the mountain, and then twisted into the clouds. The clouds began to lift, revealing an astonishing view of the mountains and their scarred bedrock. Clouds piled on top of each other at the summit of Mt. Marcy. Lakes shimmered to the south. Blue skies made a valiant attempt to drive the clouds away, but the clouds hung on in the valleys and cols. The wind heaved against the massive buttresses of the mountains as it gathered within the vast gulf of the valley below. Everything was in motion. Everything was alive.

Wes noticed a lone peregrine falcon dancing across the wind and through the mist. It was in complete control as it sliced through the air with precision, soaring up with ease and defying gravity's pull. The falcon sailed and surfed along invisible currents, positioning and angling its wings to control its flight. It was one of the most beautiful things I had ever seen.

One of the first photos of the Adirondacks I remember seeing as a kid was the view from Indian Head, looking down Lower Ausable Lake, and I wanted to see it in person. We continued to climb as gray clouds covered the sky. We reached Indian Head, and it was breathtaking. The narrow lake seemed to stretch for the horizon, squeezed by towering mountains and cliffs. The lake acted like a wind tunnel, and the gales blasted us. If only I were a peregrine falcon.

37. Northville–Placid Trail

Length: 133-mile linear trail.

Direction of description: South to north.

Duration: 6 to 14 days.

Difficulty: Moderate.

Trail conditions: The trail is known for its muddy and wet conditions. Most streams have bridges, but some do not. The trail is well established and most trail junctures have signs. There are many boardwalks along the trail.

Blazes: Blue.

Water: Generally plentiful.

Vegetation: Northern hardwoods, with hemlock, pine, and spruce.

Highlights: Numerous lakes and ponds, scenic streams, wetlands, a few cascades, isolation, superb camping and lean-tos, Cold River, Wanika Falls. Loons are often heard on the lakes and ponds. The locals tend to be friendly and many are familiar with the trail.

Issues: Sections of the trail are very isolated. Few resupply options directly along the trail. The trail is often muddy and wet. Some stream crossings do not have bridges, and will be difficult and dangerous in high water. The trail is often wet, or even flooded, due to beaver dams.

Location: The trail is near the following towns: Northville, Piseco, Blue Mountain Lake, Long Lake, and Lake Placid.

The Northville–Placid Trail (NPT) is New York's singular, premier backpacking trail. First established in 1922, it is one of the oldest long-distance hiking trails in the country. It is also New York's longest traditional footpath. The Finger Lakes Trail, North Country Trail, and Long Path are far longer, but require much more road walking. The

NPT is longer than New York's section of the Appalachian Trail. No other backpacking trail in New York is as isolated, or passes as many lakes and ponds. Finishing this trail represents the premier backpacking accomplishment in New York, and it attracts hikers from across the United States and Canada.

While the NPT traverses the heart of the vast Adirondack Park, it is not a mountainous trail. The trail keeps to drainages, valleys, swamps, and lakes. Its highest elevation, between Lake Durant and Long Lake, just barely exceeds 3,000 feet. This spot is also the trail's most significant climb and descent. However, the NPT is not easy. The trail is notoriously hilly, and long stretches of level hiking are the exception, not the norm.

Many people wonder which direction they should hike the trail. Most people thru-hike south to north, and that is the direction I took. By hiking north, the sun is usually at your back. The northern area of the trail has some of the best scenery, and ending at Lake Placid, with its numerous restaurants and hotels, is a fine reward. Hiking south will enable you to cross paths with more hikers. Furthermore, for south-bounders, the Piseco post office is ideal for a resupply package since the trail passes right in front of it.

The NPT is a fine trail that should be on any backpacker's list. It offers a long-distance experience very different from any other trail in New York, or maybe the entire United States. It is a trail where you can challenge yourself, relax at a sublime wilderness lake, contemplate your life or someone else's, marvel at the scenery far from the crush of society, or get lost in the infinite layers of stars and constellations as a loon calls in the distance.

Let's begin.

Section 1: Upper Benson to Piseco (Silver Lake Wilderness)

Length: 25.3 miles.

Duration: 1 1/2 to 3 days.

Difficulty: Easy to moderate.

Trail conditions: Trail is generally in good shape, although muddy and wet in sections. Some stream crossings do not have bridges, and boardwalks are common. Most climbs and ascents are between 100 and 300 vertical feet. The long descent from Mud Lake to the West Branch Sacandaga River is about 700 vertical feet.

Highlights: Silver Lake, Canary Pond, West Branch Sacandaga River, isolation, Silver Lake Wilderness.

Issues: No bridge across the West Branch Sacandaga River, between Rock and Meco Lakes.

Location: This section begins at Upper Benson and ends in Piseco.

The NPT technically begins in Northville; however, a significant amount of road walking is required to reach the traditional beginning at Upper Benson. Be aware that a spur of the NPT, also blazed blue and considered part of the same trail, has been built from West Stony Creek, where it meets the traditional NPT; it ends east of Woods Lake at County Route 6. You will pass this small trailhead while driving to Upper Benson. Do not begin here, unless you want to add 9 miles to your journey. This new trail is a meandering woodland trail that winds in and out of valleys and drainages and crosses streams. It was built to reduce the road walking from Northville.

This section of the NPT crosses the vast Silver Lake Wilderness, which covers over 106,000 acres. From the Upper Benson trailhead, the NPT gradually ascends along an old forest grade and enters a clearing next to West Stony Creek. Follow the beautiful creek upstream, passing rapids, pools, and boulders, as well as some campsites. Cross the creek over a bridge as the water cascades below. Do not be confused by the next trail juncture; the blue NPT joins from the right. This is the new spur trail to County Route 6. Continue left. Hike a gradual ascent along a rocky, eroded grade. Reach scenic Goldmine Creek, where there is a nice campsite on the right. The trail climbs gradually, occasionally descending slightly to cross small streams. Pass a side trail that goes down to scenic Rock Lake, another place to camp. Level hiking follows, and then the trail gradually descends, crossing more small streams. Reach the first main challenge of the trail—crossing the West Branch Sacandaga River without a bridge. Do not be confused, the NPT crosses this same river further north, where it is far larger and has a long suspension bridge. Here, the river is the size of a creek, but can still be dangerous to cross in high water.

Hike up along the river, enjoying its beautiful cascades, rapids, falls, and a stunning swimming hole. Reach the shore of sublime Meco Lake. The trail is close to the water, but the steep terrain prevents camping. Soon thereafter, reach the south end of gorgeous Silver Lake, surrounded by rolling hills as it stretches into the distance. There are a lean-to and campsites at this lake, and it's a beautiful place to relax and camp. The NPT soon leaves the lake, continues on hilly terrain, and descends to a wetland where there is a bridge. Climb to beautiful Canary Lake, where there is a superb campsite left of the trail. Descend to a stream valley and follow level trail along the base of a hill, with meadows and wetlands off to the right. The trail curves around the west end of Mud Lake on boardwalks across wetlands. Mud Lake lives up to its name, since its shore is marshy. Reach the lean-to in a nice grove of hemlock and spruce.

After a short climb, the NPT makes a long, 700-foot vertical descent to the West Branch Sacandaga River along old grades. This time cross the river over a long suspension bridge, enjoying the views of this large river and its whitewater rapids. The river is an ideal place to take

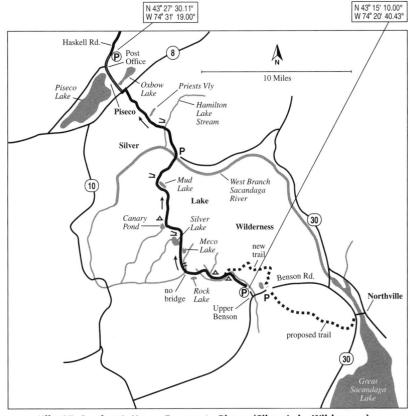

Hike 37, Section 1: Upper Benson to Piseco (Silver Lake Wilderness)

a break, and there is a campsite on the north side of the river. Reach an intersection at an old grade and trail register. Off to the right, there is a road and parking area, making this part of the trail somewhat popular. Follow the grade to the left and climb gradually to rolling terrain where the trail crosses small streams. Descend and cross Hamilton Lake Stream with a bridge. A campsite is on the left above the stream. Cross another small stream and climb a bank to Hamilton Lake lean-to on the right. Rolling, wet terrain continues to Priests Vly, a wetland to the right. Hike up a gradual climb, and then descend to the cascading outlet of Buckhorn Lake. An unofficial side trail goes up to the lake, which is somewhat swampy. Hilly terrain follows as the trail gradually descends along meadows to Route 8.

Turn left on the road and make the next right to Piseco, passing a fire hall, the outlet of Oxbow Lake, and the town hall. The road passes cottages and homes, but offers no views of Piseco Lake. Hike past the post office and turn right onto Haskell Road. Climb gradually, passing more homes, until the trail ends at a stream and a sketchy parking area.

· · ·

I originally had a different thru-hike in mind. In 2014, I faced the possibility of a career change, and I began to think that if that were to happen, I might thru-hike the Appalachian Trail. It looked like more than just a journey—it looked like freedom.

I thought I never knew what true freedom felt like. I began to mow lawns in the seventh or eighth grade, worked every summer, and attended school or held a job continuously ever since. I would stare at a road atlas and imagine all the parks and places I would visit if I had several months off, roaming the country on an endless road trip.

But, as luck would have it, I kept my job, and the Appalachian Trail was put on hold. My thru-hike aspirations settled on the Northville–Placid Trail through the Adirondacks instead. While it wasn't 2,000 miles, it would still be the longest hike I ever attempted. The mileage wasn't my only concern. My prior long hike was on the rugged Standing Stone Trail, where my Achilles tendon flared up and my knee hurt with each step. I didn't know how my body would hold up. I didn't give much thought to my mind.

I'd be hiking the Northville–Placid Trail during one of the most popular times of the year, and I hoped to meet some other thru-hikers, maybe even get a taste of a hiking community as we shared our experiences, challenges, or just a campfire.

My girlfriend, Leigh Ann, and her sister, Melissa, drove me to the southern trailhead. I got my gear together, feeling the nervous electricity of being on the cusp of the vast unknown. I couldn't fully comprehend the miles ahead of me. I said my goodbyes with a pit in my stomach and began my hike like any other, one step after the other, each foot on dirt or rock. I lost sight of Leigh Ann and Melissa through the trees as I crossed the boundary of loneliness.

The trail meandered through the woods, over log bridges across cascading streams, and into valleys. I found a nice campsite along Goldmine Creek and washed off in the frigid stream as my skin became armored with goose bumps. I crawled into my bag in the deep, dark, silent black of night.

I awoke and returned to the trail as the morning sun illuminated the leaves with a fluorescent green glow. I hiked along Meco Lake. The sun lit the mirrored surface of the lake as veils of mist rose and disappeared into the air. I soon reached beautiful Silver Lake, where I saw some campers, but there were still no other thru-hikers. The trail dropped down and crossed the West Branch Sacandaga River as it filled the forests with the roar of rapids. A large suspension bridge offered passage with views up and down the river.

I reached a trail register and read that two girls were ahead of me, also thru-hiking north. They were less than a day ahead of me, and I hoped I would catch up to them.

When I reached Route 8, my feet were burning. I sat down to take in the sun along the road as my feet cooled off, free of the putrid socks and boots. Cars and trucks tore past me. I could hear them a few miles away, with the bass of rushing air and rumbling echoes across the asphalt that grew in intensity as they came nearer. They approached like an oncoming shockwave, shredding the wind into an instantaneous tornado and a high-pitched whistle as they passed. Then the cars and trucks would shrink, disappearing down the road as quickly as they had arrived. These vehicles had so much power and consumed so much energy to perform as we demanded. Taking a step with my own body felt effortless by comparison.

I walked through the small town of Piseco. People were outside, grilling or doing yard work, enjoying the end of the summer. A young kid gave a quick wave as he sped past me, burning his tires on the road in an old, beat up Camaro. The air had a chill as the sun set behind the pine trees. I was soon back in the woods after walking through the first—and last—town along the trail.

Section 2: Piseco to Cedar River Flow/Wakely Dam
(West Canada Lakes Wilderness)

Length: 32.8 miles.

Duration: 1$\frac{1}{2}$ to 3 days.

Difficulty: Moderate.

Trail conditions: This section is quite hilly, with most climbs and descents between 100 and 300 vertical feet. This section is notorious for its wet and muddy conditions. The trail is well established, and most trail junctures have signs. The trail crosses several boardwalks.

Highlights: West Canada Lakes Wilderness, isolation, Spruce Lake, West Canada Lakes, Cedar Lakes, Cedar River, superb camping, spruce forests.

Issues: The trail is often muddy and wet. There are no bridges across the Jessup River or the outlet of West Lake.

Location: This section is between Piseco and Wakely Dam.

This section, along with Cold River at the north end of the trail, is widely considered to be among the most scenic along the NPT. The trail traverses the 156,000-acre West Canada Lakes Wilderness, the second largest wilderness area in the Adirondacks. Here, you will find some of the most isolated hiking in New York, numerous beautiful lakes and ponds, diverse forest types, and scenic streams. The NPT traverses a hilly plateau that is colder than surrounding areas. As a result, expect snowier conditions. The colder climate also supports extensive spruce forests. Keep in mind that this section is even hillier than the topographic maps indicate.

From Piseco, the trail passes a register and follows an old grade, crossing several small streams. Begin a steeper ascent up an eroded and rocky grade. Reach Fall Stream where there are several nice campsites. Cross the stream and continue the gradual ascent on the old grade, which is often wet and boggy. Reach the top of a ridge and hike through a col before making a descent into another drainage. The NPT drops down to the scenic, boulder-studded Jessup River. Although it's only the size of a large creek, there is no bridge here, so cross as best you can. Be very careful in high water. The trail coincides with an old forest road and passes a campsite to the right. A long 400-foot vertical climb follows as the trail goes up along Bloodgood Brook. Descend again to wet and muddy conditions as the trail passes a lean-to on the left. Spruce Lake comes into view, although the trail does not get close to it. Pass a side trail to Spruce Lake No. 2 lean-to, which sits above the lake. The best lean-to is the most northern, Spruce Lake No. 3, since it is close to the water and affords beautiful views across this stunning lake. Boulders dot the shore, and rolling forested ridges create the horizon.

Rolling terrain and wet conditions continue north of Spruce Lake. A mile or so from the lake, hike along the edge of a wet bog. Climb up a hill and descend to the outlet of Sampson Bog, a beautiful, serene setting with a waterfall and bridge. The next 2 miles, north to Mud Lake, are very hilly, muddy, and wet as the trail goes through spruce forests and climbs in and out of drainages. Pass a juncture with the French Louie Trail, which makes for a nice loop, and cross West Canada Creek

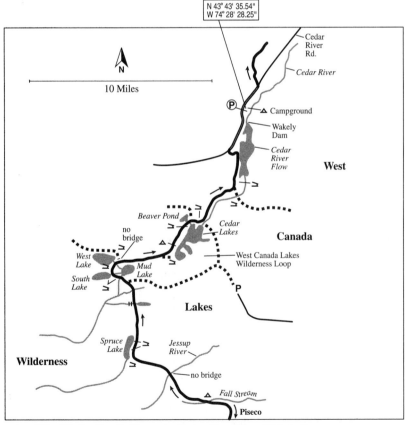

**Hike 37, Section 2: Piseco to Cedar River Flow/Wakely Dam
(West Canada Lakes Wilderness)**

at the outlet of Mud Lake. Soon pass the West Canada Creek lean-to. Climb over a small hill and descend gradually to a side trail on the left that leads to the South Lake lean-to, a fine place to camp with views of the shallow, sandy lake. Enter a meadow and cross a long wooden bridge over the outlet of South Lake. Enjoy views of the wetlands and rolling mountains. This is one of the few open areas with views along the NPT.

After a few more small hills, the trail arrives at West Lake, a popular destination. The trail does not get close to the lake, and the two side trails to the two lean-tos are to the left, and are inconspicuous. Hike into a meadow, where you will reach a register and trail sign. Reenter the woods and cross the rocky outlet of West Lake as best you can, since there is not a bridge. For the next three quarters of a mile, the trail is a difficult mix of water, mud, roots, and rock, as it circumvents a wetland and Mud Lake. There is no way to keep your feet dry. Drier conditions return as you hike over a few low hills and descend into the grassy valley of Mud Creek. Cross the bridge and begin a meandering, hilly climb in scenic forests. Pass the outlet of discreet Kings Pond and continue along the hilly terrain until the trail drops down to sublime Cedar Lakes. A side trail to the right leads to a lean-to on a peninsula. As the lake comes into view you'll notice some superb campsites on a small bay.

The trail soon leaves the lake to make a rather steep 200-foot vertical climb up Cobble Hill. Descend steeply to another side trail on the right that goes to a lean-to on the lake. Cross a slanted and somewhat rickety wooden bridge at the outlet of Beaver Pond. Enjoy views of both the pond and Cedar Lakes. Pick up an old, level grade and turn right as the NPT passes a side trail to Lost Lake. Continue on the old grade through a deep, dark forest. The terrain is rolling and hilly. Another lean-to soon comes into view on the right; it is in an overgrown meadow with a trail that goes down to the water. A superb campsite is just ahead, also on the right. The NPT goes through some high grass and reaches the Cedar Lakes dam, a register, and a trail sign. The Cedar Lakes Trail is to the right and crosses the Cedar River. Together with the French Louie Trail, it makes for a fine weekend backpacking trip into the West Canada Lakes Wilderness.

The NPT proceeds on an old grade, but keeps its distance from the rapids and boulders of the beautiful Cedar River, although it comes briefly into view. Leave the river again to make a climb up Lamphere Ridge. The descent is very gradual and the trail levels through grassy areas. Reach a trail sign and juncture, with a side trail on the right that goes to the Carry lean-to. The NPT continues on the old grade. Turn right onto a gravel road as the Cedar River Flow comes into view through the trees. The road climbs above the lake and reaches a gate and register at the Cedar River Road. Turn right onto this gravel road and descend for 1.3 miles to a small campground and picnic area at Wakely Dam. This is a fine place to relax, or even spend the night. The view south across the lake to the distant mountains is a beautiful sight. There is a particularly fine view of Lewey Mountain as it rises on the southern horizon.

• • •

The trail entered the woods, and I found a place to camp along a small stream. The cold water felt good on my feet. I no longer saw the two girls' names in the registers. I must now be ahead of them, I thought. I ate quickly and went to bed when there was still light in the woods. I stared at the tent fabric until it became dark. My body felt all right, but the aches and pains were growing. Blisters tried to form on my feet, and I battled them with pieces of duct tape.

I woke to another sunny day and hiked into the West Canada Lakes Wilderness, one of the most isolated areas in the Adirondacks. It was my toughest day. The day became very warm as the bright sun speckled the forest floor. The terrain was endless ups and downs, meandering around wetlands, bogs, and marshes. A highlight was the northern lean-to of glorious Spruce Lake, with great views across the water to the boulder-dotted shores. The rolling green hills exposed an occasional flash of red or orange from maples in the sunlight. I enjoyed the sun and the breeze while I ate lunch. This place felt so peaceful and isolated; the only sound was the breeze blowing through the trees. My ears searched for something more, maybe a plane or distant car, but all I heard was nature's delicate symphony. It felt surreal to witness a place as it has always been. I continued along the trail toward South and West Lakes as I tried to avoid depressions of black, gelatinous mud. I was getting tired and could feel the sweat, dirt, and grime enter every crevice of my body.

The trail crossed a long bridge at the outlet of South Lake, with views of the vast sedges, marshes, and wet meadows. A rocky creek crossing over swamp water brought me to Mud Lake, which lived up to its name with a tortuous muddy and rocky trail. By this point, I simply surrendered and walked in the muck with my soaked boots and mud-plastered legs. The mud was so pervasive it splashed up my shorts, adding a final, uncomfortable insult.

The forests began to change to spruce, pine, and fir, which cast the woods in twilight even though it was only midday. I found a place to camp at Cedar Lakes and noticed a couple from Syracuse, the Schmidts, were ahead of me in the registers. They were also thru-hiking to the north, and I hoped I would catch them. Loons echoed across the lake as the sun set. Being alone for so many miles gave me time to think about anything and everything. I half expected an epiphany or a wellspring of personal peace and contentment. But my thoughts came up short. Maybe my body was so tired, so demanding of energy, that my soul was denied nirvana and my mind was denied thinking about anything deeper than food and a shower.

The next morning I was up early and on the trail by 6:30 A.M. The sunlight streamed through the forest with shafts of light that glittered on the dew covering the grass and brush. The trail followed the Cedar River briefly as mist danced across the mirrored water and rose into a light fog that veiled the deep green canopy of the forest. The morning was slowly unwrapping itself in the warm silence of a late summer day.

Section 3: Cedar River Flow/Wakely Dam to Long Lake/Route 28N

Length: 27 miles.

Duration: 1$^1/_2$ to 3 days.

Difficulty: Moderate to difficult.

Trail conditions: Trail is well established and blazed. There are wet and muddy areas.

Highlights: Lake Durant, Tirrell Pond.

Issues: Long ascent and descent over the ridge in the Blue Mountain Wild Forest, the highest point on the trail. From Cedar River Road to Stephens Pond, the trail meanders quite a bit on sidehill, so expect it to take longer than you might have thought.

Location: Lake Durant, Blue Mountain Village, and Long Lake.

This section is most notable for the big climb and descent over a ridge in the Blue Mountain Wild Forest. Another highlight is the beautiful Lake Durant Campground, with its very welcome showers. The campground is near the halfway point of the trail.

From Wakely Dam, follow the road for a mile. The NPT leaves the road and goes left, following an old woods road. The climb is gradual, and blazes are infrequent. The trail continues to follow the grade as it bends left, but then leaves the old grade due to wet conditions. Cross a few small streams along rolling terrain on the side of the mountain. The trail meanders quite a bit over hilly and rolling terrain. Pass an

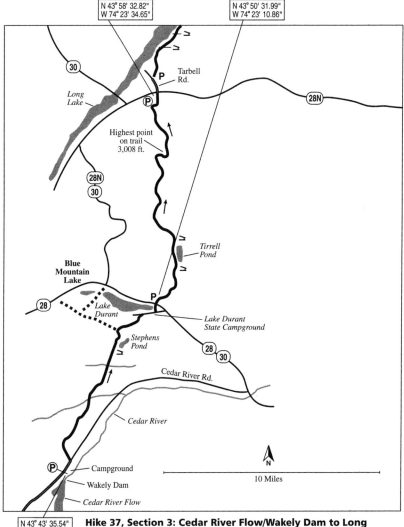

Hike 37, Section 3: Cedar River Flow/Wakely Dam to Long Lake/Route 28N

area with large, long ledge walls and outcrops, offering a nice change of scenery. The trail climbs to a ridge and descends to scenic Browns Brook, which has boulders and rapids. Continue along meandering sidehill as the trail gradually loses elevation. Hike across several small streams and drainages. Pick up an old forest road and continue to descend, entering a wet and muddy area. Soon thereafter, Stephens Pond comes into view, and there is a lean-to off to the right. Climb away from the pond on the old grade and reach a trail juncture; Cascade Pond and Blue Mountain Lake are to the left, but the NPT goes right to Lake Durant. The descent is long and gradual. Enter the campground and bear right onto the campground road. Pass a bathroom and showers, which require a fee to use. Nearby is a small beach and fine views of the beautiful lake. Bear left on an old road and cross the dam and outlet of Lake Durant. The trail continues along behind some houses and reaches Route 28/30 at a pull-off parking area. Cross Route 28/30. The village of Blue Mountain Lake is nearly 3 miles to the left if you need supplies.

The NPT traverses rolling terrain with several small stream crossings. About 3.5 miles from Route 28/30, gorgeous Tirrell Pond comes into view. The pond is one of the most scenic along the entire trail. It is surrounded by mountains and features small beaches on its north and south ends. If you can, spend some time here. A discreet side trail to the right leads to the O'Neill Flow lean-to. The trail stays in close proximity to the shore, offering many views over the water, and there are some campsites along the way. Expect wet and muddy conditions. Reach the north end of the pond as the trail passes behind a narrow beach and then leads directly to the Tirrell Pond lean-to.

Hike across hilly, wet terrain as the trail skirts the edges of wetlands until it reaches a dirt road. Turn right on the road and cross the small Salmon River, where there is a campsite on the left, right along the road. Hike up the road and enter private land. Turn left off the road and follow an old grade along a very gradual ascent. This marks the beginning of the highest climb of the trail: a long 1,000-foot vertical ascent over 2.8 miles. The climb begins easily enough along the gentle grade that enters a scenic glen; there are waterfalls off to the left of the trail. Pass some old beaver ponds and meadows, and the trail soon enters a vast, wet, high-grass meadow offering great views of the surrounding mountains. Cross a creek in the meadow and proceed across it; expect your feet to get wet in the sodden soil. Enter the woods as the grade becomes steeper, rockier, and more eroded. Springs fill the grade. The climb is in tiers, with level areas separated by steeper climbs, and this makes the climb feel longer than it is. Trail conditions continue to be very wet and muddy at the level areas. Just when you think you might be at the top, there is another climb. The trail gets steeper as you climb, and soon the ridge comes into view. Turn right at the top of the ridge, where the wet conditions persist. The climbing isn't quite over, as the trail makes a gradual ascent along the ridgeline into a forest of spruce. This is the highest point of the NPT, at just over 3,000 feet, and there is no view to reward your efforts.

The trail bears left and promptly descends. At first, there are some steep and rocky sections, but the terrain becomes easier as the NPT follows an old grade. I found the descent to be quite easy, if not enjoyable, as compared to the climb. Cross Sandy Creek and continue to follow the old grade. Enjoy some very large maple and birch trees along this area of the trail. Soon the grade becomes nearly level, until the trail suddenly branches off to the right. Rolling terrain follows as the trail crosses a few small streams with camping potential; cross-country ski trails also cross the NPT. Enter an eerie spruce forest along an extensive series of boardwalks. Ascend to a parking area and Route 28N. The village of Long Lake is 1.5 miles to the left if you need to resupply.

● ● ●

I reached Cedar River Flow and Wakely Dam in bright sunshine as the lake babbled with ripples. As I sat down to eat some lunch, everything, for a moment, was in perfect balance. The sun was warm, but not hot; the breeze was cool, but not cold. I could sit there forever. The excited voices of two children soon rang out. A brother and sister were racing their bikes on the road across the dam, their bulbous helmets bobbing up and down. One would win a race, and the other would then change the rules. Their happiness was intoxicating.

Eating became difficult. I needed the energy, but I didn't feel hungry. I had to chew forever and force the food down my throat, at times nearly gagging. I got up, lifting my pack onto my shoulders. My body was stiff and resistant as I followed the trail down the road. I was excited to reach Lake Durant, a beautiful campground with showers. It had been four days without a shower, and I was really beginning to stink. I tried to find a comparison for the smell. The best I could come up with was last summer's grease on a hot charcoal grill.

The hike down to Lake Durant was painful on my burning feet. The campground host was friendly and even lent me a towel so I could take a shower. As the brown water ran off of me, it felt so good, and I realized I take so much for granted. Nevertheless, I was losing my motivation. I expected the hike to be some kind of life-affirming journey, but it had turned out to only be a long walk through the woods. I even began to imagine excuses to end the hike. There was no one to share the experience. The freedom I sought had proven to be elusive.

I then noticed a man hobbling out of the bathroom. He asked me where he could wash some dishes. His was a classic hiker hobble, and I asked if he was hiking the NPT. He said he was, heading north on a thru-hike with his wife. They were the Schmidts! We talked for a while about the trail. The Schmidts were friendly and easygoing. I hoped to hike with them, but they were going slower and added a day to their trip. I hid my disappointment. I wouldn't see them again. At most registers, I would write a few words of encouragement for them to read.

The following morning revealed low, wispy clouds as I hiked along beautiful Tirrell Pond. The higher ridges were cloaked in clouds. Standing on the narrow beach at the north end of the pond and looking over the gorgeous panorama, I began to feel that I couldn't give up.

I hiked away from the pond and was approaching a lean-to when I noticed someone. His name was George and he was from Cleveland; he was thru-hiking, but heading south. George was a kind, free spirit. He was at home in the woods, in the lean-to, living a simple life on his own terms. George asked where I was from, and I said Pennsylvania. George mentioned how Pennsylvania has lots of good trails, and we discussed some of them. He then said, "Yeah, my friends keep telling me to get the *Backpacking Pennsylvania* book." I didn't show it, but I was shocked that this would come up in conversation between two strangers, one of them being the author, in the middle of the Adirondacks. Maybe it was wrong of me, but I didn't tell him I wrote that book. I decided to keep that moment to myself. Besides, it happened so fast, so unexpectedly, I really didn't know how to respond before we moved on to a different topic. Those few seconds provided a measure of magical coincidence that would help me continue the hike. I said goodbye to George and wished him luck on his journey. I felt light and unburdened as I sailed down the trail. I now knew I could finish.

I reached the top of the ridge, the highest point of the trail. Shafts of sun separated the lifting clouds. I had crossed over the mental and physical barrier of the trail. Before me, to the north, Long Lake, Cold River, Duck Hole, and Lake Placid patiently awaited my arrival.

Section 4: Long Lake to Lake Placid/Averyville Road (High Peaks Wilderness)

Length: 36.5 miles.

Duration: 2 to 4 days.

Difficulty: Moderate.

Trail conditions: Trail is well established, with signs at most trail junctures. Expect wet and muddy areas. Blowdowns are a problem between Big Eddy and Seward lean-to.

Highlights: Long Lake, Cold River, rapids, cascades, pools, Duck Hole, Wanika Falls, isolation, High Peaks Wilderness, beautiful lean-to and camping locations.

Issues: This section is very isolated, with no road crossings. If there is an emergency, it will be a significant amount of time before help arrives.

Location: Long Lake, Lake Placid.

For many, this is the NPT at its best, and I would have to agree. While this section does not have as many lakes and ponds as others, it does feature the huge, beautiful Long Lake, the stunning rapids, cascades, and pools of the spectacular Cold River, Duck Hole, and the impressive Wanika Falls. This section is also the most isolated of the entire trail, and explores the most isolated region in the Adirondacks, if not all of New York. Here you will find some of the finest backpacking in New York that has an added bonus of being a relatively tame trail that is easy to moderate in difficulty.

From Route 28N, follow Tarbell Road for .7 mile as it gradually climbs a hill, passing homes along the way. Crest the top of the hill and start to descend to a small parking area and trail sign on the right. Here, the NPT reenters the woods. This spot is significant, as it marks the trail's entry into the famous—and vast—High Peaks Wilderness. This is the largest wilderness area in the state, covering about 200,000 acres. The remainder of the NPT is within this wilderness as the trail completely traverses its western zone. This spot also marks the last contact with civilization until the end of the trail. Not a single road or highway is crossed. You will hike through a very isolated region of the Adirondacks. Be sure that you are prepared, because if you need help, it will be a long time coming.

Don't be completely intimidated, though. This section is fairly easy, with long level and rolling sections, although it does get quite hilly between Ouluska lean-to and Wanika Falls.

Descend from Tarbell Road and circumvent a bog. Climb over a small hill, descend to another stream, and cross the stream where there are two lean-tos off to the left. Long Lake can be seen through the trees. For the next 7 miles, the NPT is level and rolling as it follows the eastern side of Long Lake. However, for most of that time, the trail keeps its distance from the water. There are a total of nine lean-tos along the lake. Keep in mind the side trails that lead to them usually have no markings or signs, so keep an eye out for trails that lead from the NPT to the left. The lean-tos are also used by boaters and anglers. Long Lake is beautiful, and I recommend camping at one of the lean-tos. In summer, the breeze off the lake is a blessing. In cold weather, it will be just the opposite.

The hike along Long Lake is rolling and easy; you will be able to make good time. The highest climb might be 100 vertical feet. The trail crosses many small streams and drainages. It also enters private land, so be sure to stay on the trail. At the Plumley lean-tos, the trail leaves the lake and climbs over a low hill in a pine forest. Descend gradually and enter a level marshy area before crossing Pine Brook on a bridge. Rolling terrain follows for a mile until the trail reaches an old road. Turn right and hike to Shattuck Clearing, a well-known spot on the trail, although it is not particularly notable. The clearing is quickly growing over; however, there is a trail sign and register here. A horse trail joins from the left. Shattuck Clearing is also the last place you can receive cell phone service. Leave the old road to the left and drop to Moose Creek, which the trail crosses on a high bridge. The NPT soon arrives at the stunning Cold River.

Cross Cold River on a high suspension bridge and be sure to enjoy the impressive views of the rapids, pools, and cascades. Be careful, though, as the bridge can be slippery. A lean-to is on the left, and an even more impressive lean-to is .3 mile farther downstream, perched on a ledge overlooking the river. You must take some time to enjoy this glorious spot. If you can, arrange your hike to camp at these lean-tos, identified as Cold River Nos. 3 and 4.

From here, the NPT climbs to an old grade and heads upstream. The hike is easy and level. Although views of the sublime river are blocked by trees, you get an occasional peek. After a mile, reach Big Eddy, a massive, swirling pool that is the size of a pond. The trail continues along the old grade, which is brushy in places. Soon you will encounter the infamous blowdowns where numerous spruce trees have fallen across the grade, creating impenetrable barriers. The trail has been rerouted up, down, and around the grade to get by these obstacles and will take some time. The trail leaves the grade and follows a footpath above the river, soon arriving at the Seward lean-to, considered to be one of the finest in the Adirondacks. This gorgeous lean-to is located next to Millers Falls, a cascading ledge rapid that feeds a large pool.

The NPT follows meandering, hilly sidehill as it traverses the banks above the river. You will pass boulders and scenic forests of spruce, cedar, and birch. Some of the cedar trees are huge and have unique root formations. The trail also offers more views of the river with its rapids, pools, and riffles. Reach Seward Brook and cross as best you can—the bridge has been pushed into the bank by a flood. Ouluska lean-to is just ahead. It is a nice shelter and usable, but is not in the

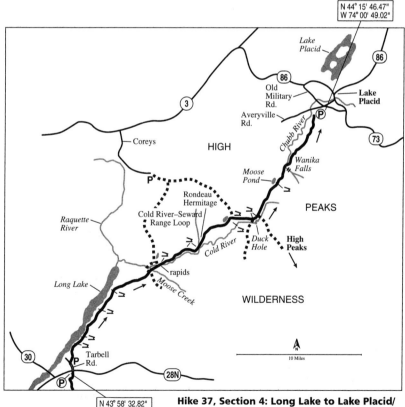

Hike 37, Section 4: Long Lake to Lake Placid/ Averyville Road (High Peaks Wilderness)

best condition. The most unique aspect of the lean-to is the transcribed journals starting from the 1980s. If you need something to read, camp here. The trail is easy and rolling until it reaches the Rondeau Hermitage, where Noah John Rondeau eschewed modern life and lived as a hermit from 1929 to 1950. Rondeau is the most famous of the Adirondack's hermits. As hikers, anglers, and hunters encountered him, his hermitage became more well known—so much so, that Rondeau was designated the "Hermit-Mayor" of "Cold River City (population 1)" and even became a local celebrity. Rondeau, at the age of 67, had to leave the hermitage in 1950 after a devastating windstorm; he moved to live in the Lake Placid region and died in 1967. Today, nothing remains of the hermitage except for some pots, pans, rusted implements, and small meadows. Prior to Rondeau, this was the site of a large logging dam, and some timbers can still be seen on the banks and in the river.

For the next 3.5 miles, the NPT explores hilly terrain and climbs in and out of stream valleys. The terrain is hillier and the trail crosses more streams than topographical maps indicate. Cross the outlet of Mountain Pond and climb above it; the trail stays away from the pond. Soon thereafter, reach an old forest road, where the NPT turns right. Descend and pass two lean-tos, one on the left and one on the right. These are Cold River Nos. 1 and 2, and they are little used. Cross Moose Creek over a bridge and begin a short, steep ascent on the old road. As the hilly ascent continues, there are some views of the Cold River to your right. Reach a trail sign and register. The NPT turns left, but trails to the right lead to popular Duck Hole, two lean-tos, and a high-grass meadow. Duck Hole used to be a large pond that reflected the distant High Peaks; however, a flood blew out the dam and the pond is a fraction of its former size. The lake bed is now changing to a meadow.

The trail stays above the reduced Duck Hole and follows scenic Roaring Brook upstream. Pass a red trail to the right that crosses Roaring Brook on a bridge. This trail can be used to access the High Peaks and end at Adirondack Loj if you so choose. Some hikers choose this option.

The NPT continues up along a rugged trail above pristine Roaring Brook, which has cascades and crystal clear pools. Leave the brook and climb gradually into a col between the mountains. Descend steeply to Moose Creek where there are beaver meadows and wet areas that must be negotiated. The trail can be hard to follow through here. Climb to the Moose Lake lean-to, which is high above the lake. This is a beautiful, serene place with views of the Sawtooth Mountains through the trees. Climb away from the lean-to through a scenic forest with a large beaver meadow below on the left. The gradual climb continues until it reaches a sharp descent to a side trail to Wanika Falls, on the right. This side hike is well worth the effort and is only .2 mile long. The creek is filled with cascades and falls, but the trail ends at the stunning Wanika Falls as it plummets down a towering cliff, slides over a sloping ledge, and then drops into a narrow pool. The falls are well over 100 feet high. There are campsites below the falls, but also signs that say camping is prohibited.

The NPT descends along the small Chubb River, and then crosses it above a beautiful chasm and cascade. Leave the river and hike rolling terrain across the gradual slope at the base of a mountain. The trail crosses several small streams and drainages in a scenic hardwood forest. Descend to a larger, muddy stream surrounded by wet meadows and beaver activity. Cross as best you can on branches. Hike across level trail, and then skirt around wetlands on boardwalks. The trail becomes hillier as it goes in and out of stream valleys with wide bridges. The trail bends left, and the placid Chubb River soon comes into view. Turn right and hike along the meandering river on an old grade. Reach a trail sign and register, and the parking area along Averyville Road. You've done it! Now go to Lake Placid, clean up, and celebrate.

• • •

I walked away from Tarbell Road and signed the register. The next road would be at the end of the hike. My determination was galvanized: I was going to finish. My body and mind were focused on achieving the goal that was about 36 miles away.

I hiked down a side trail that descended to Long Lake and the Hidden Cove lean-to. The scene was beautiful as the green forests contrasted with the deep blue skies and white clouds. A small island sat in the cove, just offshore, and tempted me to explore. I looked at my watch and realized I would otherwise be at work. Work felt like it belonged in another life. I sat on a rounded rock along the shore as the water lapped my legs, my feet consumed by the loose, cool gravel of the lake bed.

I looked over the sparkling water and tried to think about things. I found myself asking questions that felt indulgent and undeserving of an answer. It didn't matter. The life I have is far better than most. Step by step, mile after mile, after facing the vast unknown and still pushing through, I began to feel the slightest shift within myself.

We live lives of shame and self-consciousness. We are embarrassed not only by what our bodies look like, but also by what they can do. Sweat, dirt, stink, and aches are things to be expunged and avoided in our sanitized, manicured, self-conscious worlds. We think we can't do something, so we don't. When movement requires confidence, pushing ourselves can be a nightmare. But we are designed to move, to explore, to experience. Freedom, it turns out, is not a place.

The next morning was cooler, and I sped down the trail, climbing hills and passing small creeks. I crossed the impressive suspension bridge over the Cold River as the current below surged through rapids into deep, frigid pools. I watched the clear water flow over a kaleidoscope of rocks, sand, and gravel at the bottom. I found joy in the stunning scenery.

The trail passed into a different land, a territory unlike any previous. The forests were deeper and darker, with spruce, fir, and cedar. The mountains were higher and more rugged as they clawed the sky with sheer ridges. The land was untamed, wild, unapologetic. My body felt stronger. Despite back-to-back high-mileage days, I felt no pain in my Achilles or knee as I had on the Standing Stone Trail.

I paused at the site of the Rondeau Hermitage and wondered what could compel a man to leave an entire world behind for a life of seclusion. Was it to seek the salve of nature after a childhood of abuse, neglect, and poverty? Was it to have a measure of control in a world where he had none? There is no control; there never is. Even Rondeau would have to permanently abandon his hermitage and return to the very world he tried to leave behind.

I reached Duck Hole in fading light to see the two lean-tos were occupied. I walked up the dark trail alone and found a hidden place to set up my tent. I fell asleep instantly as all of my aches and pains were numbed. My sleep was absolute. When I awoke, it was sudden, it was daylight, and I felt like I had been in a time warp. Refreshed, I began my last day on the trail.

My hike brought me to the Moose Pond lean-to, where an older man named Jim was making breakfast. He encouraged me to sit down and offered me something to eat. Jim's words, and the way his eyes looked over the landscape, exuded a deep love of the Adirondacks. He wistfully told me he had been coming up here for forty years, longer than I had been alive. Jim was proud of the secret gems he had seen in the Adirondacks over the decades. Jim spoke about them in vague terms, as if they were mythical, his eyes electrified by his memories. I could feel the magic of these places through him. When it was time for me to go, Jim told me, as if imparting a lesson, that I needed to see Wanika Falls. I assured him I would.

I reached the side trail to the falls and dropped my pack. I hiked up the trail unburdened. I felt free. I stopped at the bottom of Wanika Falls. The angle of the sun cut through the length of the falls, transforming it into a blinding gown of descending crystals. I sat there alone as the sunlight reached me, warming my skin.

I continued my journey north, and the end began to feel tangible. Two older women, weighed down with monstrous packs, passed me. They were thru-hiking to the south, led by a giant, silent, gentle dog that stopped when I approached and patiently waited for me to pet him. Once I did, he promptly resumed walking down the trail, as if one of us had paid a toll. I told them I was almost done with my thru-hike, and they looked at me with kind, knowing smiles that communicated far more than their words. I tried to keep my distance from them, to save them from my putrid smell. In reality, it was a badge of honor.

The NPT followed the languid Chubb River for a short distance. I could see the end through the trees—the parking area with cars, Leigh Ann sitting on a rock in the sun, reading a book. I walked up to the trail register and signed it, writing the Schmidts one last note congratulating them. I reached the trail sign and hesitated for a second, then walked by it. I was done. I hugged Leigh Ann, who did her best to ignore my smell. Next to us was George's car, an old Corolla with Ohio plates, waiting patiently for its next adventure. The end felt new.

We drove home on I-81 the following day. As we neared our exit, I looked off to the left to see the newspaper plant where I worked eighteen years ago. I would be covered in ink and paper dust, operating machines that stuffed papers with ads. Working the night shift, I would sit in my old, tan Ford Escort during my break, eating a day-old hoagie I bought at the nearby grocery store. I'd look across to see I-81 and the continuous flow of cars, trucks, journeys, experiences, and lives. I wondered where all those people were going, what they were doing. I imagined what it would be like to be on that interstate, driving away.

I looked at that plant and parking lot as we drove by, heading home on the interstate. I could now clearly see the distance of those eighteen years. As it turned out, I was right where I always wanted to be, I was living the life I always hoped I would.

I have always been free.

About the Author

Jeff Mitchell resides near Tunkhannock, Pennsylvania, where he works as the District Attorney of Wyoming County. He is a board member of the Keystone Trails Association and author of *Hiking the Endless Mountains*, *Backpacking Pennsylvania*, *Hiking the Allegheny National Forest*, and *Paddling Pennsylvania*.

Also by Jeff Mitchell . . .

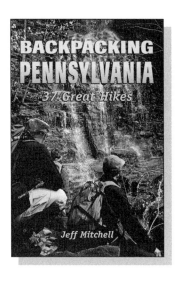

BACKPACKING
PENNSYLVANIA
37 GREAT HIKES

PB • 272 pages • 52 maps
978-0-8117-3180-5

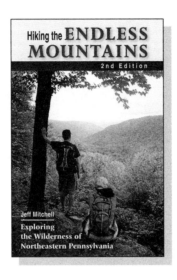

Also by Jeff Mitchell . . .

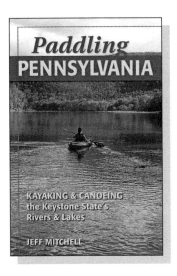

PADDLING
PENNSYLVANIA

KAYAKING & CANOEING
THE KEYSTONE STATE'S RIVERS & LAKES

PB • 320 pages • 230 maps • 8-pg. color section
978-0-8117-3626-8

WWW.STACKPOLEBOOKS.COM
1-800-732-3669